Application of Biotechnology

AAAS Selected Symposia Series

 Published by Westview Press, Inc.
5500 Central Avenue, Boulder, Colorado

 for the

American Association for the Advancement of Science
1333 H Street, N.W., Washington, D.C.

Application of Biotechnology

Environmental and Policy Issues

Edited by John R. Fowle III

AAAS Selected Symposium **106**

AAAS Selected Symposia Series

Published in 1987 in the United States of America by Westview Press, Inc.; Frederick A. Praeger, Publisher; 5500 Central Avenue, Boulder, Colorado 80301

Library of Congress Catalog Card Number: 87-51000
ISBN: 0-8133-7468-5

Composition for this book was provided by the editor.
This book was produced without formal editing by the publisher.

Printed and bound in the United States of America

The paper used in this publication meets the requirements of the American National Standard for Permanence of Paper for Printed Library Materials Z39.48-1984.

6 5 4 3 2 1

About the Series

The *AAAS Selected Symposia Series* was begun in 1977 to provide a means for more permanently recording and more widely disseminating some of the valuable material that is discussed at the AAAS Annual National Meetings. The volumes in this series are based on symposia held at the Meetings that address topics of current and continuing significance, both within and among the sciences, and in the areas in which science and technology have an impact on public policy. The series format is designed to provide for rapid dissemination of information, so the papers are reproduced directly from camera-ready copy. The papers published in the series are organized and edited by the symposium arrangers, who then become the editors of the various volumes. Most papers published in the series are original contributions that have not been previously published, although in some cases additional papers from other sources have been added by an editor to provide a more comprehensive view of a particular topic. Symposia may be reports of new research or reviews of established work, particularly work of an interdisciplinary nature, since the AAAS Annual Meetings typically embrace the full range of the sciences and their societal implications.

ARTHUR HERSCHMAN
Head, Meetings and Publications,
American Association for the
Advancement of Science

Contents

PART THREE: THE FUTURE OF BIOTECHNOLOGY--SIX PERSPECTIVES

Tables

Figures

Acknowledgments

The success of this book belongs to the organizers and participants of the AAAS symposium held in 1985 and especially to the authors of the chapters in this book. I would like to thank my fellow co-organizers of the symposium, Gregory Daneke, Morris Levin, and Philip Regal, for their help and guidance. Thanks are also due to David Andow, Terri Goldberg, Bernadine Healy, Bruce Levin, George Rathmann, Stephen Risch, Anthony Robbins, and Frances Sharples for giving up their Memorial Day to participate in the conference and to Sheldon Krimsky, Richard Lenski, Elizabeth Milewski, and Lidia Watrud, who generously contributed chapters essential for the broad coverage of this book. Finally, I would like to thank Eastern Research Group, Inc., particularly Brana Lobel, for their invaluable assistance in the editing and preparation of this book.

John R. Fowle III

Introduction

This volume is the product of a symposium held at the 1985 annual meeting of the American Association for the Advancement of Science (AAAS). The symposium provided a forum to discuss from various perspectives--scientific, economic, social, legislative--the safety and desirability of releasing genetically engineered organisms into the environment.

Until 1980, all genetic engineering experiments using recombinant DNA (rDNA) were conducted under "contained" conditions, and no genetically engineered organism had been proposed for deliberate release. Containment meant, first, that physical barriers were used to make the likelihood of release very small, and second, that the organisms were bred to have many special requirements for growth, so that their chance of survival, if accidentally released into the environment, would be very low. Containment was required because there was no body of experience about the health and environmental effects from genetically engineered organisms.

In spite of containment, there was widespread apprehension about the use of rDNA. One concern was that genetic engineering might make otherwise innocuous organisms infectious, raising the specter of an "Andromeda Strain" being released on an unsuspecting and unprepared public. Other issues were raised, including religious arguments against exploiting nature and questions about the ethics surrounding human gene therapy. In 1976, scientists who were concerned about the ethical issues and potential hazards developed guidelines for research using organisms made by rDNA techniques. They were joined later by others from the public, industry, and government (see Chapter 3). These guidelines were written for research funded by grants from the National Institutes of Health (NIH). However, others who utilized rDNA techniques, such as industrial scientists not covered by the guidelines, complied voluntarily. At this time, there was much discussion and often bitter debate about whether or not to allow rDNA techniques to be used at all (see Chapter 2), but cautious and deliberate experiments with the new technology allowed experience to develop and provided a basis for judging the safety of the contained use of rDNA.

Now products have been developed specifically to be used in the environment without physical containment. The organisms that comprise these products (such as microbial pesticides and drain cleaners) are designed to survive, at least long enough to perform their intended function. Potentially, they are capable of growing, replicating, and transferring their genetic information to other organisms. Replication and genetic exchange can magnify the scale of release of even the smallest number of engineered organisms. If these organisms have a selective advantage in a given environment, their effects could be great.

The issues surrounding deliberate release raise questions analogous to those that arose in the initial rDNA debates (see Chapters 8 and 11). Until April 1987, litigation at the national and state levels and local government action halted efforts to apply genetically engineered organisms to the environment (well-publicized examples are federal and California state injunctions against the field testing of ice nucleation minus [INA⁻] bacteria for frost control). On April 25, 1987, the first authorized outdoor test of a genetically engineered bacteria (Frostban™) was conducted by Advanced Genetic Sciences (AGS), Inc. in Contra Costa County, California. It employed modified forms of Pseudomonas syringae and Pseudomonas fluorescens to confirm their effectiveness in reducing crop losses from frost damage. The strains were engineered by deleting genes responsible for an ice-nucleating protein. The release came three and a half years after permission was first requested from NIH's rDNA Advisory Committee, and was not without protest. Vandals tore many of the strawberry plants from the ground before the bacteria were applied. A few days later, Steven Lindow, discoverer of the ice-nucleating gene, and the first person to engineer Pseudomonas species lacking the INA gene, sprayed Frostban™ on potato plants in Tulelake, California. There were no demonstrators in Tulelake before or during the field test. Does this mean the issue of potential hazard from environmental releases is laid to rest? Critics say no. They point out, as others have done before, that Frostban™ represents the least likely type of genetically engineered organism to cause adverse effects, because the organisms were modified by deletion of a gene. Other approaches, such as the transfer of the pesticidal toxin gene from Bacillus thuringiensis to P. fluorescens for insect control, are of greater concerns to public interest groups and federal agencies as well.

We now stand at a crossroads in the development of biotechnology. The central issue is how to encourage the growth of industrial applications of various biotechnology processes (see Chapters 9, 10, and 12) while adequately protecting against unreasonable adverse effects (see Chapters 5 and 6). This book explores the issue through essays that describe what "industrial biotechnology" is, what its likely benefits are, what our current knowledge allows us to say about levels of risk, what information is needed for providing risk assessment data, and, most important in light of our incomplete knowledge, how we can best proceed with respect to risk assessment and risk management.

WHAT IS BIOTECHNOLOGY?

Loosely defined, biotechnology is the willful harnessing of life forms for human use. In the past ten years, biotechnology has come to mean the commercialization of the tools of molecular biology, mainly rDNA and hybridoma or cell fusion technologies. In one sense, modern biotechnology processes are the most recent in a long line of techniques dating back over ten thousand years to the first known evidence of agriculture through the domestication of crops and animals. Beer, wine, and cheese making are familiar biotechnology industries that also date to antiquity. More recent but still familiar biotechnology applications include the use of microbes for sewage treatment (starting in the late nineteenth century) and the production of antibiotics (starting in the 1930s). Until recently, these advances occurred relatively gradually, representing an evolution in our ability to use organisms to make products for our benefit.

WHAT ARE THE ISSUES?

Modern biotechnology, specifically the use of rDNA, has brought about a revolution in our ability to control and use life forms. In some ways, it has also brought about the social upheaval associated with revolutions, forcing us to examine the ways in which we think about scientific, social, and policy issues. There are many interested parties grappling with these issues--scientists, industrialists, government officials, and the public at large. Each has his or her own perspective about what is important; there are inherent tensions about how to proceed with the new technology, and there are even those who question whether we should proceed at all. The major issue is: what is an acceptable risk?

There are risks associated with every technology; the classic applications of biotechnology have not been exempt. The introduction of agriculture has destroyed ecosystems, causing, for example, the dust bowl of the American Midwest in the 1930s. Beer and wine consumption can lead to severe illness or death, as can allergies to antibiotics administered to combat infections. We are familiar with these problems; we have a long history of experience to show us that, on balance, the benefits of these technologies outweigh their risks. But what of modern biotechnology, based on advances in molecular biology? What applications will be beneficial? How can we tell?

There is no precise answer to these questions. Information is still at an early stage. Without a sound information base, those who can argue most forcibly and articulately will sway decision making. Major decisions in most fields of endeavor are based to some extent on past experience. While we have analogous past experience to guide our decisions in biotechnology (see Chapter 4), we have no certainty that the experience is relevant. This uncertainty is a major factor in the much-publicized and painful first decade for the modern biotechnology industry. A lesson to be learned is that all those concerned about the future directions of biotechnology should be identified, engaged in discussion, and actively involved in the decision-making process as soon as possible. That this is not an easy lesson is evidenced by the public reaction to initial experimental work done with rDNA in the early 1970s, and the recent lawsuits over the release of genetically engineered organisms into the environment. In both cases, proponents of the technology proceeded with good intentions, but without the early involvement of those who seriously questioned the safety and propriety of the work.

ORGANIZATION OF THIS VOLUME

The first part of this volume (Chapters 1, 2, and 3) provides the technical background and a historical perspective. It contains a primer on molecular biology and describes the science underlying modern biotechnology, providing the information needed to understand technical points discussed in later chapters. This part also prepares the reader for subsequent discussion about the social issues by recounting the important events in the development of national and local governmental policies for evaluating the risks of biotechnology.

The second part of the volume (Chapters 4-7) examines scientific questions about the assessment of risk for the release of genetically engineered organisms into the environment. It contains descriptions of the overall process for assessing these risks and the types of questions that need to be asked to effectively monitor and evaluate the risks. Current knowledge about transfer of genetic information from species to species is examined as a basis for evaluating the impact of genetic transfer, and hypothetical case studies are presented to illustrate relevant concepts and concerns. The ecological consequences of the introduction of a nonindigenous species into a new habitat are described and evaluated for their potential as a predictive model for the release of genetically engineered organisms. Differences in opinion between molecular biologists and ecologists in thinking about the risk of the environmental releases are described, and the need for coordinated efforts between disciplines is emphasized to ensure the availability of people properly trained to evaluate potential risks.

The final part of the volume (Chapters 8-12) contains perspectives from academic, government, industry, and public interest representatives about the role each should have in fostering industrial growth and preventing adverse consequences.

REGULATORY ACTIVITIES

As this volume went to press, many important policy decisions were being made at both the national and international levels that will set the stage for future actions.

The promulgators of these policies have made attempts to hear from all major affected parties. U.S. policy about the regulation of biotechnology is coordinated among several agencies by the White House Domestic Policy Council Work Group in Biotechnology. This group is responsible for developing the Coordinated Framework for Regulation of Biotechnology (OSTP 1986) and will continue to monitor the field and make recommendations for administrative and legislative action as required. Under its aegis, a Biotechnology Science Coordinating Committee (BSCC) has been established as part of a Federal Coordinating Council for Science Engineering and Technology (FCCSET) in the Office of Science and Technology Policy, Executive Office of the President. The mission of this group is to coordinate federal science activities among federal agencies. Because of these activities, jurisdiction over the use of biotechnology has expanded beyond the original NIH Recombinant DNA Advisory Committee overview. It is important for persons and organizations interested in the growth and development of biotechnology, and in the assessment of potential risks, to follow the activities of these groups closely and to participate in their deliberations.

While coordinating activities through the BSCC, each federal agency is individually regulating biotechnology products. Those to be deliberately released into the environment are primarily under the jurisdiction of the U.S. Department of Agriculture and the U.S. Environmental Protection Agency (EPA). Most genetically engineered products proposed for deliberate release to date have fallen into traditional categories for regulatory review (for instance, plant seeds, animal biologics, microbial pesticides). Betz et al. (1987) have written an article discussing the approaches taken by EPA in addressing the scientific and regulatory questions associated with implementing EPA's policy for small-scale field testing of microbial pesticide products. Until recently, EPA limited its regulatory purview to microbial pesticide products. In the spring of 1987, however, EPA officials began to consider extending this regulatory purview to genetically engineered macroorganisms, since it was industry's stated intent to genetically engineer macroorganisms for pesticide control (for instance, by transferring Bacillus thuringiensis toxin genes from bacteria to crop plants). As the science and application of genetic engineering evolve, it is likely that many such situations will arise, creating paradoxes with respect to regulatory statutes. Questions about safety, such as food contamination, and regulatory jurisdiction (for instance, Food and Drug Administration versus Environmental Protection Agency or United States Department of Agriculture oversight), and standard setting (for example, establishment of food tolerances) will also likely arise.

INTERNATIONAL ACTIVITIES

The material contained in the 1986 OSTP document takes into account broad goals promulgated by the Organization for Economic Cooperation and Development (OECD). An ad hoc work group of government experts from member countries was formed by OECD to work to eliminate the possibility of non-tariff trade barriers preventing free trade. Internationally accepted principles have been prepared for consideration in the use and development of biotechnology. Other organizations, such as the World Health Organization, may soon begin biotechnology work efforts. It will be important for those interested in biotechnology to watch international developments closely, because actions taken abroad can have profound impact on the regulation of biotechnology in the United States.

Public Perception

In the fall of 1986, the Office of Technology Assessment commissioned Louis Harris and Associates to conduct a survey of the public's perception about genetic engineering (OTA 1987). Opinion was assessed on a number of topics, including: release of genetically engineered organisms into the environment, the credibility of different sources of risk information, and the impact of technology on the environment.

The findings were that the public is willing to accept some risks to the environment for the benefits of genetically engineered products. For small-scale, experimental field tests, eighty-two percent of Americans were in favor of the use of genetically engineered organisms. Were such tests to be conducted in their community, fifty-three percent would be in favor, fourteen percent would not care, twenty-one percent would somewhat oppose, and eleven percent would strongly oppose. Large-scale release of genetically engineered organisms by commercial firms was only favored by forty-two percent of Americans.

Assessments of risk were more believable from university scientists, public health officials, and environmental groups than from federal agencies. According to the survey, where there is disagreement over potential risks, environmental groups are believed over federal agencies sixty-three to twenty-six percent.

The implications of this survey are clear. Care must be taken in weighing the risks versus the benefits for environmental application of genetically engineered products by involving all affected parties in the process and by communicating the decisions to the public in a straightforward way.

This volume is intended to define the most salient points in the debate about the most appropriate use of genetically engineered organisms for environmental purposes. Ideas and issues from key participants in the debate have been assembled to stimulate thought and discussion, and to serve policy makers, scientists, industrialists, and the public in defining the issues, weighing the alternatives, and selecting the most appropriate courses of action.

REFERENCES

Betz, F., A. Rispin, and W. Schneider. 1987. Biotechnology Products Related to Agriculture. Overview of Regulatory Decisions at the U.S. Environmental Protection Agency. In: Biotechnology in Agricultural Chemistry ACS Symposium Series 334. Ed. H.M. LeBaron, R.O. Mumma, R.C. Honeycutt, J.H. Duesing, J.F. Phillips, and M.J. Haas. Washington DC: American Chemical Society

OSTP. 1986. Coordinated Framework for Regulation of Biotechnology; Announcement of Policy and Notice for Public Comment. Office of Science and Technology Policy. June 26. Federal Register. 51(123): 23302-23393.

OTA. 1987. New Developments in Biotechnology: Public Perceptions of Biotechnology. Office of Technology Assessment. U.S. Congress, Washington, DC. GPO 052-003-01068-2.

Part One

The Historical Context

1. The Biological Revolution: Tools and Products of Biotechnology

INTRODUCTION

Just as the ABC's or alphabets form the basis for the millions of words that constitute the world's many languages, the deoxyribonucleic acid (DNA) which constitutes the genetic alphabet of man, animals, plants, and microbes similarly contributes to the vast genetic diversity evident in living organisms. Following is a brief review of how DNA was determined to be the hereditary material. The role of past, current, and developing methodologies which use information about DNA to create useful products for diverse applications will also be discussed.

A Historical Perspective: Learning the Language

Widespread scientific acceptance that DNA is the hereditary material did not occur until after the landmark experiments of Avery, MacLeod, and McCarty and Hershey in the 1940s and 1950s (Avery et al. 1944; Hershey and Chase 1952). In those experiments, it was convincingly demonstrated that DNA, not protein, was the "transforming principle" which produced heritable changes. Tools and techniques used to isolate, characterize, and manipulate DNA, the substance of which genes are made, and proteins, the products encoded by genes, will be discussed later.

Avery and coworkers demonstrated that DNA isolated from virulent strains of the pneumonia-causing bacterium Diplococcus pneumoniae was able to produce heritable changes or transform a nonvirulent D. pneumoniae strain. The progeny of the transformed strain were virulent, causing

11

pneumonia upon injection into mice. By the use of radio-active phosphorus (^{32}P) for labeling DNA, and radioactive sulfur (^{35}S) for labeling protein, Hershey clearly demonstrated that in the bacterial virus or bacteriophage known as T2, the coat protein became labeled with ^{35}S, and DNA had the ^{32}P label (Hershey and Chase 1952).

In the early 1950s, Chargaff demonstrated that regardless of the source of the DNA, it always contained equal proportions of some of its chemical constituents (Chargaff 1950). That is, the amount of two sets of nucleotide bases called adenine and thymine, and guanine and cytosine, was always equal. Using this and additional chemical compositional and physical information obtained from X-ray diffraction patterns, Watson and Crick in 1953 published their now classic work which earned them a Nobel Prize for elucidating the helical, symmetrical structure of DNA.

DNA contains four nucleotide bases: the purines adenine and guanine, and the pyrimidines thymine and cytosine. As noted previously, the amount of adenine (A) always equals or matches the amount of thymine (T), and the amount of guanine (G) always equals or matches the amount of cytosine (C). The matching or pairing between A and T or between G and C is by relatively loose hydrogen bonding. Two hydrogen bonds link A to T; three hydrogen bonds link G to C. The concept of equal proportions and hydrogen bonding of A to T and of G to C is an important and central one in molecular biology. It is critical to the faithful transfer of genetic information to new generations. It forms the basis of molecular biology techniques such as hybridization of nucleic acids. Applications of these techniques in isolating or cloning genes will be discussed later.

In addition to the nucleotides A, T, G, and C, DNA contains a backbone made up of sugar (deoxyribose) molecules linked to phosphate by phosphodiester bonds. The ladderlike sides (or backbone) of DNA are thus made up of alternating sugar-phosphate molecules linked to the nucleotide bases A, T, G, or C. The nucleotides in turn are loosely linked by hydrogen bonds, which form the rungs of the DNA ladder. The entire ladder is itself twisted into a helical (alpha-helix) conformation.

Subsequent work led by Nirenberg, Holley, and Khorana formed the basis for deciphering the so-called genetic code (Nirenberg and Matthei 1961; Holley 1966; Khorana 1966-67). Just as DNA from very diverse biological sources generally contains only the four nucleotides A, T, G, and C, proteins from diverse sources are commonly made up of only twenty amino acids (the building blocks of proteins). The question then became: how could only four nucleotides code for twenty amino acids? That is, how long a sequence of nucleotides, and which arrangements of the nucleotides, were necessary to code for the twenty amino acids? Mathematically, one could argue that all possible combinations of four bases, taken one or two at a time, could account for only four or sixteen amino acids respectively; taken as triplets (codons), (4^3) or sixty-four arrangements could be predicted. This is more than enough to code for the twenty amino acids. However, the triplet code also provided for more than one code for a given amino acid. Some codons which did not code for amino acids were called "nonsense" or "missense" codons; it was hypothesized that they served as punctuations for the genetic alphabet or code. The finding that more than one codon could code for a given amino acid is referred to as "degeneracy" or "redundance" in the genetic code.

The concepts of degeneracy, missense, and nonsense are significant ones, since they provide an understanding of how the DNA of different organisms may code for the same amino acids. They also provide numerous ways to code not only for the composition but also for the unique arrangements or sequences of amino acids in the diverse proteins of those organisms. Researchers have the potential, by specifically rearranging, inserting, deleting, synthesizing, or transferring DNA sequences, to create novel research tools and useful products. Some of the key methods used by genetic engineers to isolate, characterize, and manipulate DNA will be discussed in the sections which follow.

Having in hand the information on the nature (that is, the composition and arrangement) of what constitutes DNA, the hereditary material, it has become possible for scientists to develop the means to further elucidate and regulate how, where, and when genes function. Genes are defined as discrete sequences of DNA which code for given biological molecules such as structural proteins and enzymes. The DNA is packaged free in bacteria and viruses, or in organelles (specialized cell parts) in eucaryotes (most DNA is in nuclei, but it is also found in mitochondria and chloroplasts). In higher organisms, DNA may additionally be located on plasmids (extrachromosomal, circular segments of self-replicating DNA) within organelles, or may be found free in the cytoplasm. In simple microbes such as bacteria, which lack a nucleus bounded by a nuclear membrane, the major cellular DNA is found in a single large circular chromosome. Microbes also commonly contain additional DNA as small, circular plasmids. Plasmids, which may code for functions such as antibiotic resistance or production, toxin production, or host range, have become the workhorses of molecular biology. They may be used in laboratory experiments as vectors which carry or introduce DNA from one organism to another. They may also be used to create "libraries" of genes, a process described later in this chapter.

Central Dogma

Scientists from many different scientific disciplines, including microbiology, biochemistry, genetics, and physics, have contributed to the development and elucidation of the central dogma of modern biology. This is that genetic information contained in the codons of DNA may be transcribed to a nucleic acid called messenger ribonucleic acid (m-RNA). Ribonucleic acid is very similar to DNA, but differs in several important ways: it is generally single-stranded, it contains the sugar ribose instead of deoxyribose, and it contains uracil (U) instead of thymine as one of the bases. Appropriate nucleotide base sequences in m-RNA can pair with and are said to be complementary to the DNA sequence. Thus, adenine in DNA will pair with uracil and guanine will pair with cytosine. The information or message in m-RNA sequences is translated or read on ribosomes. Ribosomes are the cellular sites for the assembly of amino acids into the peptides which comprise proteins. Thus, the messages in DNA sequences are transcribed into m-RNA sequences, which ultimately contain the information used to make given proteins. (Readers interested in more detailed information on DNA and RNA structure and on the processes of transcription and translation are referred to Darnell 1985; Doolittle 1985; and Felsenfeld 1985.) Figure 1.1 summarizes the concept of the central dogma.

ISOLATING GENES

Knowledge of the physical and chemical characteristics of desired DNA fragments--their sizes, shapes, and conformation--can aid in the selection of methods used to isolate and purify those fragments. Methods used to isolate and purify DNA are described in the following section.

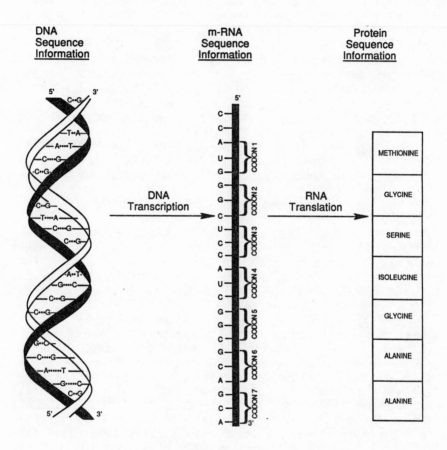

Figure 1.1 Central dogma. The genetic message contained in the nucleotides of DNA is transcribed into a strand of messenger RNA (m-RNA). The information in RNA is translated into sequences of amino acids which make up the protein encoded by the DNA. From "DNA" by G. Felsenfeld. Copyright 1985 by Scientific American, Inc. All rights reserved.

Isolating the DNA

Whether isolating DNA from the linear chromosomes of plant or animal cells or from simple bacteria, the cells must be broken open to release the DNA. Methods used to achieve that desired breakage may be physical (homogenization or pressure) or biochemical. The latter treatments may include solubilization with detergents or enzymes. Choice of the enzymes is based on the composition of the particular cells that are used. Cellulases and proteases may be used for plant materials; chitinase might be included for fungal samples; lysozyme is commonly used for both bacterial and animal tissue samples.

The DNA must then be separated from the cell walls, membranes, and other cellular debris. Methods commonly used to achieve that separation include simple centrifugation, often followed by density gradient centrifugation. Thus, if one takes a homogenate or fraction of a given cell or organellar type and applies it to a dense solution of sucrose or cesium chloride and spins the samples in a centrifuge, different cellular fractions of their component DNAs may "band out" on the gradient. Depending upon the degree of purification of the starting materials, and on the specific type of gradient used, the DNA may be seen with or without instrumental aid.

Localization of DNAs in the gradient may be by instrumental means (absorption at 260 nanometers [nm]) or visually, by means of fluorescence. In the latter case, ethidium bromide initially mixed with the cesium chloride binds to DNA. Since the DNA bound to ethidium bromide will fluoresce upon exposure to ultraviolet (uv) light, scientists can isolate particular size classes or conformations of DNAs on the gradients. The isolations are made by inserting a syringe into the side of soft plastic tubes used for centrifugation and withdrawing the bands visible in uv light. Alternatively, the tube bottom can be punctured to collect drops manually or mechanically. The fractions containing the highest uv absorbance (260 nm) are those containing the DNA.

Depending upon the degree of purity of the DNA that is required for given experimental needs, the gradient-purified DNA may be further purified and physically characterized (for example, for size) by means of electrophoresis in gels made up of agarose or of acrylamide. In the electrophoresis process, samples containing DNA are inserted into slots in a precast gel. A solution of a buffer contained in the wells of the electrophoresis apparatus acts as the conductant or electrolyte for the DNA molecules. As in the sucrose and cesium chloride density gradient methods, ethidium bromide DNA may also be added to the DNA sample, or later to the gel, to allow visualization and localization of desired DNA fragments upon exposure to uv light. Upon application of an electrical charge to the buffer in the electrophoresis apparatus, the DNA in the samples can be fractionated by size. Based on the purity, pretreatments, and size of the DNA, one or more bands of DNA may be seen upon examination under ultraviolet light, due to fluorescence of the DNA-ethidium bromide complexes and faster migration of smaller DNA fragments than of larger ones.

Characterizing the DNA

Once a genetic engineer has isolated DNA, it is often necessary to characterize or cut that DNA into specific, well-defined fragments. The tools that genetic engineers use to precisely cut DNAs are called restriction enzymes.

Restriction enzymes cut at specific places within given nucleotide sequences. For example, the restriction enzyme EcoRI, which is obtained from the bacterium Escherichia coli, recognizes the sequence GAATTC. The restriction enzyme BamHI, which is obtained from Bacillus amyloliquefaciens, recognizes GGATCC, and the restriction enzyme HindIII, which is obtained rom Haemophilus influenzae, recognizes the sequence AAGCTT. Similarly, other restriction enzymes recognize other nucleotide sequences.

By successfully cutting given DNA fragments with specific restriction enzymes, scientists can establish whether certain restriction sites or nucleotide sequences exist in a particular fragment of DNA. By sequentially using a series of restriction enzymes on a DNA fragment, the presence and order of the sites, as well as the size of the fragment, can be determined to create what is known as a restriction enzyme map. Restriction maps of plasmids commonly used as carriers or vectors to transfer genetic information from one piece of DNA to another or from one cell to another are well known. Characteristics used to describe plasmids include size, locations of restriction sites, promoters, antibiotic resistance genes, and ribosome binding sites.

Joining DNAs to Create Libraries of Genes

Knowledge of a vector's restriction map helps genetic engineers to decide which specific restriction enzymes to use to cut the DNA fragments both of the donor strain and of the plasmid or bacteriophage being used as a vector. By cutting both the donor DNA and the vector DNA with the same restriction enzyme, matching "sticky ends" or overhangs may be created in the donor and vector DNAs. By mixing the cut fragments of the donor and vector DNAs and allowing them to anneal (A will bind to T, G to C, as in the DNA double helix) a population of hybrid vector plasmids or fragments, collectively called a gene library, can be created. An enzyme called ligase, obtained from a bacterial virus (bacteriophage T4), is often used as a glue to seal the cut ends, thus annealing or splicing the donor and vector fragments to create hybrid or recombinant DNA (rDNA). Figure 1.2 depicts the use of a restriction enzyme and ligase to create rDNA fragments.

In order to identify the hybrid vector(s) which contain the desired genes from the donor DNA, methods are available to distinguish those vectors which have received inserts of the donor DNA (that is, have been transformed), and to distinguish which transformants actually contain the gene of interest. To identify the presumptive transformants, genetic engineers use methods which are amenable to screening large numbers of samples. These include the use of media selective for the growth of strains which have certain characteristics. Examples of selective media would be those which contain one or more antibiotics. Only strains carrying the genes which confer resistance to those antibiotics will be able to grow on those media. Thus, if the vector carried genes for resistance to ampicillin and tetracycline and the tetracycline site contained a unique BamHI site into which the donor DNA had been inserted or cloned, presumptive transformants would be resistant to ampicillin, but would have lost the resistance to tetracycline that was characteristic of the parental vector. Once presumptive transformants have been identified, those clones or colonies containing the donor DNA fragments must be screened to determine which ones actually contain the gene of interest. Screening of this so-called library of genes contained within the various presumptive transformant clones may require the use of nucleotide or immunological probes as "bait" to "fish out" or identify the desired clones or transformants.

Screening Gene Libraries

Screening of gene libraries is typically based on the use of specific probes to identify or isolate the clone of interest by binding to their DNA or RNA (nucleotide probe),

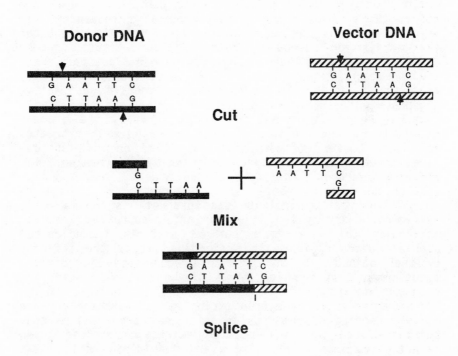

Donor DNA

Vector DNA

Cut

Mix

Splice

Figure 1.2 Use of a restriction enzyme and ligase to create a recombinant DNA fragment. The restriction enzyme EcoRI which recognizes the sequence GAATTC can make a jagged cut between A and G. When donor and vector DNA are cut with EcoRI "sticky ends" consisting of single strand overhangs of complementary bases are created. If donor and vector DNA are mixed, hydrogen bonds can form between the complementary bases. The enzyme ligase is used to splice together donor and vector DNA, creating recombinant DNA. From "The Molecules of Life" by R.A. Weinberg. Copyright 1985 by Scientific American, Inc. All rights reserved.

or to their protein product (immunological probe), respectively. The concept of nucleotide or hybridization probes is based in part on the specificity of the binding between A and T and G and C in DNA, or between A and U and G and C in RNA. It is also based on finding sequences of DNA that are unique enough to code for parts of given gene sequences which code for specific and unique parts of given proteins. Thus, knowledge of the amino acid sequence of a unique part of a desired protein gives a genetic engineer the information needed to synthesize a nucleotide probe coding for that unique sequence. Oligonucleotide probes (constructed of a chain of several nucleotides) chemically synthesized in the laboratory commonly contain radioactive phosphate and may be only twelve to twenty-four nucleotides long. Longer DNA probes may be prepared by the process known as nick-translation, in which isolated DNA is treated in liquid buffer containing a mixture of one ^{32}P nucleotide, three unlabeled nucleotides, and DNA polymerase. The radioactive DNA can then be isolated from the reaction mixture and used as a probe.

If the desired protein (gene product) is available in sufficient quantity for injection into laboratory animals, antibodies to the protein can be used as immunological probes. When probing with antibodies, it is the affinity of the antibody to the protein produced by the desired transformed clones which forms the basis of identifying clones of interest.

There are colony hybridization methods available which allow screening of numerous colonies of microorganisms containing cloned gene sequences by extracting nucleic acids directly onto membrane filters and hybridizing colony extracts with given nucleotide probes. The probes will bond only to those colonies containing exactly the same genetic information as that of the probe. Commonly used hybridization methods to confirm the identity of clones of interest are Southern blots (based on DNA-DNA hybridizations) and Northern blots (based on DNA-RNA hybridizations).

Immunological methods for the detection of clones producing proteins of interest include Western blots and dot-blotting methods. In Western blots, proteins from clones of interest are isolated and separated by polyacrylamide gel electrophoresis (PAGE), a procedure conceptually very similar to separation of DNA fragments on agarose gels, described earlier in this chapter. When the electrophoresis is completed, part of the gel typically is stained with a protein-specific dye. Following transfer of proteins in the remainder of the gel to special filters, the filters are flooded with an antibody solution. Clones which produce the desired protein will produce visible bands upon reaction with the antibody solution. The dot-blot immunological method assays total protein extracts rather than separated protein bands. Immunological detection methods may also include the use of radioactive iodine or linkage to enzymes (horseradish peroxidase or phosphatase) to enhance visualization and quantitation of the protein products of interest.

SYNTHESIZING AND ANALYZING GENES AND PROTEINS

Along with the conceptual and research advances of modern biology has come improved equipment to aid research and development efforts. Use of centrifuges and electrophoresis equipment have already been discussed. The following examples illustrate how knowledge of DNA and protein structure are being used to enhance genetic engineering efforts by both manual and automated procedures.

Synthesizing DNA

Short radioactively labeled sequences of DNA (for example, one to two dozen nucleotides long) are often used as probes for screening gene libraries. They may also be used to create defined genetic changes. Resultant mutations causing altered or shorter peptide sequences may result in proteins with a different specificity, with a higher desired level of activity, or in a higher level of production of a given protein. The knowledge which biochemists and genetic engineers use to create and introduce these sequences is based on the structure, particularly the sequences of nucleotides in DNA itself. If the restriction map of a given plasmid or donor DNA fragment has been determined, candidate sites for potential insertions or rearrangements can be selected. Prior to actually making a desired insertion, it may be necessary to treat either or both the incoming (donor) and recipient (vector) DNA fragments so that they may become joined or ligated. Such steps may include using a nuclease to make blunt end cuts and prevent the formation of sticky overhangs, using fill-in reactions to add given nucleotides, and adding given sequences of nucleotide linker fragments. The latter are particularly useful, since they may permit the joining of specific sequences of DNA overhangs, and thereby result in the creation of desired (unique) restriction sites for subsequent manipulations, including the insertion of synthetic and/or natural sequences.

Actual synthesis of given sequences can be done manually or automatically. In either case, the reactants are the same, as is the chemistry which governs the linkage of the major components: adenine, guanine, thymine, and cytosine. By attaching the first nucleotide to a solid support (for example, silica), and washing the solid support between reaction steps, nucleotides can be added stepwise. In repeated cycles consisting of condensation of 5' protected or 3' protected nucleotides and removal of a blocking group from one end, oligonucleotides of desired compositions and lengths can be constructed.

Sequencing DNA

Sequencing DNA is useful for identifying critical areas of genes and for confirming the quality of synthesized DNA. Sequencing can also provide information used to regulate gene expression, that is, to identify promoter and terminator sequences which may result in higher levels of production of desired gene products. Although restriction mapping can give some information about the sequence of given restriction sites in a DNA fragment, two methods (Maxam-Gilbert and Sanger) are among those commonly employed to determine the actual nucleotide sequence in given DNA fragments.

In the Maxam-Gilbert procedure, DNA with a radioactive label on one end of one of the strands is produced. A chemical agent (piperidine) is then used to cleave the DNA strand, which under different sets of reaction conditions creates a series of labeled fragments which differ in length. Following separation of the different size DNA fragments by polyacrylamide gel electrophoresis, their positions on the gel can be seen on X-ray film exposed by radiation emitted by the labeled DNA fragments. The sequence of bases on the analyzed strand of DNA is then used to determine the DNA sequence on the complementary strand.

In the Sanger procedure, the products of four separate DNA polymerization reactions are separated on a polyacrylamide gel. In each, one of the normal nucleotides is replaced by the corresponding 2',3'-dideoxynucleotides. The dideoxynucleotides cannot form a phosphodiester bond with the next incoming dinucleotide triphosphate, resulting in a cessation of growth of those particular DNA chains. In the presence of DNA polymerase, a short primer strand of DNA, complementary to the end of the DNA strand to be sequenced, initiates normal polymerization of dinucleotide-triphosphates. However, when dideoxynucleotide triphosphates included in the reaction mix are incorporated, elongation of the DNA ceases. By sizing the DNA fragments produced in these controlled reaction mixtures, the sequence of DNA in the fragment of interest can be deduced. The method typically uses the single-stranded bacteriophage M13 as the gene vector.

Synthesizing and Analyzing Peptides

Just as nucleotides are the building blocks of nucleic acids, amino acids are the building blocks of peptides and proteins. Knowledge and manipulation of DNA sequences can be used to create desired peptides. Alternatively, knowledge of protein or peptide structure can be used to deduce the DNA sequence required to code for given peptide sequences. With such information about proteins, genetic engineers can synthesize probes to isolate the genes coding for those sequences. They may also use that information to code for specific variants of those peptides. By analyzing the activity of proteins produced by altering the DNA sequence, it may ultimately be possible to produce useful novel drugs, hormones, pesticides, etc.

Analysis of the sequence of amino acids in a peptide involves the creation of chemical derivatives, phenylthiohydantoin (PTH) amino acids, to remove amino acids one at a time from the N-terminal portion of a protein. The PTH amino acids can be analyzed by various analytical means, including high-performance liquid chromatography (HPLC).

Synthesis of peptides is effected by sequentially joining amino acids. By stopping and starting reactions, desired sequences can be synthesized and later analyzed to confirm their sequence and purity. Key features of automated peptide synthesizers include synthesis on high-purity solid resin supports, creation of highly reactive symmetric anhydrides from the component amino acids, and automation of solvent washing and coupling steps. If bioassays of synthetic peptides produce desired effects, nucleotide sequences coding for those peptides can be synthesized and spliced into the DNA of organisms engineered to produce the desired useful novel peptides.

PRODUCTION AND USES OF MONOCLONAL ANTIBODIES

Injection of a protein antigen into a mouse results in the production of a mixture of (polyclonal) antibodies in the serum of the immunized mouse. If cultured mouse tumor (myeloma) cells are fused to normal spleen cells from immunized mice, hybrid cells result which produce a single type of antibody against the original protein antigen injected into the mouse. Continued growth of these somatic hybrid (hybridoma) cells in culture results in a homogeneous, indefinite supply of antibody to the original protein antigen. The resultant monoclonal antibodies are often superior to less specific mixtures of (polyclonal) antibodies which are produced simply by direct injection of the antigen into laboratory animals such as mice and rabbits.

Benefits associated with the use of monoclonal antibodies are the consistent, long-term production of a given antibody, rather than a mixture, and the specificity of their affinity or recognition of given protein antigens. It is this latter feature of high specificity that makes monoclonal antibodies attractive for use in genetic engineering research as well. Thus, following an initial screening of the protein products of a gene library with polyclonal antibodies or with a mixture of monoclonal antibodies, positive reaction with a monoclonal antibody would help pinpoint clones producing specific protein variants of interest. Antibodies are additionally useful in assays aimed at quantifying the level of expression of a desired protein from candidate clones. The effects of additional genetic manipulations, culture modifications, etc., could also be assessed in immunological assays which could help to precisely quantify the amount of desired protein produced by given clones.

ADVANTAGES AND APPLICATIONS OF RECOMBINANT DNA TECHNIQUES

If a single word could be chosen to summarize both the advantages and applications of rDNA and monoclonal antibody techniques, it would be specificity. In contrast to classical methods of mutagenesis, microbial, plant, or animal breeding and the standard production of polyclonal antibodies, rDNA and monoclonal antibody techniques offer greater specificity and predictability. Recombinant DNA technology offers the opportunity to cross formerly impenetrable genetic barriers to combine desirable characteristics within individual lines of microbes or cell lines of plants or animals. Specific applications of rDNA and monoclonal antibody technology lie not only in academic, medical, and industrial research laboratories, but in the marketplace as well.

Applications which have been proposed are for human and animal health care, food processing, plant agriculture, mining, waste management, and environmental cleanup. Specific examples in the health care area are insulin, growth hormones, interferons, anticlotting factors, vaccines, and antibiotics. In the veterinary area, growth hormones and vaccines are of particular interest. Food and beverage processing applications include using enzymes or biological additives from engineered microbes to improve taste, texture, or nutrient qualities. Diagnostic products are of interest for human, animal, and plant diseases. In plant agriculture, engineering of plants and microbes may increase the quantity and quality of crop yields by affording plants protection from diseases, insects, and environmental stresses. Environmental cleanup and reclamation applications include wipe-up or detoxification of accidental spills or waste streams, recovery of reusable resources, leaching of mining wastes, and biological conversion of biomass to provide energy sources. In summary, the applications of genetic engineering and immunological techniques are of high current and future interest for the diverse potential benefits they offer mankind.

REFERENCES

Avery, O.T., C.M. MacLeod, and M. McCarty. 1944. Studies on the Chemical Nature of the Substance Inducing Transformation of Pneumococcal Types. Induction of Transformation by a Deoxyribonucleic Acid Fraction Isolated from Pneumococcus Type III. Journal of Experimental Medicine 79:137-158.

Chargaff, E. 1950. Chemical Specificity of the Nucleic Acids and Mechanism of Their Enzymatic Degradation. Experimentia 6:201-209.

Darnell, J.E. 1985. RNA. Scientific American 253:68-78.

Doolittle, R.F. 1985. Proteins. Scientific American 253:8-99.

Felsenfeld, G. 1985. DNA. Scientific American 253:58-67.

Hershey, A.D., and M. Chase. 1952. Independent Functions of Viral Protein and Nucleic Acid in Growth of Bacteriophage. Journal of General Physiology 366:39-56.

Holley, R.W. 1966. The Nucleotide Sequence of a Nucleic Acid. Scientific American 214(2): 30-39.

Khorana, H.G. 1966-67. Polynucleotide Synthesis and the Genetic Code. Harvey Lectures 62:79-105.

Nirenberg, M.W., and J.H. Matthei. 1961. The Dependence of Cell-Free Protein Synthesis in E. coli upon Naturally Occurring or Synthetic Polyribonucleotides. Proceedings of the National Academy of Sciences 47:1588-1602.

Weinberg, R.A. 1985. The Molecules of Life. Scientific American 253:48-57.

ADDITIONAL SUGGESTED READINGS

Maniatis, T., E.F. Fritsch, and J. Sambrook. 1982. Molecular Cloning--A Laboratory Manual. Cold Spring Harbor Laboratory. Cold Spring Harbor, New York.

Old, R.W., and S.B. Primrose. 1980. Principles of Gene Manipulation--An Introduction to Genetic Engineering. Blackwell Scientific Publications. University of California Press, Berkeley and Los Angeles.

U.S. Congress. Office of Technology Assessment. 1984. Commercial Biotechnology--An International Analysis. Washington, DC.

Watson, J.D., J. Tooze, and D.T. Kurz. 1983. Recombinant DNA-- A Short Course. Scientific American Books. Distributor: W.H. Freeman and Co., New York.

Williamson, R. 1981-1983. Genetic Engineering. Vols. 1-4. London: Academic Press.

2. Gene Splicing Enters the Environment: The Socio-Historical Context of the Debate over Deliberate Release

Social controversy over genetic engineering has a lineage that dates back to the discovery of plasmid-mediated gene transfer (otherwise known as recombinant DNA molecule technology) by Stanley Cohen and Herbert Boyer in 1973. Subsequently, public debates have branched off in several directions, including the risks of laboratory hazards, ethical concerns over human gene therapy, anxiety over the development of biological weapons, the corporate transformation of academic biology, and the potential for adverse effects on humans or the biosphere by releasing genetically engineered life forms into the environment.

Over the past several years, industry and university proposals for field-testing genetically modified plants and organisms have triggered a major science policy debate in the United States that has spilled over to the European community. Those who have followed the recombinant DNA (rDNA) controversy from its inception will recognize that the current configuration of policy alternatives is a result of a ten-year historical process. Initially, molecular geneticists cast the problem of genetic engineering in technological terms. Gradually, public perception of the problems associated with applied genetics incorporated social, ethical, and ecological issues. The emergence of a second generation of genetics policy debates has brought participation from new disciplines, new communities, and new federal agencies. Safety concerns have shifted from the laboratory to the environment. And while these changes were taking place, regulatory oversight of biotechnology also shifted from the National Institutes of Health to other governmental bodies.

In this chapter, I shall place the debate over the deliberate release of genetically modified organisms into a

27

historical and sociopolitical context. First, I shall describe the path from Asilomar to the current state of regulations, highlighting key policy changes. Second, I shall
explore the factors that have propelled the issue to
national prominence. Third, I shall compare the earlier
and later genetics debates on issues such as community and
public interest involvement, the role of scientists in risk
assessment, and the normalization of regulatory control. I
shall begin by examining how the issue of deliberate release evolved out of the earlier rDNA controversy.

THE ROLE OF CONTAINMENT IN THE DEVELOPMENT OF THE rDNA GUIDELINES

For nearly a decade, the agency which assumed primary
responsibility for the safe uses of genetic engineering was
the National Institutes of Health (NIH). Essentially a
science-funding agency under the Department of Health and
Human Services, NIH established the Recombinant DNA Advisory Committee (RAC) in 1974 at the recommendation of Paul
Berg, the Stanford biologist who provided leadership in the
early efforts to assess the risks of rDNA research.
According to Berg's plan, an international meeting of
biologists (held at the Asilomar Center, Pacific Grove,
California) would result in a set of principles for safe
handling of rDNA molecules. Those principles were then to
be used by NIH's newly formed scientific advisory committee
to establish guidelines for all genetic experiments involving the cutting and splicing of foreign genetic material.
Berg, along with other scientists who organized the Asilomar meeting, sensed that if NIH did not act with dispatch
in responding to the potential risks of gene splicing, Congress might pass restrictive legislation. They viewed the
passage of such legislation as detrimental to the interests
of biology. First, biologists would lose influence over
the risk assessment and risk management process. Second,
the field of molecular genetics would become stigmatized as
the only discipline whose principal research method was
regulated. Third, there was considerable concern that rDNA
legislation would be inflexible and difficult to amend.
Asilomar organizers feared that biology would be saddled
with irrational requirements.
Written by scientists for scientists, the NIH guidelines were introduced in June 1976. No explicit references
were made to industrial processes or non-NIH-supported uses
of rDNA. The guiding principle behind the development of

the guidelines was containment. Since one could not predict with any reasonable degree of certitude that a foreign
gene introduced into an organism could not inadvertently
transform it into an epidemic pathogen, the consensus at
Asilomar was to construct a set of containment provisions
consisting of physical barriers, safety operations, and
carefully selected host organisms chosen because they do
not survive well outside of the laboratory setting. Each
containment level was matched with a class of experiments
that was permissible under the stipulated conditions. As
scientists on the RAC and elsewhere became more confident
in the safety of rDNA techniques, containment requirements
were substantially relaxed.

The early NIH guidelines contained a provision that
restricted industrial applications of rDNA technology.
Cultures of rDNA organisms produced or handled in volumes
greater than ten liters were classified as large scale and
prohibited for NIH grant recipients. The large-scale prohibition was not based upon a scientific assessment of
risk. It was a convenient threshold introduced by academic
scientists to protect the use of standard laboratory beak-
ers in basic research.

A second provision of the NIH guidelines restricted
industrial activity by explicitly proscribing the intentional release of an rDNA organism into the environment.
Since absolute containment was nothing more than an ideal-
ization, unintentional releases were considered unavoid-
able. However, by limiting the volume of rDNA culture, the
probability of escape could be minimized. Also, since the
volume of agent released is correlated to survival and
propagation, the large-scale prohibition also supported the
general containment strategy.

Commercial interests in rDNA techniques grew rapidly
in the mid-1970s (Kenney 1986). Inventories of industry
growth vary. My own count discloses that a minimum of
fourteen new biotechnology firms were formed in 1976, the
year the NIH guidelines were introduced. By 1979, biotechnology firms grew by at least twenty-six; and in 1981, a
minimum of sixty-six new firms entered the biotechnology
industry (Krimsky 1984; compare OTA 1984, p. 93).

NIH had no legal jurisdiction over the research in
private companies. In practice, however, firms were not
willing to risk the negative publicity that might arise if
they violated the NIH guidelines. This was an industry
comprised of small firms started by young scientists and
seasoned molecular geneticists. The close link between
academia and industry may help explain the high degree of

compliance among new biotechnology firms with the standards adopted by NIH. Despite a watchful media, there is no evidence that the NIH guidelines were flaunted by the biotechnology industry. The few cases where violations of the guidelines were reported took place at universities.

Between 1976 and 1979, the NIH process for overseeing rDNA research was put to its severest test. First, the city of Cambridge, Massachusetts issued a moratorium on rDNA experiments requiring moderately high physical and biological containment. After a widely publicized citizen review process, the city passed the country's first rDNA law in 1977. The law departed from the NIH guidelines in a few minor ways. More important, it symbolized the city's right to exercise control over this new area of research.

After the Cambridge rDNA law was passed, nearly two dozen states and local communities debated the issues. Legislation was enacted in about half the jurisdictions. In response to local events and a national mood of concern toward gene splicing, more than a dozen bills were filed in Congress to regulate rDNA research. Some of these bills would have shifted the regulatory authority from NIH to a national commission. These bills also varied in the degree to which local laws were subject to federal preemption. Congress spent two years debating the issue of an rDNA law. A compromise bill finally was voted out of committee early in 1978, but, for lack of congressional interest, it failed to reach the House or Senate floor for a vote.

Congressional forfeiture to enact legislation strengthened NIH's position as the sole agency overseeing rDNA activities. Responding to a continuing public concern over the research, the Department of Health, Education, and Welfare (DHEW, currently Health and Human Services) rewrote the RAC's charter and increased the size of the committee from sixteen to twenty-five. The new charter, issued in 1978, stipulated that one-third of the committee was to consist of individuals with expertise and interest in public health and the environment. The change in the composition of the RAC drew sharp criticism from prominent scientists who argued that rationality was being compromised by including nonscientists in what was essentially a technical process. When the expanded RAC met in early 1979, its agenda was filled with petitions for relaxing containment requirements and approving additional host-vector systems.

Over the next few years, three policy changes at NIH led the way to a review of deliberate release experiments: the introduction of a voluntary compliance program; the end of the list of prohibitions, including large-scale rDNA activities; and the intentional release of genetically altered strains into the environment.

VOLUNTARY COMPLIANCE PROGRAM

After the defeat of federal legislation, there was a strong residue of public and congressional criticism that federal rDNA rules were not designed to protect society from the potential adverse consequences of commercial gene splicing. In response, NIH developed a voluntary compliance program. This initiative gave the fledgling biotechnology industry the opportunity to gain the imprimatur from NIH for both laboratory- and commercial-scale rDNA work. A firm wishing to participate in the program first submitted the composition of its institutional biosafety committee (IBC) to NIH's Office of Recombinant DNA Activities for approval. Once IBC approval came, a firm could file requests with the RAC, following procedures similar to those of university petitioners.

One difference between academic and industry proposals is that, on the occasion of the latter, the RAC went into closed session. Members were required to sign confidentiality pledges for the protection of information deemed proprietary by the firm. Some RAC members were opposed to having the committee review proposals in closed session. They argued that the oversight of the private sector was the responsibility of those agencies of government with statutory authority to protect workers, public health, and the environment. NIH lacked authority to carry out these functions.

A firm that registered its IBC with NIH under the voluntary compliance program was under no legal requirement to submit its rDNA experiments for RAC review. Nevertheless, many biotechnology companies considered it in their long-term interest to secure RAC approval for their rDNA activities. Regardless of how the firm's management felt about the potential risks of gene splicing, submitting experiments for NIH approval was excellent public relations. The voluntary compliance program helped the biotechnology industry respond to the criticism that the private sector was operating without regulations. When pressed by local communities to justify the safety of genetic experiments, a company's most compelling response was that it complied with the NIH guidelines.

In the wake of sporadic episodes of local opposition to genetic engineering research, the biotechnology industry sought a predictable and stable regulatory climate, but one that would not impede research and development. NIH contributed to this goal, but with limited success. The voluntary compliance program proved functional to the industry during its early years of development when there was intense competition, investment instability, and the uncertainties of local regulation. As the commercial activities progressed from laboratory research to product development, NIH policies accommodated the new stage of industrial activity. But a new initiative of public activism also emerged.

LARGE-SCALE PROHIBITIONS

Provisions were built into the early NIH guidelines for waiving the large-scale prohibition in cases where minimal risks were balanced against important societal benefits. The wording of the prohibition was clarified in the 1978 version of the NIH guidelines. No exceptions to the prohibition against the production of large-scale cultures were permitted "unless the recombinant DNAs are rigorously characterized and the absence of harmful sequences established" (DHEW 1978).

For a short period of time, the NIH gave serious attention to all phases of large-scale work with rDNA molecules. Proposals submitted to the RAC were required to include a description of laboratory practices, specifications on physical and biological containment, risk data, characterization of genes, and the design of the fermentation equipment in conjunction with the physical description of the facility. In 1980, the RAC published a standard that it planned to use for reviewing large-scale proposals (DHEW 1980).

The committee's role in evaluating plant design and operations for large-scale fermentation drew criticism from some members. They argued that the RAC should confine itself to advising NIH on the nature of biological procedures and not on plant operations. The committee, after all, had no special expertise in bioprocess safety engineering. It depended on outside consultants for guidance in this area. Also, it was a matter of no insignificance that molecular biologists on the RAC found the review of plant design boring and uninformative.

Other RAC members contended that if the voluntary compliance program was to mean anything, a comprehensive review of large-scale operations was essential. Since no other federal agency was engaging in this review, they believed that it was NIH's responsibility to fill the regulatory void.

The internal debates over this issue were a poignant reminder of NIH's ambivalence in serving as overseer of commercial genetic engineering. These debates also cast doubt on NIH's capacity to guide a nascent industry exclusively through a system of voluntary measures. The peculiar nature of this regulatory program began to reveal its contradictions. For example, within the RAC, opposing factions exchanged positions. Initially, the group most skeptical about the safety of genetic engineering expressed opposition to the RAC's review of industrial proposals, particularly large-scale ones. They reasoned that NIH was acting as de facto regulator without enforcement powers or congressionally derived authority. If the RAC refused to serve this function, members of this faction believed that agencies like the Occupational Safety and Health Administration (OSHA) and the Environmental Protection Agency (EPA) would enter the field.

Concurrently, there were other members of the RAC who opposed broader federal involvement in biotechnology, particularly legislative or rule-making actions. They viewed NIH's continued role in overseeing commercial rDNA work as essential to preempting such initiatives.

An unexpected reversal took place among committee members around 1980. The pro-regulatory group grew less sanguine about the involvement of other agencies in regulating biotechnology. As a consequence, this faction began supporting a stronger role for the RAC. Meanwhile, the committee's regulatory minimalists, also confident that broader agency involvement was unlikely, backed an NIH role over commercial rDNA activities that was limited to issues of pure genetics, namely, sequence characterization and approval of host-vector systems.

The regulatory minimalists succeeded in limiting the RAC's review of the safety of rDNA products exclusively to the science. By 1981, firms taking part in NIH's voluntary compliance program no longer were obligated to submit data on sterilization of their fermentation system or on procedures for disposal of rDNA cultures. This policy change was expressed in a proposition adopted at the September 1980 RAC meeting (RAC 1980): "The RAC will determine if a

given recombinant DNA-containing strain is rigorously characterized and the absence of harmful sequences is established. Such a determination shall include specification
of a containment level. These determinations should not in
any way be construed as RAC certification of safe laboratory procedures for industrial scale-up."

The potential release of rDNA organisms through the
effluent of bioreactors did not attract any public attention. While EPA had jurisdiction over such biological releases under the Clean Water Act, a constituency for agency
action did not develop. The newly formed Committee for
Responsible Genetics published an article on biogenetic
waste in its public interest bulletin GeneWatch (Vogel
1985). However, the issue of biogenetic waste was not a
rallying point among environmentalists or the general public. It seemed to lack some important features. First, it
did not impart a clear and present environmental danger.
Second, the waste stream, even if it carried genetically
engineered organisms, did not excite the media. Bioef-
fluent was not intentionally designed to alter nature.
Since science writers are captivated by the frontiers of
science, there wasn't much of a story in fermentation
sludge.

Quite a different media and public reaction took place
when proposals appeared before the RAC requesting approval
to field test genetically modified plants and bacteria.
There is an informative distinction to be made in the public reaction between intentional and nonintentional releases of genetically modified life forms. To fully grasp
the distinction, we have to look at the kinds of experiments proposed, the types of media coverage they were
given, the role of scientists in raising safety concerns,
and the development of a public interest constituency.

DELIBERATE RELEASE

As the RAC reduced its oversight over industrial bio-
processes, it became more active in reviewing environmental
releases of organisms produced by rDNA techniques. As a
consequence, field testing was given greater visibility in
the media. From 1980 to 1984, when companies and university scientists were preparing to field test their products, NIH was the only federal agency with active responsibility over deliberate release experiments involving genetically altered plants or microorganisms.

Progressive relaxation of the rDNA rules finally led to the removal of barriers to field testing. The revised NIH guidelines of 1982 eliminated the entire list of proscribed experiments. The prohibition against intentional release of rDNA organisms was replaced by a multitiered review process. Submissions for deliberate release required approval by the RAC, the IBC, and the NIH director, in addition to various subcommittees.

Agricultural applications of biotechnology, widely publicized in the media, were being readied for field trials. By December 1983, the RAC had reviewed and approved three proposals for releasing genetically altered life forms. In each case, the committee concluded that the tests contributed no significant risk to health or the environment (Milewski and Talbot 1983).

The first three proposals for deliberate release came from university scientists and therefore did not involve proprietary information. In March 1980, a Stanford University scientist requested approval from the RAC to field test a corn plant into which had been inserted the corn storage protein gene with modified sequences. The new corn protein gene encodes all the amino acids essential to humans (including an enhancement of lysine and methionine, in which corn is deficient). By genetically engineering the new corn protein with the full complement of the essential amino acids, its value to the human diet would be improved. The RAC failed to come up with a hazard scenario for the genetically modified corn; nevertheless, the investigators were required to detassel the plant to prevent pollen dispersion during the field trials. Permission for the test was granted on August 1981. There was no significant public reaction to the decision.

A second proposal for field testing was brought to the RAC by a Cornell University scientist in June 1982. Tomato and tobacco plants were transformed with DNA from yeast and Escherichia coli to confer them with antibiotic resistance. In reviewing the experiment, the RAC raised concerns about the possible spread of antibiotic resistance and the effect of an itinerant plant on the ecology. Neither of these concerns delayed the committee's approval, which it gave on October 25, 1982. When the recommendation reached the director of NIH, he referred the proposal to the U.S. Department of Agriculture (USDA) for a reading. After USDA approval was given on February 1983, NIH approved the field test in April 1983, nearly a year after the proposal was first brought to the RAC.

The third of the early field-trial proposals for genetically modified life forms proved to be the most controversial. Ironically, it was viewed by some experts to be among the safest deliberate release experiments one could perform in the environment. There was one important distinction between the first two proposals and the third: the latter consisted of genetically altering a soil bacterium. The difference between plants and bacteria proved to be a critical factor in the public perception of risk. Also, there was an established tradition of introducing hybridized plants into the environment. However, no analogous tradition existed for microorganisms. The relative novelty of this field test was reflected in the RAC's review.

In September 1982, scientists at the University of California at Berkeley proposed to field test two soil organisms (Pseudomonas syringae pv. syringae and Erwinia herbicola) from which about a thousand base pairs of DNA sequences had been deleted. In their natural state these organisms synthesize a protein that provides a nucleation point for ice crystallization. By excising the genes responsible for ice nucleation and establishing the genetically modified organism in the environment, scientists believed they could reduce the temperature at which frost begins to form on crops.

When the proposal for field testing the microbes with the deleted ice crystallization gene (denoted by INA⁻ or ice minus) was first brought before the RAC, one member expressed concern about the role the organisms might play in the environment. Questions raised about the effect of INA⁻ on precipitation patterns were based on some theories that INA⁺ plays a role in atmospheric weather. The precipitation issue was not resolved by the committee. Nevertheless, the RAC approved the field test, although by a small plurality (seven yes, five no, two abstentions). When the recommendation was transmitted to the director of NIH, more data along with additional safeguards were requested. Several months later, on the second round of review, the RAC approved the proposal unanimously. NIH gave the final go-ahead for the field test on June 1983, some nine months after it had initially received the proposal.

Investigators agreed to mark the strains of the ice minus organism with antibiotic resistance, which allowed them to monitor the dispersal of the organism. They also agreed to limit field testing to a single location, the University of California agricultural field station at

Tulelake in Northern California, a site isolated from the major fruit tree and citrus growing regions of the state. Despite these precautions, the RAC's decision on the field test for ice minus proved to be a poor predictor of community response.

GENETIC ACTIVISM THEN AND NOW

In the mid-1970s, when rDNA molecule research was still an exotic technique, the public entry into the debate over its safe uses was determined by several factors. First and foremost, a group of distinguished biologists called attention to the new technique by publishing letters in science journals that caught the attention of the popular press. The international meeting at Asilomar was attended by science writers, whose coverage of the events dramatized the disagreements among biologists at the meeting. In drawing attention to the new discovery, the Asilomar organizers did not intend the fate of the new technology to be decided by popular acclamation or democratic process. However, some biologists, frustrated by NIH's role in setting safety standards, brought their concerns to university campuses and local communities. To the public, it appeared that scientists were polarized on the dangers of rDNA research.

Second, the issues were dramatized through the world press in the controversy that erupted in Cambridge, Massachusetts, which pitted community values against the interests of national science (Krimsky 1986). The 1976 Cambridge rDNA controversy represented the birth of public involvement in genetic engineering. Prior to that, the issues were debated on university campuses, notably the University of Michigan.

Third, national environmental groups such as Friends of the Earth, the Environmental Defense Fund, and the Sierra Club devoted some attention to genetics issues between 1976 and 1979. But the commitment by these groups was limited to a single staff person. Their activities were met with skepticism, and in some cases, disapproval by some board members.

Fourth, but to a lesser extent, litigation had drawn public attention to the issues. Two suits were filed against DHEW/NIH in 1977. A resident of Frederick, Maryland petitioned the court to enjoin NIH from performing a risk assessment experiment until an environmental impact statement was prepared. A second suit filed by Friends of the Earth alleged that DHEW failed to comply with the requirements of the National Environmental Policy Act when it established policies for rDNA research.

Fifth, congressional interest in the safety of rDNA research intensified in the mid-to-late 1970s. House and Senate hearings provided a forum for activist scientists and environmental lobbyists. The accumulated effect of these factors resulted in heavy media coverage for both local and national events related to gene splicing experiments.

The public debate over the deliberate release of genetically engineered organisms has been fostered by a similar configuration of factors, namely, scientist-critics, litigation, environmental coalitions, local opposition to experiments, and congressional interest. However, the old and new rDNA debates differ in the weighting of these factors. For example, on deliberate release, Jeremy Rifkin, head of the Washington, D.C.-based Foundation on Economic Trends, has been remarkably effective in drawing public attention to the environmental and ethical issues associated with genetic engineering. Operating with the modest resources of his non-profit public interest organization, Rifkin has utilized a variety of organizing techniques, including confrontational protests, litigation, and short-term coalition building, to dramatize breaking issues in genetics and public policy.

Rifkin's philosophical opposition to genetic engineering: "Genetic engineering represents the ultimate negation of nature" (Rifkin 1983, p. 252; 1985, p. 74) can be found in his writings and media accounts that feature his work. On genetics policy, he has had more impact on the media than any single group or individual in the United States. His notable success as a publicist and genetics critic can be explained by several factors. Rifkin can act quickly, since he is not accountable to a board of overseers or a mass organization. He is able to identify and capitalize on the weakest link of any policy process. With properly timed and targeted litigation, Rifkin can strike at the jugular of the bureaucracy. He has proven time and again that a well-placed lawsuit is a magnet for media attention. Rifkin made his national debut as a genetics activist in 1977 when he and a group of supporters invaded a meeting at the National Academy of Sciences (NAS) devoted to rDNA science and policy. His strategy at the Academy is best described by the 1960s term "guerrilla theater," a dramatically staged political confrontation. Fearing major disruption of its conference, the Academy allotted Rifkin time at the start of the program for a statement (NAS 1977, pp. 18-21). Meanwhile his associates, donning silk stocking face masks, stood like motionless icons, projecting a grotesque apparition of human mutants.

On another occasion, Rifkin organized a signature campaign of scientists and religious leaders who were asked to support a statement against genetic manipulation of the human germ line. The list of supporters included individuals of vastly different ideological persuasion. To have such a politically diverse group on the same side of an issue was itself a news event. It proved worthy of a front page story in the New York Times.

In the fall of 1983, when the RAC was reviewing a proposal for field testing ice minus, Rifkin brought national attention to the problem of deliberate release by filing suit against NIH on the grounds that its approval was given prior to a full study of the environmental consequences. His suit was supported by two organizations, Environmental Action and the Environmental Task Force. To strengthen his case, Rifkin received sworn affidavits from leading ecologists who opposed the release of the ice minus strains, at least until more could be learned about the environmental consequences.

Rifkin's lawsuits have been rallying points for critical debate on genetics issues. Philosophically, he personifies the modern genetics Luddite. But on a practical level, he has made effective use of environmental law to impose a greater burden of responsibility for risk assessment. Ironically, he is secretly applauded by many who, while they might differ with him philosophically, find a certain degree of relief in slowing down the clock of regulation. Environmental groups, skeptical about deliberate release, have been hesitant to act more aggressively because the hazards of genetic engineering are still hypothetical. For Rifkin, it is less important to prove that the hazards exist than to rally support against the hubris of science. In his view, it is a question of who knows best, nature or science.

There is a striking comparison between the old and new genetics controversies on the role of scientific participation. In 1976, the molecular geneticists were taken to task for not calling upon infectious disease epidemiologists to evaluate the risks of transforming E. coli into an epidemic pathogen. Subsequently, the infectious disease community did participate in the risk evaluation.

Similarly, ecologists played no role in the rDNA debate until the controversy over deliberate release erupted. Their entry into the discussion over deliberate release came when the social and political context was ripe for their participation. Ecologists are viewed as natural allies to environmentalists; when the latter became involved in the debate over field tests, they sought advice from the former. Also, the House Committee on Science and Technology made specific recommendations to NIH and USDA that they revise the memberships of their advisory committees to include individuals specifically trained in ecology and environmental sciences (U.S. House of Representatives 1984).

Finally, EPA began developing its own policy on deliberate release in the early 1980s. The agency is accustomed to working with ecologists, for example, in evaluating pest control methods. The first genetically engineered organisms planned for environmental release were classified as biological control agents. EPA began hiring consultants to study the potential environmental problems of releasing such agents. A terrestrial ecologist from Oak Ridge National Laboratory, Frances Sharples, completed a study for EPA in 1982 on the effects of the introduction of organisms with novel genotypes into the environment (see Chapter 4). Microbial ecologist Martin Alexander of Cornell University chaired an EPA study group on biotechnology. In 1984, ecologists participated in an EPA-sponsored workshop at the Banbury Center at Cold Spring Harbor, New York, on the evolutionary consequences of biotechnology. Also in 1985, with support from EPA, USDA, national environmental organizations, and corporations, ecologists, geneticists, public interest representatives, and federal regulators met for four days at Cornell's biological field station in Bridgeport, New York to develop principles of containment for genetically engineered organisms tested under field conditions (Gillett 1987).

By raising the issues of biotechnology in the national media, the Foundation on Economic Trends also helped catalyze the concerns and perspectives of ecologists on the problems of deliberate release, particularly those who had not been brought in as consultants to the major agencies. Eventually, letters from ecologists appeared in Science (Colwell et al. 1985; Odum 1985), followed by responses from geneticists (Brill 1985; Szybalski 1985). A dialogue was opened between molecular geneticists, microbiologists, and ecologists on their approaches to risk assessment

(Halvorson et al. 1985; Sharples 1987; Davis 1987). Soon it became evident that the issues over ice minus had unfolded into a larger debate about scientific culture, epistemology, and disciplinary hegemony.

EARLY COMMUNITY REACTIONS TO FIELD TESTS

The Cambridge rDNA controversy was ignited by a newspaper article describing plans by Harvard University to build a new containment laboratory for genetics research. Ten years later, residents of Monterey County, California learned from reports in the media that their community was the site of a field test for a genetically engineered soil bacterium, under the trade name Frostban^{TM}. The subsequent events in these cases were similar in several key respects. The local authorities in both communities expressed dismay that they were not fully informed of the planned events and that their consent had not been sought. Neither community was persuaded by the fact that federal approval was given for the respective activities. Both in Cambridge and Monterey County, local residents perceived gaps or inconsistencies in the regulatory process. In evaluating the potential risks, citizens were drawn to worst-case scenarios. Finally, both communities sought a moratorium on the experiments to provide sufficient time for local residents to review the risks and benefits. The Cambridge rDNA controversy is discussed in Krimsky (1982).

Monterey County reacted to the field test of ice minus out of a general mood of apprehension to genetic engineering that existed throughout the country. The media emphasized that this was an experiment with unknown risks. Jeremy Rifkin, already an international personality, communicated concerns that Frostban^{TM} could alter rainfall patterns. The general population reads about a public activist suing industry and the government to prevent the release of organisms. Stories are carried in the leading dailies such as the New York Times and the Washington Post. Most people who are not intimately acquainted with the issue and do not have a financial interest in the industry are likely to respond rather conservatively, particularly if their community is the chosen site for the field test.

Residents of Monterey County were in a reactive position when they learned about the field trials of

Frostban™, since they were uninformed about the test untilshortly before it was supposed to take place. The site of the release was kept confidential, according to the company, on the grounds that a genetic pirate could obtain a sample of the microorganism. The elaborate discussions evaluating ice minus that took place at the RAC and EPA were of little consequence to a community that wished to satisfy itself about the risks. Beyond the skepticism that local governments have exhibited toward federal protection of health and environmental quality, there were additional factors that reinforced local reaction. The Monterey County Board of Supervisors received a letter from twenty-seven members of the West German Parliament which advised the board to forbid the release of ice minus. The German Green Party transformed the field test of Frostban™ into an event of international environmental significance. These conditions were more than sufficient to fan the fires of public apprehension.

When the issue broke in the local press, the media carried quotes from Monterey residents expressing a cultural view about risk that was not represented at the federal level. One resident wrote that "the new technology conjures up images of a science fiction thriller where the creation of mad scientists threaten the delicate balance of nature and our ecosystem" (Manning 1986). Other technological episodes in Monterey's history were recounted as a warning against the field test. Some residents recalled EPA's approval of the pesticide DBCP, a carcinogen that caused sterility among male factory workers. The pesticide contaminated several sources of drinking water in the county. Although DBCP has a mode of action quite distinct from that of ice minus and was subject to a very different kind of risk assessment, the episode of its misuse, etched in the consciousness of an environmentally sensitive community, provided an important context within which the field test of Frostban™ was viewed. The Board of Supervisors eventually voted to postpone the test until the county completed its own assessment.

The EPA, in conjunction with state environmental agencies, has exclusive authority over pesticide regulation under federal pesticide statutes. Nevertheless, citing its legal powers over land use, the Monterey Board of Supervisors issued an interim ordinance restricting any field testing of genetically engineered products. In the aftermath of its study, the Board of Supervisors debated passage of a county ordinance governing the deliberate release of genetically engineered organisms. To date, no action on the resolution has been reported.

When the City of Cambridge passed an ordinance regulating rDNA research, about a dozen cities and towns and two states responded with their own laws (Krimsky 1979). Monterey County's opposition to the field test also had an effect on other communities. The town of Tulelake, California, near the Oregon border, was chosen as a site to test another strain of ice minus developed by a team of University of California scientists. Apprised of the Monterey events, local residents of Tulelake opposed the spring 1986 testing date. Initially postponed for three months, the field test was eventually delayed for a year while caught up in litigation. Local farmers spoke out against the test not because they believed the organism was harmful, rather, they feared that the public might boycott farm products from the area, by associating the deliberate release of genetically engineered products with events like Chernobyl and Three Mile Island.

A simulation of the field test was carried out at Tulelake in northern California in late July 1986. Scientists released the naturally occurring INA$^+$ of Pseudomonas syringae with an antibiotic resistance gene for monitoring its dispersal. The plan called for monitoring the organism in air, soil, water, and on plants. The release of INA$^-$, scheduled for Tulelake on University of California land, was challenged by Rifkin in state court. He won a suspension of the release on grounds that state environmental agencies did not issue a permit or an environmental impact assessment for releasing and transporting the genetically modified organisms.

Public opposition to the field tests in Monterey County were also being monitored by residents in St. Charles, Missouri. This city was chosen by Monsanto to field test a genetically engineered pesticide. The organism is a strain of Pseudomonas fluorescens with an added gene that synthesizes a toxin which kills corn rootworms and cutworms. In March 1986, the St. Charles City Council unanimously approved a resolution requesting Monsanto to move the test site from that community.

One month after an EPA scientific advisory panel voted favorably on the Monsanto field test (Schneider 1986a), the agency announced that it would not permit the company to initiate the experiment until additional safety tests were completed (Schneider 1986b). The Monsanto field test is still on hold as the company decides whether it will continue to develop its biological pesticide. The California nia protests made EPA somewhat more cautious in its approval of an environmental release.

When scientists from the University of California at Berkeley and Advanced Genetic Sciences (AGS) in Oakland, California finally received EPA approval for field testing ice minus, they became entangled with community politics and litigation. In response to a court settlement, the University of California issued an Environmental Impact Review on February 20, 1987. Meanwhile, AGS turned away from Monterey County as a site for the field test. The company approached several other communities in different California counties, publicly announcing that it would not test in any area where there was local opposition. Support for AGS came from the Contra Costa County Board of Supervisors for a test site near Brentwood, California.

A coalition of groups including Earth First, the Berkeley Greens, and the Foundation on Economic Trends sought an injunction to block the field test, but their challenge was denied by a California Superior Court. On the morning of April 24, 1987, amidst a torrent of media coverage, a scientist at AGS sprayed genetically modified ice minus bacteria on strawberry plants in a field near Brentwood, California, culminating a five-year effort that began with the first governmental review. Less than a week later, University of California at Berkeley scientists supervised a parallel test on potato plants at Tulelake. The second test was barely noted in the national media, confirming the threshold hypothesis--namely, that after the first precedent-setting deliberate-release experiment, media attention will rapidly decline.

Public images of genetically engineered organisms running amok are strikingly similar for the older and newer genetics controversies. However, the emphasis of risk perception changed from human health to ecology. One of the early concerns of the rDNA controversy was the creation of a carcinogenic organism that could run rampant among the human population. For ice minus, the worst-case risks were described as changes in precipitation patterns.

As genetic technology moved from the laboratory to the field, the ecological, regulatory, and social environments have become more complex. In response to the increasing levels of complexity, a new policy was issued by the Executive Office of the President on June 26, 1986. The purpose of this policy was to provide a unified and coordinated framework for regulating products of the new technology (see Chapter 10).

SCIENCE POLICY AND BIOTECHNOLOGY

For a half-dozen years, the National Institutes of Health served as the exclusive regulatory body over genetic experiments, although it had no legal jurisdiction over the private sector. Starting in 1984, when EPA issued its interim policy on microbial pesticides, federal agencies began to articulate more clearly their policies toward biotechnology. EPA asserted its authority over deliberate releases of genetically modified organisms, including release in field tests. FDA developed a policy covering rDNA-produced drugs. USDA has worked closely with NIH in reviewing genetically engineered plants, but has not found it necessary to develop any additional regulations beyond those it already uses for conventional products. A report issued by the U.S. General Accounting Office (GAO) in 1985 estimated that eighty-seven projects involving genetically engineered plants and organisms funded by USDA would be ready for environmental release within a few years (GAO 1985).

The problems of regulating biotechnology are manifold. They range from incomplete or inadequate laws, to imprecise definitions, to a lack of scientific basis for risk assessment. For example, EPA has cited the Toxic Substances Control Act (TSCA) as one of its strongest instruments for regulating deliberate releases of genetically engineered products. However, EPA's authority under the Act is contingent upon whether the term "chemical substance and mixtures" can be interpreted to cover biological agents (McGarity 1985). Thus far, EPA's interpretation of TSCA's relevance to the products of biotechnology has not been subject to legal challenge.

Beyond the legal issue of jurisdiction, all the rules under TSCA were made for chemicals. If TSCA is applied to biologicals, an entirely new set of definitions and standards must be developed in response to questions such as: What constitutes a release into the environment? What organisms should be regulated and under what criteria? What changes in an organism constitute a new entity? How do we assess the risks of releasing novel organisms into the environment?

Another obstacle to sound regulation is that "predictive ecology" is in its infancy. Ecologists generally agree that there is an insufficient scientific basis for predicting how genetically modified organisms will behave in the environment. EPA's Study Group on Biotechnology stated that the principles governing dispersal and persistence of genetically engineered organisms are not known.

Only after these principles are discovered, they added, might it be possible to develop reliable risk assessments (EPA 1986). It remains unclear, however, whether generalized theories that can predict the ecological consequences of released organisms are discoverable. While these issues are being debated among scientists, ecologists and regulators have advocated a case-by-case approach to environmental assessment. Some have argued that broad exemptions should be applied to the case-by-case approach to avoid cumbersome regulations (Miller 1987).

Another difficulty that has plagued the regulatory process is the lack of consistency and coordination among the responsible agencies. The history of chemical regulation is testimony to the confusion that arises when each agency operates under a different standard of risk analysis (NAS 1985).

To address these problems, the Office of Science and Technology Policy (OSTP) issued a Coordinated Framework for Regulation of Biotechnology (OSTP 1986) (see Chapter 10). Several years in the making, the framework is the first serious effort by OSTP to provide guidance to the regulatory sector. OSTP set overall regulatory responsibilities for each agency without recommending new laws. The framework established the Biotechnology Science Coordinating Committee (BSCC), which is responsible for "coordination and consistency of scientific policy and reviews." Thus, as part of its role, the BSCC has initiated a scientific vernacular for biotechnology that is recommended but not mandatory for all agencies. It has proposed definitions for "new organism," "pathogen," "release into the environment," and "genetically engineered organism." OSTP outlined four responsibilities of the coordinating committee (OSTP 1985):

- Serve as a forum for addressing scientific problems, sharing information, and developing consensus.

- Promote consistency in the development of federal agencies' review procedures and assessments.

- Facilitate continuing cooperation among federal agencies on emerging scientific issues.

- Identify gaps in scientific knowledge.

The BSCC does not stand above the independent regulatory bodies. It is comprised of high-level administrators from the agencies with jurisdiction over biotechnology. The coordinating committee can conduct analyses that extend beyond the scope of any individual agency; it can hold public hearings and issue recommendations. However, it does not have the status of a "Super RAC" as originally conceived in the first draft of the OSTP proposal.

What is gained by the OSTP coordinated biotechnology framework? From the standpoint of the administration, it communicates to Congress that the executive branch has given serious attention to the regulatory problems of biotechnology. The OSTP initiative is likely to diminish the chances of congressional action, such as the establishment of an independent commission on biotechnology or the passage of new laws. By establishing formal lines of communication among the key agencies and fixing regulatory boundaries, the new framework is designed to reduce the chances of interagency squabbles. Finally, the OSTP plan places a burden on the agencies with statutory responsibility over biotechnology to complete the task of their policy development.

How will the coordinated framework affect public confidence in biotechnology? As regards the openness of the process, the new structure was not designed to broaden public participation in the policy review. Under the proposed framework published in 1984, the Biotechnology Science Board, colloquially referred to as the Super RAC, was to be comprised exclusively of scientists. Critics of that structure emphasized the importance of mixing public members with scientists. For example, McGarity (1985, p. 54) argued: "Because it will inevitably have a direct role in setting public policy for biotechnology, the 'Super RAC' should include persons with expertise in public policy and lay persons...." In the final OSTP proposal, the Biotechnology Science Board was replaced by the BSCC. Thus, a second-tier scientific advisory committee was jettisoned in favor of an interagency coordinating group. The question of public representation on this body became moot.

Within each of the individual agencies, a biotechnology advisory committee, like that of the RAC for NIH, might have public members. For example, in its biotechnology policy USDA has inaugurated several new administrative entities. The Agriculture Biotechnology Recombinant DNA Advisory Committee (ABRAC) is supposed to parallel the role of the RAC for the Department of Agriculture. But the agency has also created the Committee on Biotechnology in Agriculture (CBA), which is designated as a scientific and policy review panel (OSTP 1986, p. 23344). Moreover, USDA does not describe public representation on either of these panels, despite the widely held conclusion that gaps in the science will be filled with policy judgments (OSTP 1986, pp. 23336-23347).

Judged by community opposition to deliberate release, there is clearly a confidence gap over biotechnology that divides the regulatory sector from ordinary citizenry living in areas designated for field tests. A survey of public attitudes toward biotechnology, which reported that sixty-seven percent of environmental organization leaders would allow field tests, fails to account for the strength of local opposition to deliberate release (Miller 1985). The early survey, however, does reflect the recent support AGS's Frostban^{TM} test received from residents and local officials in those communities where informed consent and public education were given high priority.

OSTP's framework offers little potential for narrowing communication barriers or risk perceptions between the technosphere and either communities or public interest/ environmental groups. The policy statements published in the coordinated framework hardly take cognizance of the warnings by ecologists that immense knowledge gaps exist in our understanding of deliberate releases of novel organisms. The risks still remain conjectural, as they were a decade ago when NIH initiated a historically unique process of technology assessment. The NIH model, which is now being emulated by other agencies, provides continuity between the old and new genetics policies. However, the intent of these policies has changed significantly over ten years. Originally, rDNA organisms were designed to be contained; now they are being prepared for release, activation, and growth in the environment.

Thus far, the public's apprehension about this technology has been expressed principally through local community protest against deliberate releases, and a call for better risk assessment by environmental/public interest groups and independent ecologists. The industrial sector interprets the local opposition as a threshold phenomenon; industrialists contend that once the first few tests are completed, the opposition will disappear and deliberate releases will become commonplace. Industry spokespersons draw their optimism in part from a bullish investment market in biotechnology, and secondarily from the fact that neither laboratory nor industrial hazards resulting from the uses of genetic engineering have been revealed. That optimism is also nourished by an administration that views biotechnology as an important area for U.S. industrial growth. Thus, while one segment of society is expressing doubts about exposing the environment to releases of genetically modified life forms, another is investing heavily in the promise of biotechnology. As investment pressure builds and new products are submitted for field tests, policy debates over the appropriate criteria for risk assessment will continue for a number of years, well after the first releases have taken place.

Social controversy is sometimes a sign of growth. This is where I find a deeper meaning to the deliberate release episode. Biotechnology is on trial because of what it represents. It is perhaps the first modern example of a technology that is being evaluated in anticipation of hazards. Until now, the social guidance of technology has been predicated on known risks or clear and present dangers. However, the rationale for the social regulation of deliberate release experiments is based upon conjectured, hypothetical, or unanticipated hazards. While we are still struggling with the problems of nuclear waste, reactor safety, and industrial chemicals, society is properly asking whether we can do better in controlling the potential adverse effects of genetic technologies. This has led to some provocative questions: Do we have the wisdom to anticipate negative consequences before damage is done or before there are irreversible effects, when the hazards are purely hypothetical? How long should we delay the development of a technology or any of its by-products to satisfy ourselves of its safety?

The deliberate release episode may be heralding the start of a new morality toward technology. The moral questions, more than the scientific, are most vexing. Science can provide us with some answers, but it cannot tell us how much science is necessary to satisfy public confidence. It is a sign of the maturation of our technological culture that these questions are arising at this time, and maturation is rarely a smooth process. The intensity of the policy debate is a measure of how serious we are in pursuing the new moral direction. The older morality would have us intervene when the hazards were obvious. In stark contrast, the new approach makes a deliberate effort to screen out potentially adverse consequences. However, this approach imposes some heavy burdens and responsibilities, including a commitment to a predictive ecology, or at least a prospective technology assessment; a set of procedures for the review of new products that draws upon broad multidisciplinary expertise and that allows for effective public participation; monitoring products for a long time after

50

they have been approved; and providing sufficient resources
to the regulatory sector for carrying out scientific
research, product review, and monitoring of ecosystems.

Genetic engineering is the first major transforming
technology to have appeared since the birth of the modern
environmental movement in the late 1960s. The potential of
the technology had been discussed for a decade before
genetically modified plants and organisms were developed
for environmental release. Final resolution of the deliberate release question will serve as an important precedent
for setting the proper balance between innovation and protection, for establishing a dialogue and a common base of
understanding among different scientific disciplines, and
for communicating the technical issues to the public.

ACKNOWLEDGMENTS

I wish to acknowledge the Center for Environmental
Management, Tufts University and the U.S. Environmental
Protection Agency for their partial support of this
research.

REFERENCES

Brill, W. 1985. Genetic Engineering in Agriculture.
(Letter.) Science 229:115-117.

Colwell, R.K., E.A. Norse, D. Pimentel, F.E. Sharples, and
D. Simberloff. 1985. Genetic Engineering in
Agriculture. Letter. Science 229:111-112.

Davis, B.D. 1987. Bacterial Domestication: Underlying
Assumptions. Science 235:1329; 1332-1335. March 13.

DHEW. 1978. Recombinant DNA Research: Revised
Guidelines. Department of Health, Education, and
Welfare. National Institutes of Health. Federal
Register 43(247): 60108-60131. December 22.
Abbreviated DHEW/NIH, 1978.

---. 1980. Physical Containment for Large-Scale Uses of
Viable Organisms Containing Recombinant DNA
Molecules. Federal Register 45(72): 24968-24971.
Abbreviated DHEW/NIH, 1980.

EPA 1986. Report of the Study Group on Biotechnology. Environmental Protection Agency. Assessing EPA's Biotechnology Information Needs. 1-8. January.

GAO. 1985. Biotechnology: The U.S. Department of Agriculture's Biotechnology Research Efforts. General Accounting Office. 1-80. October.

Gillett, J.W. (Ed.). 1987. Prospects for Physical and Biological Containment of Genetically Engineered Organisms. Proceedings of the Shackelton Point Workshop on Biotechnology Impact Assessment, October 1-4, 1985. Ithaca, NY: Ecosystems Research Center, Cornell University. March.

Halvorson, H.O., D. Pramer, and M. Rogul (Eds.). 1985. Engineered Organisms in the Environment: Scientific Issues. Proceedings of a symposium held in Philadelphia, PA, June 10-13, 1985. Washington, DC.: American Society for Microbiology.

Kenney, Martin. 1986. Biotechnology: The University-Industrial Complex. New Haven: Yale University Press.

Krimsky, Sheldon. 1979. A Comparative View of State and Municipal Laws Regulating the Use of Recombinant DNA Molecule Technology. The Recombinant DNA Technical Bulletin 2(3): 121-125.

---. 1982. Genetic Alchemy. Cambridge, MA: MIT Press.

---. 1984. Corporate-Academic Ties in Biotechnology. GeneWatch 1(5&6): 3-5.

---. 1986. Research Under Community Standards: Three Case Studies. Science, Technology & Human Values 11(3): 14-33.

Manning, William W. 1986. Letter. Salinas Californian. January 22.

McGarity, Thomas O. 1985. Regulating Biotechnology. Issues in Science and Technology 1(3): 40-56. Spring.

Milewski, E., and B. Talbot. 1983. Proposals Involving Field Testing of Recombinant DNA-Containing

Organisms. Recombinant DNA Technical Bulletin 6(4): 141-145.

Miller, H. 1987. The Case for Qualifying "Case by Case". Science 236-133.

Miller, J.D. 1985. The Attitudes of Religious, Environmental and Science Policy Leaders Toward Biotechnology. 1-68. Dekalb, IL: Public Opinion Laboratory, Northern Illinois University. April 8.

NAS (National Academy of Sciences). 1977. Research with Recombinant DNA. Washington, DC: National Academy of Sciences.

---. 1985. Risk Assessment in the Federal Government: Managing the Process. Washington, DC: National Academy Press.

Odum, E.P. 1985. Biotechnology and the Biosphere. Letter. Science 229:1338.

OSTP. 1985. Coordinated Framework for Regulation of Biotechnology; Establishment of the Biotechnology Science Coordinating Committee. Office of Science and Technology Policy, Executive Office of the President. Federal Register 50(220): 47174-47176.

---. 1986. Coordinated Framework for Regulation of Biotechnology. Federal Register 51(123): 23302-23350.

OTA. 1984. Commercial Biotechnology: An International Analysis. Office of Technology Assessment. Washington, DC: U.S. Government Printing Office. January.

RAC. 1980. Minutes of Meeting. Recombinant DNA Advisory Committee. September. Abbreviated: RAC 1980.

Rifkin, J. 1983. Algeny. New York: Viking Press.

---. 1985. Declaration of a Heretic. Boston: Routledge and Kegan Paul.

Schneider, K. 1986a. Panel Endorses Field Test of Gene-Altered Pesticide. New York Times. April 26.

———. 1986b. U.S. Delays Test of Gene-Altered Pesticide. New York Times. May 21.

Sharples, F.E. 1987. Regulation of Products from Biotechnology. Science 235:1329-1332.

Szybalski, W. 1985. Genetic Engineering in Agriculture, Letter. Science 229:112-113.

U.S. House of Representatives, Committee on Science and Technology, Subcommittee on Investigations and Oversight. 1984. The Environmental Implications of Genetic Engineering. Washington, DC: U.S. Government Printing Office.

Vogel, S. 1985. Biogenetic Waste: A Federal and Local Problem. GeneWatch 2(4-6): 7-9.

3. The NIH Guidelines and Field Testing of Genetically Engineered Plants and Microorganisms

INTRODUCTION

The technique known as recombinant DNA (rDNA) or gene cloning was developed in the early 1970s. Using this technique, genetic information from virtually any source, no matter how unrelated, may be recombined and introduced into living cells. Recipient cells are potentially capable of maintaining and expressing this information and passing the information to their progeny.

Although humans have been manipulating the genetic information of other species for over 10,000 years to develop a vast array of crop plants, domesticated animals, and microbes, with rare exceptions the genetic information exchanged has been limited to members of the same or closely related species. The rDNA technique, however, can be used to overcome or circumvent phylogenetic constraints which previously restricted the transfer of genetic material.

The considerable potential of this powerful technique was immediately apparent and led thoughtful scientists, aware that similar breakthroughs in chemistry and physics had negative as well as positive impacts, to raise questions about possible hazards and to request guidelines for the use of rDNA technology. The National Institutes of Health (NIH) responded by developing its Guidelines for Research Involving Recombinant DNA Molecules.

The original NIH guidelines were directed to laboratory research utilizing the rDNA technique, since the earliest applications were laboratory experiments to address and elucidate basic questions in biology. Other uses of the technology soon became apparent, however. Some of these uses involved application in the environment of modified plants, animals, and microbes. As the number of these proposed environmental applications increased, the NIH guidelines were modified to address field testing of modified organisms, and documents indicating the type of information which should be submitted for review were developed. This chapter reviews the history of the NIH guidelines, with particular emphasis on environmental applications.

HISTORY OF THE NIH GUIDELINES FOR RESEARCH INVOLVING RECOMBINANT DNA MOLECULES

The initial discussions about the potential impact of rDNA technology began before the technique had been used enough to permit the ramifications of employing the technique to be evaluated from a strong data base. The discussions, however, raised enough concern that scientists asked first for a moratorium on some types of experiments; second, for the development of guidelines for the use of rDNA technology; and third, for the convening of an international conference of experts to discuss the issues.[1,2]

The international conference was convened in February 1975 at the Asilomar Conference Center in California. The final report of the conference suggested that rDNA experiments in the laboratory might proceed, but biological and physical containment standards should be assigned to each experimental protocol on the basis of perceived conjectural risk.

The Recombinant DNA Advisory Committee (RAC), which had been chartered in 1974 by the NIH to provide advice on rDNA technology, met on the day following the Asilomar meeting and proceeded to develop guidelines for rDNA research. These guidelines were intended to apply to laboratory research, and included biological and physical containment standards. The NIH called a public meeting to discuss the proposed guidelines. Many distinguished scientists and public representatives were invited to participate, and others came voluntarily to testify. The proposed guidelines, testimony, public comments, and observations were analyzed by the NIH, and the initial version of the NIH Guidelines for Research Involving Recombinant DNA Molecules was issued in July 1976.[3]

Approximately two and one-half years elapsed between the issuance of the original guidelines in 1976 and the first major revision in December 1978. During that period, a series of scientific and public meetings demonstrated a consensus that the guidelines were needlessly restrictive. To reflect this consensus, the NIH in December 1977 proposed to revise the guidelines. Scientific experts participated in the revision process, and a new version of the guidelines was published for public comment in July 1978.[4] A public hearing chaired by the General Counsel of the Department of Health, Education, and Welfare (then DHEW, now Department of Health and Human Services [DHHS]) was held in September 1978 to examine this revised document. The guidelines, modified to reflect these two and one-half years of discussion, were reissued on December 22, 1978.[5]

The revised version of the guidelines contained a major procedural modification which provided flexibility: a mechanism by which to amend and modify the guidelines. Under this mechanism, a proposal to modify any section or to introduce new language into the guidelines must be published for public comment in the Federal Register at least 30 days before a RAC meeting. The proposal and any public comments are then discussed by the RAC in open public session. A final decision on the proposal is rendered by the Director of NIH after consideration of RAC recommendations.

Using these procedures, modifications in the guidelines have been made following most RAC meetings held since December 1978. Several major revisions of the guidelines have been issued since 1978:

- In January 1980, a revision which substantially modified the status of the host-vector systems (Escherichia coli K-12, Saccharomyces cerevisiae) used at that time in the majority of rDNA experiments necessitated the reissuance of the guidelines.[6]

- In November 1980, the guidelines were reissued when the procedures to register rDNA experiments were modified.[7]

- In July 1981, the guidelines were reissued to reflect a revision exempting from the guidelines those host-vector systems (E. coli K-12, S. cerevisiae, asporogenic Bacillus subtilis) used at that time in approximately eighty to ninety percent of laboratory rDNA experiments.[8]

- In April 1982, a major revision resulted in a general lowering of containment requirements. This revision originated from an April 1981 proposal to convert the NIH guidelines into a "code of standard practice."[9] The proposal would have reduced containment to the P1 level for most rDNA experiments, with the exception of prohibited experiments, and would have eliminated the mandatory aspect of the guidelines. Although the RAC did not endorse this proposal when it was presented, there appeared to be some agreement that a major reevaluation and reorganization of the guidelines should be undertaken. A Working Group on Revision of the Guidelines was convened in June and July of 1981 to develop a proposal to modify the guidelines. The proposal advanced by the working group recommended a general lowering of containment requirements, but suggested the mandatory aspect of the guidelines be maintained. The proposal was presented to the RAC in September 1981.[10] During the discussion, the RAC developed a proposal which amalgamated portions of the earlier April 1981 proposal with the working group proposal. This proposal was published in the Federal Register of December 4, 1981 to elicit public comment on the concept of converting the guidelines to a code of standard parctice.[11] An alternative proposal developed by the chairperson of the Working Group on Revision of the Guidelines appeared in the December 7, 1981 Federal Register.[12] This proposal was based on the document, "Evaluation of the Risks Associated with Recombinant DNA Research," which had been generated by the working group.[13]

Although the proposals differed in several features, the major distinctions between them were whether the guidelines would continue to be mandatory for institutions receiving NIH funding and whether the institutional biosafety committees (IBCs) would continue their oversight function.[14] At the February 1982 meeting,[15] the RAC endorsed the latter proposal. NIH accepted the RAC recommendation to maintain the mandatory nature of the guidelines[16] and issued revised guidelines.[17]

● In August 1982, the guidelines were reissued[18] to fulfill the recommendation the RAC made at the February 1982 meeting that the Working Group on Revision of the Guidelines simplify further and modify the April 1982 version of the guidelines.

- A June 1983 revision added to the guidelines Appendix K, Physical Containment for Large-Scale Uses of Organisms Containing Recombinant DNA Molecules, and Appendix L, Release into the Environment of Certain Plants.[19]

- In the November 1984 revision, Appendix G, Physical Containment, was modified, and a new section III-A-4 addressing transfer of rDNA into humans was added.[20]

Table 3.1 (see pp. 75-78) describes the salient differences between the major revisions of the guidelines.

APPLICABILITY OF THE GUIDELINES

The original 1976 guidelines were binding on investigators whose research was supported by the NIH. Investigators receiving funds from other sources, including other federal agencies, were not obligated to adhere to the NIH guidelines. In July 1976, Senators Jacob Javits (D-NY) and Edward Kennedy (D-MA) wrote to President Gerald Ford urging that "every possible measure be explored for assuring that the NIH guidelines are adhered to in all sectors of the research community." In reply, President Ford described the creation of the Federal Interagency Committee on Recombinant DNA Research. The Committee was composed of all the federal agencies which might either fund or regulate rDNA research (Table 3.2), and provided the communication necessary to coordinate activities related to rDNA research. All the federal agencies participating in the committee endorsed the NIH guidelines, and departments which supported or conducted rDNA research agreed to abide by the NIH guidelines.

The 1976 guidelines were also silent concerning compliance by industry or other private institutions. Efforts were made in the 95th Congress to legislate national regulation of rDNA. Such legislation would have uniformly affected rDNA research in both the public and private sectors. These efforts, however, did not result in legislation. In the absence of national legislation, the NIH, with the endorsement of the Federal Interagency Committee, provided a mechanism for voluntary compliance by the private sector. Part VI of the guidelines, Voluntary Compliance, which was added in January 1980, formally encouraged voluntary compliance by the private sector and specified

60

TABLE 3.2
Departments and Agencies Which Participated in the Federal
Interagency Committee on Research Involving Recombinant DNA
Activities*

Arms Control and Disarmament Agency	Department of the Interior
	Department of Justice
Department of Agriculture	Department of Labor
Department of Commerce	Department of State
Department of Defense	Department of Transportation
Department of Energy	Environmental Protection Agency
Department of Health and Human Services	Executive Office of the President
• Office of the Assistant Secretary for Health	National Aeronautics and Space Administration
• Centers for Disease Control	National Science Foundation
• Food and Drug Administration	Nuclear Regulatory Commission
• National Institutes of Health	Veterans Administration

* As of December 1980.

how NIH would protect proprietary information voluntarily
submitted. No penalties are specified in Part VI of the
guidelines for noncompliance.

INTERAGENCY COORDINATION AND EFFECT OF ACTIVITIES IN OTHER
AGENCIES

As the pace of commercial applications accelerated,
activities in agencies other than NIH influenced oversight
of rDNA technology. In 1984, the Cabinet Council on Natural Resources and the Environment established an inter-

agency working group (the Cabinet Council Working Group on Biotechnology, which has since been reorganized under the Domestic Policy Council) to study and coordinate the government's policy for regulating products of rDNA technology. On December 31, 1984, this interagency working group published a _Federal Register_ notice which, among other things, was to provide a concise index of U.S. laws related to biotechnology and to clarify the policies of the major regulatory agencies that would be involved in reviewing research and products of biotechnology.[21]

In the December 31, 1984 _Federal Register_, the U.S. Environmental Protection Agency (EPA) described its intention to regulate certain microbial products of biotechnology under the Federal Insecticide, Fungicide, and Rodenticide Act (FIFRA) and the Toxic Substances Control Act (TSCA).[21] The U.S. Department of Agriculture (USDA) described its intention to regulate biotechnology products under the following statutes: the Virus Serum Toxic Act of 1913 (21 USC 151-158), the Federal Plant Pest Act of May 23, 1957 (7 USC 150aa-150jj), the Plant Quarantine Act of August 20, 1912 (7 USC 1551-164, 166, 167), the Organic Act of September 21, 1944 (7 USC 147a), the Noxious Weed Act of 1974 (7 USC 2801 et seq.), the Federal Seed Act (7 USC 551 et seq.), the Plant Variety Act (7 USC 2321 et seq.), the Federal Meat Inspection Act (21 USC 601 et seq.), and the Poultry Products Inspection Act (921 USC 451 et seq.). These two agencies would regulate environmental releases of genetically modified organisms.

Because other federal agencies had begun to assume new roles in the review of proposals, NIH announced its intention in the November 22, 1985 _Federal Register_ to exercise the option of deferring to the review and approval of other agencies on proposals involving rDNA molecules.[22] If experiments in this category were submitted for review to a federal agency (other than NIH), the submitter was to notify NIH; NIH would then determine whether such review served the same purpose as NIH review.

THE NIH GUIDELINES AND FIELD TESTING OF GENETICALLY MODIFIED PLANTS AND MICROORGANISMS

Intentional release, including field testing, of organisms containing rDNA is considered a special category of experiments under the NIH guidelines. The original version of the NIH guidelines issued in 1976 specified that experiments involving "deliberate release into the environment of any organism containing a recombinant DNA molecule" were "not to be initiated at the present time." In the first revision of the guidelines in 1978, this specification became section I-D-4, which prohibited "deliberate release into the environment of any organism containing recombinant DNA," but which allowed individual waivers to be approved by the Director of NIH following publication of proposals in the Federal Register for comment and review by the RAC. In the April 1982 version of the guidelines, section I-D-4 became section III-A-2; experiments under this section had to have "RAC review and NIH and IBC approval before initiation."

Several proposals involving the field testing of organisms modified through the rDNA techniques were received, reviewed, and approved by the NIH during the years 1980 through 1985.[23,24,25] The proposals reviewed by NIH are listed in Table 3.3.

DEVELOPMENT OF GUIDELINES FOR FIELD TESTING OF CERTAIN PLANTS

With the growing recognition that genetic engineering systems were being developed to modify plants genetically and that field testing of modified plants was a necessary step in developing novel varieties, over a two-year period the RAC and its working groups constructed guidelines for field testing of certain modified plants.

At its January 21, 1983 meeting, the RAC Working Group on Revision of the Guidelines recommended that guidelines for field experimentation involving plants modified by rDNA techniques be developed for consideration at the April 11, 1983 RAC meeting.[26] In response to this recommendation, the RAC Plant Working Group prepared a document which was published in the March 4, 1983 Federal Register.[27] The proposed language described conditions under which certain types of modified plants could be field tested and the review procedures which would be followed.

The guidelines in force at the time the proposal was constructed required RAC review and NIH approval, as well as the approval of the local IBC for the "deliberate release into the environment of any organism containing recombinant DNA." The proposal developed by the Plant Working Group would have changed this requirement, so that if investigators met certain criteria, field testing of certain plants modified in specific ways by rDNA techniques could proceed with IBC approval under section III-B without

TABLE 3.3 Proposals Involving Field Testing of Modified Organisms Submitted to NIH for Review[a]

Proposal	Submitter	Date of Submission	Date of RAC Review	Date of NIH Approval
A request to field test corn plants (Zea mays) which had been transformed by corn DNA or modified corn sequences cloned in E. coli or S. cerevisiae host-vector systems.	Stanford University	02/09/1980	06/06/1980	08/07/1981
A request to field test tomato and tobacco plants transformed with bacterial and yeast DNA. Pollen would be used to mediate transformation of the plants with plasmid vectors.	Cornell University	06/09/1980	10/25/1982	04/15/1983
A request to construct and field test Pseudomonas syringae pv. syringae and Erwinia herbicola to biologically control frost damage in plants. All or part of the genes involved in ice nucleation would be deleted.	University of California, Berkeley	09/17/1982	10/25/1982 04/11/1982	06/01/1983
A request to construct and field test Pseudomonas strains to biologically control frost damage in plants.	Advanced Genetic Sciences, Inc.	03/22/1984	06/01/1984	Voluntarily withdrawn
A request to field test tobacco plants grown from seeds containing recombinant DNA for resistance to crowngall disease.	Cetus Madison Corporation (now Agracetus, Inc.)	05/05/1983	09/19/1983	11/13/1985

[a]These proposals all involve field tests in defined locations under specified conditions.

RAC review and NIH approval. The IBC would be required to notify the NIH Office of Recombinant DNA Activities of all approvals.

Plants covered by the proposed action would be annual species of a cultivated crop of a genus that has no species known to be a noxious weed; the latter specification was included because the tendency of a plant to develop "weedy" characteristics might follow taxonomic classifications. Cultivated crops were specified because more is known of their genetics and behavior when they are introduced into the environment. The vector could consist of DNA from (1) host-vector systems exempt under Appendix C of the NIH guidelines, (2) plants of the same or closely related species, (3) non-pathogenic prokaryotes or non-pathogenic lower eukaryotic plants, (4) plant pathogens, if sequences known to cause disease symptoms had been deleted, or (5) a combination of (1) to (4). The DNA to be introduced into the plants would be well-characterized and contain no sequences harmful to humans, animals, or plants. The proposal indicated that antibiotic resistance genes might be introduced as selectable marker traits if stable integration into the host DNA was known to occur. Most crop plants with the exception of potatoes and rice would be covered by the proposal.

The RAC considered the proposal at its April 11, 1983 meeting and discussed it extensively.[28] The RAC modified several specific scientific and procedural criteria of the proposal. One modification eliminated the language limiting the use of antibiotic resistance traits as selectable markers to situations in which integration into the host DNA was known to occur; the RAC reasoned that the restriction specified by the guidelines on the introduction of antibiotic resistance markers into microbial pathogens was reasonable, but the logic of the restriction could not be applied to plants. Language limiting the species to annuals was deleted because of potential ambiguity--crops exhibit varied growth habits (e.g., perennial, biannual), and no greater risk to the environment could be envisaged by modified longer-season crops. The RAC also added language to the document that required the investigator to develop procedures to assess "spread" of plants containing rDNA. In modifying the procedural aspects of the proposal, the RAC recommended creation of a new appendix to the guidelines, Appendix L. Appendix L would require review and approval of experiments both by the IBC and by the RAC Plant Working Group.

The exact language of Appendix L was subsequently developed by NIH staff based on the recommendations made at the April 11, 1983 RAC meeting. At the request of NIH, the USDA Recombinant DNA Committee reviewed the RAC recommendation, including proposed Appendix L, and unanimously endorsed adoption. The NIH subsequently accepted these recommendations.[29] In June 1983, Appendix L was added to the guidelines, and section III-A-2 was modified to require RAC review and NIH and IBC approval before initiation of experiments involving "deliberate release into the environment of any organism containing recombinant DNA, except certain plants as described in Appendix L."

Subsequently, the RAC Plant Working Group proposed an amendment of Appendix L-II-C. Appendix L-II-C describes the type of vector which might be used to introduce DNA into plants. The working group requested a modification of the specification that the vector may consist of DNA "...from plant pathogens only if sequences causing disease have been deleted...." The proposed modification would specify that the vector may consist of DNA "...from plant pathogens only if sequences resulting in production of disease symptoms have been deleted...."

The proposed amendment of Appendix L-II-C was published in the August 16, 1983 <u>Federal Register</u> for comment.[30] The RAC discussed this proposed modification at its September 19, 1983 meeting.[31] At that meeting, it was noted that under the original language, review by the Plant Working Group might have to be conducted using the strictest interpretation of the word "disease." A strict definition might preclude use of some plasmid and virus-derived nucleic acids as vectors under Appendix L, since the simple replication of the DNA might be construed as a disease process, even though no symptoms would develop in the plants. Furthermore, in some cases, DNA sequences causing disease symptoms might be necessary to introduce the rDNA into the plant; these symptom-causing sequences can be removed from the plants before the plants are tested in the field. Under the proposed modification, data showing these sequences had been eliminated would be evaluated by the Plant Working Group. The RAC agreed that if all other stipulations of Appendix L were satisfied, this minor change would result in no greater probability of risk to the environment from field testing plants containing rDNA than from testing the same plants without rDNA. The RAC recommended the proposed modification, and the NIH modified Appendix L-II-C of the guidelines.[32] Appendix L currently reads as shown in Table 3.4 (see pp. 79-80). It should be noted that proposals involving plants which are not covered by Appendix L may be reviewed on a case-by-case basis under section III-A-2 of the NIH guidelines.

DEVELOPMENT OF A "GUIDANCE DOCUMENT" FOR SUBMISSIONS UNDER APPENDIX L

In order to provide guidance for individuals preparing submissions under Appendix L of the guidelines, the RAC Plant Working Group subsequently began to prepare a "working" document outlining the type of information the working group would require of the investigator. The first version of the guidance document listed requirements which included--but were not limited to--common and scientific names, data on plant homogeneity, strain designations, methods by which vectors would be constructed, the use of host organisms, and monitoring. The first version of the "working" guidance document was sent by the Plant Working Group to the RAC for its consideration at the February 6, 1984 RAC meeting.[33] During the discussion, several comments and recommendations were made concerning the requirements specified in the document. The document was then sent for review to the RAC Working Group on Release into the Environment. This group, at its April 9, 1984 meeting, introduced several modifications into the document.[34] At this meeting, the concept that the document should deal only with submissions under Appendix L was firmly implemented; other documents dealing with microorganisms or with weeds would be developed by the NIH at a later date. The working group categorized submission requirements under three major headings: description of plant materials, vectors and method of introduction, and characteristics and monitoring of plants.

Although the guidance document was not envisaged as being incorporated into the NIH guidelines, interested parties requested that the document be published for public comment prior to the June 1, 1984 RAC meeting. In response to that request, the guidance document was published in the April 24, 1984 Federal Register.[35]

The document was again reviewed and modified by the Working Group on Release into the Environment at its May 31, 1984 meeting.[36] As the document developed, several concepts were further clarified. In discussing the use of disabled pathogens to transmit the vector to the plant, the working group felt consideration should be given to intrinsic characteristics of the vector, as well as to any physical measures that might be used to prevent these microorganisms from regaining or acquiring pathogenic potential. The working group modified the language of the guidance document to reflect this concern. The group also modified the document to require that morphological data gathered over two generations be supplied where feasible. This requirement was qualified to indicate such information be supplied where feasible or appropriate because in some crop plants, such as pine trees, the generation time is long, and data generated over two generational cycles would be difficult to obtain in the career span of a single investigator. In discussing the earlier versions of the document, the working group emphasized that the word "abnormality" was not used in the sense of pathology, but rather in the sense of abnormalities in physiology. In order to clarify this concept, the working group deleted the word "abnormality" and requested submission of physiological data.

The document, as modified at the May 31, 1984 meeting, was discussed by the RAC at its June 1, 1984 meeting.[37] Some minor modifications were introduced by the RAC, and the document was titled "Points to Consider for Submissions Under Appendix L." The RAC indicated that this document was to serve as advice to individuals or groups submitting proposals for review under Appendix L of the guidelines. The guidance document currently reads as shown in Table 3.5 (see pp. 81-83).

A "GUIDANCE DOCUMENT" ADDRESSING FIELD TESTING OF
GENETICALLY MODIFIED MICROORGANISMS

Proposals involving field testing of modified microorganisms fall under section III-A-2 of the guidelines, which requires RAC review and NIH and IBC approval of proposals before initiation. In order to provide guidance for individuals preparing submissions involving field testing of microorganisms modified using rDNA techniques, in the fall of 1984 the RAC Working Group on Release into the Environment began to prepare a "working" document outlining the types of information which would be appropriate for submission review. This document, generated over a nine-month period, is shown in Table 3.6 (see pp. 84-90).

The first meeting at which the group would approach the task of developing a points-to-consider document for field testing of microorganisms was scheduled for October 5, 1984. Prior to this meeting, a subgroup of the Working Group on Release into the Environment constructed a preliminary draft "strawman" document by telephone conference calls on September 14 and September 21, 1984. The following points were included in the preliminary draft: a summary of the experiment, including objectives, significance, and justification; a description of the parental organism; the genetic manipulation, the inserted DNA, and the method of introduction; the characteristics of the modified organisms; the properties of the modified organism as compared to the wild-type parental strain; and the effect of the modified organism on target and non-target plants, animals, and inanimate objects.[38]

The full working group met on October 5, 1984, and considered the concepts offered in the preliminary document.[38] The working group restructured the points-to-consider document, basing the new document on portions of the subgroup preliminary draft, and portions of a draft version of the "Points to Consider in the Preparation of TSCA Premanufacture Notices for Genetically Engineered Microorganisms" which the EPA had offered to the working group to elicit comment and to cooperate with the group.

At this early stage of development, the working group document was sent to the RAC at its October 29, 1984 meeting in order to inform the RAC of the working group's activities.[39] At that meeting, it was noted that the document would not contain standard protocols and criteria for evaluation, and would not constitute an environmental assessment on field testing experiments. On October 30, 1984, the working group met to continue to develop the points-to-consider document.[40] The group met again on February 11, 1985 to complete work on the document.[41] The document was officially presented to the RAC at the May 3, 1985 meeting.[42] At that meeting, the RAC unanimously accepted with thanks the "Points to Consider for the Environmental Testing of Microorganisms" developed by the Working Group on Release into the Environment. RAC requested that the full committee be consulted concerning any major changes in the document. A brief history of "testing in environment" and the NIH guidelines is shown in Table 3.7.

MAJOR CONSIDERATIONS IN DEVELOPING A GUIDANCE DOCUMENT
FOR FIELD TESTING OF MICROORGANISMS

The points-to-consider document was originally conceived in terms of microorganisms (such as bacteria, fungi, and viruses) in agriculture (for example, nitrogen fixation, vaccines, protection against frost damage, and pest control), but the concepts outlined in the document were felt to be applicable to a variety of other uses (for example, ore leaching, oil recovery, and pollution control).

Because of the great diversity of organisms, test sites, and techniques, the working group felt that each proposal involving environmental testing would initially have to be reviewed on a case-by-case basis. The infinite range of possible combinations indicated that no single set of tests was likely to be appropriate in all circumstances. Some common considerations exist, however, and were set forth in the points-to-consider document.

The points-to-consider document developed by the Working Group on Release into the Environment is a working document which outlines scientific considerations in the evaluation of small-scale field testing of modified organisms.

TABLE 3.7 The NIH Guidelines and Testing in the Environment

Year	Activity
1976	Original version of the guidelines specified that experiments involving "deliberate release into the environment of any organism containing a recombinant DNA molecules are not to be initiated at the present time."
1978	"Deliberate release into the environment of any organism containing recombinant DNA" is prohibited, but individual waivers are possible.
1982	Experiments involving deliberate release into the environment of any organism containing DNA must have RAC review and NIH and IBC approval before initiation.
1983	Appendix L, <u>Release into the Environment of Certain Plants</u>, is added to the guidelines.
1984	RAC accepts with thanks the "Points to Consider for Submissions Under Appendix L."
1985	RAC accepts with thanks the "Points to Consider for the Environmental Testing of Microorganisms."

Different considerations might be called for in large-scale testing. The language of the "points to consider" is often open-ended; that is, the data requests are stated in general rather than specific terms. This open-endedness was purposely structured into the document to permit investigators and reviewers a greater degree of latitude in determining what information would be relevant in evaluating a particular application. For example, the document requests information on "relevant genetics." Since information on genetics relevant in one application may be irrelevant in another, listing specific "relevant genetics" would be rigid and counterproductive.

The points-to-consider document encompasses the perceptions of individuals with training in molecular biology and those with training in ecology. The compromises reached between these two groups contributed to the development of a flexible document to which individuals can respond as appropriate.

The "points to consider" were intended to be as flexible to modification as possible as data accumulate, and were thus not developed for inclusion in the NIH Guidelines for Research Involving Recombinant DNA Molecules.

NOTES

1. M. Singer and D. Soll, Guidelines for DNA Hybrid Molecules, Science 181:1114, 1973.

2. P. Berg et al., Potential Hazards of Recombinant DNA Molecules, Science 185:303, 1974.

3. Federal Register 41:27902, 1976, Recombinant DNA Research; Guidelines.

4. Federal Register 43:33042, 1978, Recombinant DNA Research; Revised Guidelines.

5. Federal Register 43:60108, 1978, Guidelines for Research Involving Recombinant DNA Molecules.

6. Federal Register 45:6724, 1980, Guidelines for Research Involving Recombinant DNA Molecules.

7. Federal Register 45:77384, 1980, Recombinant DNA Research; Proposed Actions Under Guidelines.

8. Federal Register 46:34462, 1981, Guidelines for Research Involving Recombinant DNA Molecules, June 1981.

9. Federal Register 46:17994, 1981, Recombinant DNA Research; Proposed Actions Under Guidelines.

10. Recombinant DNA Advisory Committee, Minutes of the Meeting, September 10-11, 1981, Department of Health and Human Services Public Health Service, National Institutes of Health (hereafter cited as DHHS, PHS, NIH), Recombinant DNA Research 7:190, December 1982.

11. Federal Register 46:59368, 1981, Recombinant DNA Research; Proposed Revised Guidelines.

12. Federal Register 46:59734, 1981, Recombinant DNA Research; Proposed Actions Under Guidelines.

13. Federal Register 46:59384, 1981, Evaluation of the Risks Associated with Recombinant DNA Research, and Recombinant DNA Technical Bulletin 4:166, 1981.

14. The NIH Guidelines for Research Involving Recombinant DNA Molecules require that each institution conducting or sponsoring recombinant DNA research covered by the guidelines ensure that the research is carried out in full conformity with the provisions of the guidelines. One specification is that each institution must establish an institutional biosafety committee (IBC). The IBC shall be constituted to collectively have the experience and expertise necessary to assess the safety of recombinant DNA experiments and to assess any potential risk to public health or the environment; at least two members of the IBC represent the surrounding community. The IBC is responsible for reviewing recombinant DNA projects for compliance with the NIH Guidelines.

15. Recombinant DNA Advisory Committee, Minutes of the Meeting, February 8-9, 1982, DHHS, PHS, NIH, Recombinant DNA Research 7:328, December 1982.

16. Federal Register 47:17166, 1982, Recombinant DNA Research; Actions Under Guidelines.

17. Federal Register 47:17180, 1982, Guidelines for Research Involving Recombinant DNA Molecules.

18. <u>Federal Register</u> 47:38048, 1982, Guidelines for Research Involving Recombinant DNA Molecules.

19. <u>Federal Register</u> 48:24556, 1983, Guidelines for Research Involving Recombinant DNA Molecules, June 1983.

20. <u>Federal Register</u> 49:46266, 1984, Guidelines for Research Involving Recombinant DNA Molecules.

21. <u>Federal Register</u> 49:50856, 1984, Proposal for a Coordinated Framework for Regulation of Biotechnology; Notice.

22. <u>Federal Register</u> 50:48344, 1985, Recombinant DNA Research; Actions Under Guidelines; Notice.

23. E. Milewski and B. Talbot, Proposals Involving Field Testing of Recombinant DNA Containing Organisms, <u>Recombinant DNA Technical Bulletin</u> 6:141, 1983.

24. Memorandum of June 19, 1985 analyzing public comment on and containing the "Environmental Assessment and Finding of No Significant Impact" concerning the application to field test ice-nucleation-minus bacteria, <u>Recombinant DNA Research</u> 10:165, May 1986.

25. <u>Federal Register</u> of November 13, 1985 promulgating an action involving field testing of plants grown from seeds containing recombinant DNA and an "Environmental Assessment and Finding of No Significant Impact," <u>Recombinant DNA Research</u> 10:486, May 1986.

26. Recombinant DNA Advisory Committee Working Group on Revision of the Guidelines, Minutes of Meeting, January 21, 1983, DHHS, PHS, NIH, <u>Recombinant DNA Research</u> 8:68, May 1986.

27. <u>Federal Register</u> 48:9346, 1983, Recombinant DNA Research; Meeting and Proposed Actions Under Guidelines.

28. Recombinant DNA Advisory Committee, Minutes of Meeting April 11, 1983, DHHS, PHS, NIH, <u>Recombinant DNA Research</u> 8:85, May 1986.

29. <u>Federal Register</u> 48:24548, 1983, Actions Under Guidelines for Research Involving Recombinant DNA Molecules.

30. *Federal Register* 48:37199, 1983, Recombinant DNA Research; Proposed Actions Under Guidelines and Advisory Committee Meeting.

31. Recombinant DNA Advisory Committee, Minutes of Meeting, September 19, 1983, DHHS, PHS, NIH, *Recombinant DNA Research* 8:184, May 1986.

32. *Federal Register* 48:53056, 1983, Recombinant DNA Research; Actions Under the Guidelines.

33. Recombinant DNA Advisory Committee, Minutes of Meeting, February 6, 1984, DHHS, PHS, NIH, *Recombinant DNA Research* 8:244, May 1986.

34. Recombinant DNA Advisory Committee Working Group on Release into the Environment, Minutes of Meeting, April 9, 1984, DHHS, PHS, NIH, *Recombinant DNA Research* 8:366, May 1986.

35. *Federal Register* 49:17672, 1984, Recombinant DNA Research; Proposed Actions Under Guidelines; Notice.

36. Recombinant DNA Advisory Committee Working Group on Release into the Environment, Minutes of Meeting, May 31, 1984, DHHS, PHS, NIH, *Recombinant DNA Research* 8:425, May 1986.

37. Recombinant DNA Advisory Committee, Minutes of Meeting, June 1, 1984, DHHS, PHS, NIH, *Recombinant DNA Research* 8:452, May 1986.

38. Recombinant DNA Advisory Committee Working Group on Release into the Environment, Minutes of Meeting, October 5, 1984, DHHS, PHS, NIH, *Recombinant DNA Research* 9:11, May 1986.

39. Recombinant DNA Advisory Committee, Minutes of Meeting, October 29, 1984, DHHS, PHS, NIH, *Recombinant DNA Research* 9:131, May 1986.

40. Recombinant DNA Advisory Committee Working Group on Release into the Environment, Minutes of Meeting, October 30, 1984, DHHS, PHS, NIH, *Recombinant DNA Research* 9:176, May 1986.

41. Recombinant DNA Advisory Committee Working Group on Release into the Environment, Minutes of Meeting, February 11, 1985, DHHS, PHS, NIH, Recombinant DNA Research 9:296, May 1986.

42. Recombinant DNA Advisory Committee, Minutes of Meeting, May 3, 1985, DHHS, PHS, NIH, Recombinant DNA Research 10:120, May 1986.

TABLE 3.1
Major Modifications to the NIH Guidelines for Research Involving Recombinant DNA Molecules

Section	Modification

June 1976 Guidelines

I.   • Specified prohibited experiments.

II.   • Described in great detail four sets of special
       practices, equipment, and laboratory instal-
       lations (P1, P2, P3, P4).

      • Defined the concept of biological containment
       for E. coli K-12 systems (EK1, EK2, EK3).

III. • Specified physical and biological containment
       levels for different classes of permitted ex-
       periments using E. coli K-12 .

IV.   • Specified roles and responsibilities of scien-
       tists, institutions, Institutional Biosafety
       Committees (IBC), and the NIH.

December 1978 Guidelines

I.   • Exempted from the guidelines certain classes
       of experiments deemed of the lowest potential
       hazard.

II.   • Generalized biological containment specifica-
       tions to include other prokaryotic and eukary-
       otic host-vector systems.

III. • In general, assigned experiments lower con-
       tainment levels. Permitted experiments with a
       larger variety of hostvector systems.

IV.   • Mandated increased representation for local
       IBCs and the RAC.

      • Incorporated into the guidelines a procedure
       by which to modify the guidelines.

      • Specified penalties for noncompliance.

TABLE 3.1 (continued)

==

Section   Modification

January and November 1980 Guidelines

   III.   • Assigned lower containment levels for many experiments.

           • Allowed lower containment specifications for most frequently utilized host-vector systems (E. coli K-12 EK1, S. cerevisiae).

   IV.   • Required only IBC review of most experiments for which containment was clearly specified in the guidelines.

   VI.   • Added voluntary compliance provision.

July 1981 Guidelines

   I.   • Expanded exempt class of experiments to include the most frequently utilized host-vector systems (E. coli K-12 EK1, S. cerevisiae, asporogenic Bacillus subtilis).

April and August 1982 Guidelines

   I.   • No longer used the term "prohibition." However, three of the prohibitions (drug resistance traits, toxin genes, and deliberate release to the environment) appeared in a new section III-A and required RAC review and approval. Two of the prohibitions (formation of rDNAs from pathogenic organisms and large-scale procedures) were listed in section III-B and were allowed to proceed following IBC review and approval.

   II.   • Deleted reference to HV3 host vector systems.

           • Certain sections became Appendices G, H, and I.

TABLE 3.1 (continued)

===

Section   Modification

April and August 1982 Guidelines, cont.

    III.   ● Greatly simplified. Lowered physical contain-
ment requirements for some classes of experiments.

           ● New section III-A contained three of the pro-
hibitions.

           ● New section III-B specified experiments re-
quiring IBC approval before initiation. They
were assigned containment levels P1 to P4.

           ● New section III-C included all experiments not
included in sections III-A, III-B, or III-D.
These experiments required IBC notification
simultaneously with initiation of experiments
and could be carried out at P1 containment.

           ● New section III-D consisted of those experi-
ments exempt from the guidelines.

           ● Amended the CDC Classification of Etiologic
Agents on the Basis of Hazard, the original
source of Appendix B, to suit the purposes of
the guidelines.

    IV.   ● Determined that the responsibilities of the
IBC need not be restricted to rDNA.

           ● Deleted requirement that 20 percent of the IBC
membership could not be affiliated with the
IBC. (The institution would still be required
to appoint two nonaffiliated members to the
IBC.)

TABLE 3.1 (continued)

Section   Modification

June 1983 Guidelines, cont.

Appendix K ● Incorporated Physical Containment Recommendations for Large-Scale Uses of Organisms Containing Recombinant DNA Molecules into the
guidelines as Appendix K, Physical Containment
for Large-Scale Uses of Organisms Containing
Recombinant DNA Molecules.

Appendix L ● Added Appendix L, Release into the Environment
of Certain Plants, to the guidelines.

November 1984 Guidelines

   III.   ● Added section III-A-4 addressing deliberate
transfer of rDNA into human subjects.

Appendix G ● Amended Appendix G, Physical Containment, to
correspond to the biosafety levels set forth
in the CDC/NIH document Biosafety in Microbiological and Biomedical Laboratories.

TABLE 3.4
NIH Guidelines for Research Involving Recombinant DNA Molecules: Appendix L, Release into the Environment of Certain Plants

Appendix L-I. General Information

Appendix L specifies conditions under which certain plants, as specified below, may be approved for release into the environment. Experiments in this category cannot be initiated without submission of relevant information on the proposed experiment to NIH, review by the RAC Plant Working Group, and specific approval by NIH. Such experiments also require the approval of the IBC before initiation. Information on specific experiments which have been approved will be available in ORDA* and will be listed in Appendix L-III when the Guidelines are republished.
Experiments which do not meet the specifications of Appendix L-II fall under Section III-A and require RAC review and NIH and IBC approval before initiation.

Appendix L-II. Criteria Allowing Review by the Plant Working Group Without the Requirement for Full RAC Review

Approval may be granted by ORDA in consultation with the RAC Plant Working Group without the requirement for full RAC review (IBC review is also necessary) for growing plants containing recombinant DNA in the field under the following conditions:

Appendix L-II-A. The plant species is a cultivated crop of a genus that has no species known to be a noxious weed.

Appendix L-II-B. The introduced DNA consists of well-characterized genes containing no sequences harmful to humans, animals, or plants.

Appendix L-II-C. The vector consists of DNA: (i) from exempt host-vector systems (Appendix C); (ii) from plants of the same or closely related species; (iii) from nonpathogenic prokaryotes or nonpathogenic lower eukaryotic plants; (iv) from plant pathogens only if sequences resulting in production of disease symptoms have been deleted; or

TABLE 3.4 (continued)

(v) chimeric vectors constructed from sequences defined in (i) to (iv) above. The DNA may be introduced by any suitable method. If sequences resulting in production of disease symptoms are retained for purposes of introducing the DNA into the plant, greenhouse-grown plants must be shown to be free of such sequences before such plants, derivatives, or seed from them can be used in field tests.

Appendix L-II-D. Plants are grown in controlled access fields under specified conditions appropriate for the plant under study and the geographical location. Such conditions should include provisions for using good cultural and pest control practices, for physical isolation from plants of the same species outside of the experimental plot in accordance with pollination characteristics of the species, and for further preventing plants containing recombinant DNA from becoming established in an environment. Review by the IBC should include an appraisal by scientists knowledgeable of the crop, its production practices, and the local geographical conditions. Procedures for assessing alterations in and the spread of organisms containing recombinant DNA must be developed. The results of the outlined tests must be submitted for review by the IBC. Copies must also be submitted to the Plant Working Group of the RAC.

---

* National Institutes of Health, Office of Recombinant DNA Activities.

TABLE 3.5
Points to Consider for Submissions under Appendix L

==

Appendix L of the Guidelines specifies conditions under which certain plants may be approved for "release into
the environment" including field tests. Experiments in
this category cannot be initiated without submission of
relevant information on the proposed experiments to NIH,
review by the RAC Plant Working Group, and specific approval by NIH.

The proposal should include a statement of objectives
and a description of materials and methods, including
methodology for monitoring the experiments, and expected
results. A summary of relevant preliminary results should
accompany the proposal. Information to be submitted should
include but not be limited to:

A. Description of Plant Materials

Give common and scientific names of plants. Identify
the specific cultivars or genetic lines to be used.
Include information on the relative homogeneity of the
plant cultivars or lines and specific genetic markers
they are known to possess.

B. Vectors and Method of Introduction

1. Describe the cloned DNA segment and its expression
in the new host.

2. Give the method(s) by which the proposed DNA vector will be or has been constructed. Diagrams are
very helpful and may be necessary for adequate
understanding of the construct. Explain the
advantages (and disadvantage(s), if appropriate) of
your vectors, if other candidate vetors could be
considered.

3. If microorganisms are used to introduce vectors or
are vectors themselves, indicate how they compare
with wild-type strains. If disabled pathogens are
used to transmit the vector, indicate factors that
will most likely prevent these microorganisms from
regaining or acquiring pathogenic potential. If
the vector is likely to survive independently of

TABLE 3.5 (continued)

the desired host(s), refer to this possibility, and provide any available data to assess the probability of such transfer to other organisms.

4. If microorganisms are used to introduce vectors, the absence of these microorganisms in the plants to be released in the field should be documented.

C. Characteristics and Monitoring of Genetically Engineered and Control Plants

1. Provide data from greenhouse and/or growth chamber studies to support prospective field studies. Data should include morphological data for at least two generations of plants as appropriate. Supply any molecular or physiological data, especially as applicable to the trait(s) under consideration.

Specify plant monitoring procedures; frequency; types of data to be obtained.

2. Field plots should meet the criteria specified in Appendix L-II-D:

Appendix L-II-D. Plants are grown in controlled access fields under specified conditions appropriate for the plant under study and the geographical location. Such conditions should include provisions for using good cultural and pest control practices, for physical isolation from plants of the same species outside of the experimental plot in accordance with pollination characteristics of the species, and for further preventing plants containing recombinant DNA from becoming established in the environment. Review by the IBC should include an appraisal by scientists knowledgeable of the crop, its production practices, and the local geographical conditions. Procedures for assessing alterations in and the spread of organisms containing recombinant DNA must be developed. The results of the outlined tests must be submitted for review

TABLE 3.5 (continued)

by the IBC. Copies must also be submitted to the Plant Working Group of the RAC.

Supporting data should include the following:

a. total area;

b. geographical location(s): where, how many locations;

c. plot design: for example, replication, row spacing, nature of border rows;

d. specify plant monitoring procedures: frequency; types of data to be obtained, including leaf, seed, fruit, or root characteristics; disease, insect and other animal population monitoring as appropriate;

e. specify techniques for monitoring the vector and/ or altered DNA; and

f. specify access and security measures.

TABLE 3.6
Points to Consider for Submissions Involving Testing in the
Environment of Microorganisms Derived by Recombinant DNA
Techniques

===

Experiments in this category require specific review
by the Recombinant DNA Advisory Committee (RAC) and approvals by the National Institutes of Health (NIH) and the
Institutional Biosafety Committee (IBC) before initiation.
The IBC is expected to make an independent evaluation although this evaluation need not occur before consideration
of an experiment by the RAC. Relevant information on the
proposed experiments should be submitted to the Office of
Recombinant DNA Activities (ORDA). The objective of this
review procedure is to evaluate the potential environmental
effects of testing of microorganisms that have been modified by recombinant DNA techniques.

These following points to consider have been developed
by the RAC Working Group on Release into the Environment as
a suggested list for scientists preparing proposals on environmental testing of microorganisms, including viruses,
that have been modified using recombinant DNA techniques.
The review of proposals for environmental testing of modified organisms is being done on a case-by-case basis because the range of possible organisms, applications, and
environments indicate that no standard set of procedures is
likely to be appropriate in all circumstances. However,
some common considerations allow the construction of points
to consider such as those below. Information on all these
points will not be necessary in all cases but will depend
on the properties of the parental organism and the effect
of the modification on these properties.

Approval of small-scale field tests will depend upon
the results of laboratory and greenhouse testing of the
properties of the modified organism. We anticipate that
monitoring of small-scale field tests will provide data on
environmental effects of the modified organism. Such data
may be a necessary part of the consideration of requests
for approval of large-scale tests and commercial applications.

TABLE 3.6 (continued)

===

I.   Summary

      Present a summary of the proposed trial including
      objectives, significance, and justification for the
      request.

II.   Genetic Considerations of Modified Organism to be
      Tested

      A. Characteristics of the Nonmodified Parental Or-
         ganism

         1. Information on identification, taxonomy,
            source, and strain.

         2. Information on organism's reproductive cycle
            and capacity for genetic transfer.

      B. Molecular Biology of the Modified Organism

         1. Introduced Genes

            a. Source and function of the DNA sequence used
               to modify the organism to be tested in the
               environment.

            b. Identification, taxonomy, source, and strain
               of organism donating the DNA.

         2. Construction of the Modified Organism

            a. Describe the method(s) by which the vector
               with insert(s) has been constructed. In-
               clude diagrams as appropriate.

            b. Describe the method of introduction of the
               vector carrying the insert into the organism
               to be modified and the procedure for selec-
               tion of the modified organism.

TABLE 3.6 (continued)

c. Specify the amount and nature of any vector and/or donor DNA remaining in the modified organism.

d. Give the laboratory containment conditions specified by the NIH guidelines for the modified organism.

3. Genetic Stability and Expression

Present results and interpretation of preliminary tests designed to measure genetic stability and expression of the introduced DNA in the modified organism.

III. Environmental Considerations

The intent of gathering ecological information is to assess the effects of survival, reproduction, and/or dispersal of the modified organism. For this purpose, information should be provided where possible and appropriate on: (i) relevant ecological characteristics of the nonmodified organism; (ii) the corresponding characteristics of the modified organism; and (iii) the physiological and ecological role of donated genetic sequences in the donor and in the modified organism(s). For the following points, provide information where possible and appropriate on the nonmodified organism and a prediction of any change that may be elicited by the modification.

A. Habitat and Geographic Distribution

B. Physical and Chemical Factors which can Affect Survival, Reproduction, and Dispersal

C. Biological Interactions

1. Host range.

TABLE 3.6 (continued)

===

2. Interactions with and effects on other organisms in the environment including effects on competitors, prey, hosts, symbionts, predators, parasites, and pathogens.

3. Pathogenicity, infectivity, toxicity, virulence, or as a carrier (vector) of pathogens.

4. Involvement in biogeochemical or in biological cycling processes (e.g., mineral cycling, cellulose and lignin degradation, nitrogen fixation, pesticide degradation).

5. Frequency with which populations undergo shifts in important ecological characteristics such as those listed in III-C points 1 through 4 above.

6. Likelihood of exchange of genetic information between the modified organism and other organisms in nature.

IV. Proposed Field Trials

A. Pre-Field Trial Considerations

Provide data related to any anticipated effects of the modified microorganism on target and nontarget organisms from microcosm, greenhouse, and/or growth chamber experiments that simulate trial conditions. The methods of detection and sensitivity of sampling techniques and periodicity of sampling should be indicated. These studies should include, where relevant, assessment of the following items:

1. Survival of the modified organism.

2. Replication of the modified organism.

TABLE 3.6 (continued)

3. Dissemination of the modified organism by wind, water, soil, mobile organisms, and other means.

B. Conditions of the Trial

Describe the trial involving release of the modified organism into the environment:

1. Numbers of organisms and methods of application.

2. Provide information including diagrams of the experimental location and the immediate surroundings. Describe characteristics of the site that would influence containment or dispersal.

3. If the modified organism has a target organism, provide the following:

   a. Identification and taxonomy.

   b. The anticipated mechanism and result of the interaction between the released microorganism and the target organism.

C. Containment

Indicate containment procedures in the event of accidental release as well as intentional release and procedures for emergency termination of the experiment. Specify access and security measures for the area(s) in which the tests will be performed.

D. Monitoring

Describe monitoring procedures and their limits of detection for survival, dissemination, and non-target interactions of the modified microorganism. Include periodicity of sampling and

TABLE 3.6 (continued)

==

rationale for monitoring procedures. Collect data
to compare the modified organisms with the nonmodified microorganism most similar to the modified
organism at the site of the trial. Results of monitoring should be submitted to the RAC according to
a schedule specified at the time of approval.

V. Risk Analysis

Results of testing in artificial contained environments together with careful consideration of the genetics, biology, and ecology of the nonmodified and
the modified organisms will enable a reasonable prediction of whether or not significant risk of environmental damage will result from the release of the
modified organism in the small-scale field test.

In this section, the information requested in Sections II, III, and IV should be summarized to present an analysis of possible risks to the environment in the test as it is proposed. The issues
addressed might include but not be limited to the
following items:

A. The Nature of the Organism

1. The role of the nonmodified organism in the environment of the test site, including any adverse effects on other organisms.

2. Evaluation of whether or not the specific genetic modification (e.g., deletion, insertion,
   modification of specific DNA sequences) would
   alter the potential for significant adverse
   effects.

3. Evaluation of results of tests conducted in
   contained environments to predict the ecological behavior of the modified organism relative
   to that of its nonmodified parent.

TABLE 3.6 (continued)

===

B. <u>The Nature of the Test</u>

Discuss the following specific features of the experiment that are designed to minimize potential adverse effects of the modified organism:

1. Test site location and area.

2. Introduction protocols.

3. Numbers of organisms and their expected reproductive capacity.

4. Emergency procedures for aborting the experiment.

5. Procedures conducted at the termination of the experiment.

Part Two

Environmental Release—Ecological Issues

4. Application of Introduced Species Models to Biotechnology Assessment

In 1981, I wrote a report for the U.S. Environmental Protection Agency (EPA) that summarized the results of an expansive search of the literature on introduced species (Sharples 1983). The motivation for the study was provided by several individuals in the agency who were asking for a preliminary judgment about whether or not it was possible to make a prediction about the likelihood of a recombinant organism becoming established in the environment and causing ecological damage. At the time, the National Institutes of Health's Guidelines for Research Involving Recombinant DNA Molecules were still directed entirely at prohibiting environmental releases. The Recombinant DNA Advisory Committee itself had set the stage for interpreting environmental releases as "worst case" events in dealing with recombinant organisms.

My report attempted to answer EPA's question by delving into what is known about the ecological processes involved in the successful introduction of a "new" or "novel" species. My conclusions, very briefly, were as follows:

- There is a great deal of information available on introduced species, although much of it is anecdotal, and most of it was collected after the fact of the introduction.

- Even with all this information, it is not possible, in general, to make quantitative predictions on the basis of historical evidence alone as to the likelihood that any particular species may become established, reproduce in its new environment, and spread. Although only a small fraction of introduced species causes ecological disruptions, it would not be possible to predict which ones out of a set of proposed introductions could cause problems without ecological evaluations directed at specific organisms before release.

- The introduced species model, or analogy, is nevertheless valid because the ability of an organism to become established and spread in a new environment is an ecological question regardless of the origin or nature of the "new" or "novel" aspects of that organism. In other words, the ecological processes that are called into play when an organism is moved from one place to another are the same whether that organism is moved from one continent to another, from one ecosystem to another on the same continent, from one environmental medium to another in the same ecosystem, or from a laboratory to an open field.

My evaluations were based not only on recorded experience with the more notorious "exotic" species such as the chestnut blight and the gypsy moth, but also on recorded experience with agricultural species, both domesticated plants and animals, as well as that provided by pest management with counterpests (biological pest control). In my mind, there is no difference between these different categories of historical observation with introductions insofar as ecological processes are concerned. Furthermore, I have never talked to another ecologist who disagrees with this point of view in any substantive way.

Unfortunately, many nonecologists, even those who are scientists, still fail to see the point the ecologists are making and reject the introduced species model as being irrelevant to the issue of ensuring environmental safety for recombinant products. They therefore dismiss or ignore the valuable information contained in the vast documentation available on introductions of exotics. Although the fact that some introduced species have caused environmental disruptions is never disputed, the validity of the exotic species analogy is frequently challenged. The kinds of objections that are reiterated over and over fall into several general groups:

<u>A recombinant organism with only one or several new genes cannot be the ecological equivalent of a completely foreign organism from another part of the globe.</u>

The presumption in this argument is that the ability of a new organism to cause ecological disruption must be proportional to the number of "new" genes it carries. We know this to be false. Many instances of drastic change in the ecological, medical, and economic status of diverse kinds of organisms are known to have been caused by changes in single genes. Examples include antibiotic resistance in bacteria, pesticide resistance in insects, and changes in the pathogenicity of viruses and fungi. This is not to say that every single gene change has this potential. Still, it is not the number of new genes that can be of ecological significance, but rather which genes and what their functions are that is important.

The problems caused by introduced species are due to the fact that they are put into new environments that lack the pests, predators, etc., that naturally kept them in check in their native homes (Brill 1985; Davis 1984; Genetic Engineering News 1984). Native species with new genes are not the same thing, and therefore couldn't become a problem.

This argument implies a belief in a delicately balanced "nature" that takes care of itself unless human interference unbalances it. This belief, however, does not match the facts as they are known to ecologists. Organisms are adequately adapted to survive, but are not optimally adapted (Regal 1986). Communities and ecosystems are not saturated with "perfected" species surviving together harmoniously. Ecological niches shift continuously, and are highly context-dependent. Regulatory mechanisms operating between different populations are sometimes very weak, and natural populations may fluctuate drastically in the absence of interference of any kind (Simberloff and Colwell 1984). Though it is sometimes true that introduced species have escaped the restraining ecological forces of their native homes, the same principle must also apply to genetically engineered species designed with certain kinds of advantages in mind. The kinds of modifications that are of interest to biotechnology (e.g., plants able to grow at lower temperatures or lower nutrient levels, microorganisms equipped to destroy a greatly expanded variety of insects on many more kinds of host plants than before, etc.) are hardly minor changes from an ecological point of view (Colwell et al. 1985). If the traits of an engineered organism give it the ability to survive in a new habitat or on a new food source, then that organism may have become very much the ecological equivalent of an introduced species in an environment where it did not exist before.

<u>Genetically engineered organisms are even less likely to cause problems than organisms developed through traditional breeding, and these don't cause problems.</u>

This argument is particularly common when the subject of crop plants is under discussion, but familiar microorganisms such as Rhizobium may also be included. Although it is true that probably the most beneficial results of experiments with new species have come in the area of introduced crops, this is not sufficient reason to assume that anything that can be called a crop plant is therefore automatically harmless and risk-free, especially in economic terms. "Crops" and "weeds" are intimately related categories. Of the world's eighteen worst weeds, which collectively cause annual agricultural losses in the billions, eleven are themselves grown as crops in several countries, and two are grown here in the United States (Holm et al. 1977). It is not uncommon for commercial varieties of crops derived from traditional breeding to be considered "noxious weeds." In addition, the ability of commercial species to hybridize with wild relatives and existing weeds could provide a handy conduit by which advantageous engineered traits, such as herbicide resistance, could find their way into surrounding plant populations to create even more hardy plant pests. Important weeds in a number of agriculturally significant genera--Avena, Hordeum, Helianthus, Solanum-Lycopersicum, Brassica, Daucus, and Sorghum, to name a few--may hybridize freely with crops. A notable example, Johnson grass (Sorghum halepense), is considered to be an extremely pernicious weed. It is known to hybridize with commercial sorghum (S. bicolor), and could greatly benefit from any engineered traits that might give it a competitive advantage in the field. Familiarity alone should therefore not necessarily be a reason to exempt "domestic" species from scrutiny until the facts of a particular case are evaluated.

I suggest that it is fruitless to argue much longer over the validity of the exotic species model as an analogy for introduced recombinants. What might be productive, however, is to probe more deeply into the various realms of experience with introduction--agriculture, biological pest control, waste treatment, and so on--and try to identify the factors that spell benign success in some instances and disaster in others. An interesting analysis by Dritschilo et al. (1985) has taken such an approach with what could be productive results. This group at the University of California at Los Angeles analyzed data on 1,263 species that have been introduced into the state of California. They identified factors that appeared to be associated with species that were minimally disruptive (e.g., narrow habitat tolerances and low dispersal capability) by statistical techniques. Further refinements of such approaches could help to develop general guidelines on where to direct the most thorough examinations in evaluating potential environmental hazards of released recombinants.

The essential next step, however, is to begin to approach the question of risk in a truly multidisciplinary way, using the appropriate kinds of available expertise. Ecologists and evolutionary biologists have this expertise, and should be brought into the process of developing recombinant organism products. Simberloff has suggested that reasonably sound advice on the likely behavior of a recombinant organism could be developed on the basis of about a Ph.D. dissertation's worth of research (Simberloff and Colwell 1984). It would, however, be much easier and more effective if an ecologist were collecting this data in concert with product development, rather than trying to backfit a risk analysis on an already developed, and about-to-be-delayed, product. The most effective new approach would be for the biotechnology community to cease regarding ecologists as suspicious characters--as "Luddites," fanatics, or just environmental activists--and recognize that their discipline has much to offer in making biotechnology the scientific and commercial success it ought to be.

REFERENCES

Brill, W. J. 1985. *Science* 227:381.

Colwell, R.K., E.A. Norse, D. Pimentel, F.E. Sharples, and D. Simberloff. 1985. *Science* 229:111.

Davis, B. 1984. *Discover* August, 24-25.

Dritschilo, W., D.E. Carpenter, O. Meyn, D. Moss, and M.N. Weinstein. 1985. *Implications of Data on Introduced*

Species in California for Field Releases of Recombinant
Organisms. Report 85-60. School of Public Health,
University of California at Los Angeles.

Genetic Engineering News. 1984. 4(no. 5): 4.

Holm, L.G., D.L. Plucknett, J.V. Pancho, and J.P.
Herberger. 1977. The World's Worst Weeds: Distribution
and Biology. Honolulu: University of Hawaii.

Regal, P.J. 1986. Models of Genetically Engineered Organisms
and Their Ecological Impact. In Ecology of Biological
Invasions of North America and Hawaii, ed. H. Mooney,
111-129. New York: Springer-Verlag.

Sharples, F.E. 1983. Recombinant DNA Technical Bulletin
6:43-56.

Simberloff, D., and R.K. Colwell. 1984. Genetic Engineering
News 4(no. 8): 4.

5. The Infectious Spread of Engineered Genes

INTRODUCTION

The deliberate release of genetically engineered organisms into the environment may provide a variety of economic and social benefits (see Chapter 1). Possible environmental applications of biotechnology include bacteria that have been engineered to degrade toxins, such as pesticides, that are contaminating soil and water (Kellogg et al. 1981; Broda et al. 1981; Chatterjee et al. 1981); pathogens that have been engineered to control pests, like weeds and insects, that are damaging forests and agricultural crops (Paul 1981; Yoder 1983; Pimentel 1985; Watrud et al. 1985); and crop plants that have been engineered for greater productivity, or to resist insects, disease, and even herbicides used to control competing weeds (Barton and Brill 1983; Hahlbrock et al., 1984; Goodman and Newell 1985; Hardy 1985). But attendant with these potential benefits are also potential risks associated with unanticipated consequences of the release of genetically engineered organisms into the environment (see Chapters 4 and 6).

Until recently, concerns over the safety of research with genetically engineered organisms were allayed by appropriate containment procedures (see Chapters 2 and 3). These procedures have limited not only the opportunities for physical transport of engineered organisms outside of research laboratories, but also the biological potential for survival and replication of these organisms should they accidentally escape physical containment. This "biological" containment has been accomplished by the use of organisms that grow well only under restricted conditions that are unlikely to be met outside research laboratories (Curtiss 1976; Curtiss et al. 1977).

But for applications requiring deliberate release, genetically engineered organisms must be chosen for their ability to survive and reproduce in natural environments, at least to an extent sufficient for them to carry out their intended functions. Thus, it is imperative to evaluate any possible risks associated with the release of genetically engineered organisms into the environment. As has been emphasized elsewhere, this evaluation should proceed on a case-by-case basis, because the complexity of ecological systems makes generalizations concerning possible risks of genetically engineered organisms difficult, if not impossible (Brown et al. 1984; Simberloff and Colwell 1985; Regal 1986). The primary foci of these evaluations, broadly stated, must be to predict the fate of the genetically engineered organism after its release into the environment (Sharples 1983; Stotzky and Babich 1984) and to anticipate the effects of the genetically engineered organism on populations of other organisms in the environment, and on important ecosystem processes, including nutrient cycling and productivity (Vitousek 1985; Flanagan 1986).

These evaluations are complicated by the possibility that an engineered organism may disappear (or otherwise have no adverse effects), but the DNA introduced during the course of its engineering may be transferred to some other organism present in the environment, where it has a different fate (or produces different effects). Although the infectious spread of an engineered gene to another organism is in some sense secondary to the direct effects of the engineered organism, it could potentially be very significant.

In this chapter, I provide several hypothetical cases where the infectious transfer of engineered genetic material results in adverse environmental consequences that would otherwise not arise. I then describe some of the mechanisms by which DNA can be infectiously transmitted from one organism to another, and I present a short review of our current understanding of the importance of infectious gene transfer in nature, drawing especially on data for bacteria. Finally, I provide a general framework which describes the information necessary to evaluate fully the likelihood of infectious transfer of an engineered gene.

HYPOTHETICAL EXAMPLES OF ADVERSE CONSEQUENCES ARISING FROM THE INFECTIOUS SPREAD OF ENGINEERED GENES

The scenarios that follow are provided only to illustrate the sorts of complications that could arise as a result of the transfer of genetic material from an engineered organism that has been deliberately released to another organism already present in the environment. They are not intended to be directly relevant to any specific applications currently being considered, nor are they intended to represent "worst case" scenarios.

Case One

Let us consider a bacterium that has been genetically engineered to degrade completely a pollutant that is present in some environment. The engineered bacteria derive energy from the degradative process, and so can use the pollutant as an ecological resource. However, the engineered bacteria are unable to compete successfully with the indigenous bacteria for naturally occurring resources. Thus, once the engineered bacteria have completed their intended biodegradative function, they should disappear from the environment without further consequence.

But let us imagine that one of the genes involved in this biodegradative process is infectiously transmitted to an indigenous bacterium. This gene permits the conversion of the pollutant into an intermediate compound. Unfortunately, the intermediate compound that is produced by the indigenous recipient of the engineered gene is even more toxic than the original pollutant.

Perhaps the engineered organism can use the highly toxic intermediate as a resource, and thus complete the intended degradation of the pollutant with no untoward consequences. This will depend on the details of the biochemistry, physiology, and ecology of the bacteria. The critical point is that it becomes necessary to answer many more questions. How many steps are involved in the degradative process, and how many of these yield net energetic gains for the bacteria? Are any of the biochemical intermediates toxic, and can bacteria take up these intermediates and complete their biodegradation? Can any or all of the engineered genes whose products are involved in the degradative process be transmitted to the indigenous bacteria?

Case Two

Now consider an insect that is a forest pest. There occurs naturally a highly specialized virus which can infect this pest, but it normally has little impact because

the insect has evolved a defense against this type of infection. The virus is genetically engineered, however, to
bypass the insect's defense. This engineered virus can
then be used successfully as a biological control agent,
thereby avoiding the need to use chemical pesticides.

However, if the trait which permits the virus to overcome the insect pest's defense can be transmitted to other
viruses that infect a broad array of insects, then many
beneficial insect species might be harmed. It is conceiv-
able that the deleterious effects of other insect pests,
released from control by their beneficial insect predators,
could be even more harmful than the effects of the pest
that was originally targeted by the engineered virus. In
fact, situations that are very similar to this have been
documented for chemical insecticides (see DeBach 1974).
Once again, the possibility that the engineered genetic material could spread to other species, each with its unique
ecological relationships, greatly increases the number of
questions that must be addressed in order to ascertain any
possible risks associated with deliberate release (see
Pimentel 1985).

Case Three

Finally, let us consider a crop plant that has been
engineered to be resistant to herbicides. Herbicides can
be applied in higher doses without adversely affecting the
crop plant, thereby permitting higher yields. One might
reasonably view crop plants as particularly safe organisms
for genetic engineering and introduction into the environment, since agricultural systems are not natural, but highly simplified and tightly managed. Crop plants are adapted
to rapid growth in environments that are tailored to their
needs, but they are unlikely to fare well in other set-
tings. Once again, consider the possible effect if the engineered herbicide resistance could be infectiously transmitted to other plant species, including weeds.

In order to evaluate the likelihood of this complica-
tion, we would again need to address many more questions
than would otherwise be necessary. Can infectious transfer
of the resistance trait, perhaps mediated by plant viruses,
occur in nature? What is the range of host plants that
these viruses can infect? What is the source of the genetic material used to engineer the herbicide resistance in
the crop plant, and could it be transmitted directly from
this source to the weed species in nature?

MECHANISMS OF INFECTIOUS TRANSFER OF GENES, AND THEIR
ECOLOGICAL AND EVOLUTIONARY SIGNIFICANCE

Mutation and recombination generate variability within
biological populations. This variability provides the genetic basis for natural selection, which is responsible for
the diversification of organisms and their adaptation to
the environment. The traditional view of evolution, which
has been based largely on higher organisms, is that genes
follow vertical lineages, or lines of descent. Sexuality,
as manifest by Mendelian segregation and reassortment, provides a mechanism for the formation of new gene combinations in conjunction with production of new individuals.
Sexual recombination of genes normally occurs only within
the confines of a single species. In fact, this traditional view is embodied in the most widely accepted definition
of biological species: "Species are groups of interbreeding
natural populations that are reproductively isolated from
other such groups" (Mayr 1970). Hybridization between
closely related species may occur under exceptional circumstances, but the traditional view of evolutionary processes
gives no consideration to the movement of genes between
organisms that is independent of the production of new
individuals.

In procaryotes (which include bacteria and blue-green
algae), the situation is dramatically different from this
traditional view. First of all, procaryotes reproduce in a
clonal manner, without sex and the resulting genetic recombination. One might therefore imagine that mutation is the
sole source of genetic variability in populations of procaryotes, but this is not true (Reanney 1976; Slater
1984). Intensive genetic studies over the last several
decades have identified a variety of mechanisms that can
result in gene exchange, especially among bacteria. In
fact, these mechanisms are utilized by molecular biologists
in their efforts to engineer the recombinant organisms
intended for biotechnological applications.

Gene exchange in bacteria operates independently of
the production of new individuals, and hence is termed
horizontal gene transfer. Mechanisms of horizontal gene
transfer are sometimes also called infectious, because they
can be mediated by semiautonomous extrachromosomal genetic
elements, which behave to varying degrees as molecular parasites. For example, transduction refers to horizontal
gene transfer that is mediated by viruses. During the
course of replication and packaging of their own DNA, viruses may pick up sequences from their host's genome, which

can then be transmitted to other hosts during subsequent infections. Certain viruses can actually integrate their genetic material into the host's genome, and such viruses are especially likely to transmit host genes. The phylogenetic distance over which virus-mediated exchange of host genes can occur is determined by the host range of the virus, which may be quite broad. For example, the virus P1 can infect cells belonging to several different genera of bacteria (Reanney 1976).

Another process by which bacteria can exchange genes is mediated by extrachromosomal elements called conjugative plasmids (Falkow 1975; Broda 1979; Day 1982; Hardy 1986). Plasmids differ from viruses in that they have no extracellular particle state. However, many plasmids are able to promote their own transfer from one bacterium to another. This process, referred to as conjugation, requires physical contact between two cells. Transfer of the plasmid is facilitated by a special structure, termed a pilus, that is produced by the plasmid-bearing cell (Bradley 1981). As with viruses, certain plasmids may become integrated into the host genome, increasing the likelihood that chromosomal genes will be transmitted along with the genes of the extrachromosomal element. Conjugative plasmids may also mobilize the transmission of other nonconjugative plasmids, which do not encode pilus formation and are not otherwise transmitted horizontally. Once again, the phylogenetic extent of plasmid-mediated recombination depends on the host range of the plasmid. This may be extremely broad, especially when one allows for indirect transmission occurring through intermediates. For example, Barkay, Fouts, and Olson (1985) have demonstrated homology in the plasmid-encoded mercury resistance genes for diverse gram-negative bacteria.

Bacteria may also exchange genes via a process known as transformation. Unlike transduction and conjugation, which are mediated by semiautonomous genetic entities, transformation involves the exchange of free DNA between cells. For some bacteria, including the widely studied Escherichia coli, transformation occurs only under restricted conditions that are unlikely to be met outside the laboratory. For other bacterial species, however, transformation may be an important form of recombination under natural conditions, as suggested by the work of Graham and Istock (1979) on Bacillus subtilis.

Genes may also be exchanged between chromosomes and extrachromosomal elements via a mechanism known as transposition. Transposons (also sometimes called mobile genetic elements or "jumping genes") contain special regions of nucleotide bases at their extremities that promote recombination with sequences elsewhere in the genome (Campbell 1983; Shapiro 1983; Levy 1985; Hardy 1986). Viruses themselves may recombine if two different types infect the same host. Similarly, plasmids may recombine when two or more forms occur together in a host cell. In a sense, these semiautonomous elements can undergo a sort of "modular" evolution, at the same time mediating the acquisition of new functions in their bacterial hosts (Reanney 1976; Botstein 1980; Muster et al. 1981).

At present, it is not clear how important analogous processes are in eucaryotes. Within the confines of a single species, sexually mediated recombination is certainly far more important than horizontal gene transfer. But there are at least occasional opportunities for infectious transmission of genes involving eucaryotic species. The Ti plasmid of Agrobacterium tumefasciens can become incorporated into the genome of infected plants, and can also be used to mediate the interspecific transfer of genetic material (Zambryski et al. 1983; Depicker et al. 1984; Horsch et al. 1984; Schell et al. 1984). Also, it has been hypothesized that the mitochondria and chloroplasts found in eucaryotic cells are themselves derived from ancient symbiotic procaryotes (Margulis 1970), which suggests additional possibilities for gene transfer between distantly related taxa (Zambryski et al. 1983; Timmis and Scott 1984; Price et al. 1986). Processes comparable to viral transduction in procaryotes can almost certainly occur in eucaryotes, and there are several instances of possible interspecific transfer of genetic material that might be explained in this way (Krieber and Rose 1986). However, it seems unlikely that horizontal gene transfer has had the evolutionary significance in eucaryotes that it has had in procaryotes.

In bacteria, genetic traits that are commonly transmitted by plasmids and viruses include resistance to antibiotics and to heavy metals, the ability to produce certain toxins, and the ability to metabolize various substrates (Reanney 1976; Day 1982; Hardy 1986). These horizontally transmitted traits typically can generate a profound selective advantage for the host bacterium under appropriate environmental conditions (e.g., in the presence of an antibiotic), and they allow a bacterium to acquire a complex function without the combination of improbable mutations that would be necessary to evolve that function de novo.

In the absence of the appropriate selective regime, however, carriage of plasmids or integrated viruses which encode these functions may have no benefit to the host bacterium, and instead may be so much "excess baggage," owing to the added costs of producing the extra DNA and proteins. Bacteria may lose plasmids and viruses via segregation of their genetic material during cell replication. These bacterial segregants may then out-compete those bacteria-carrying plasmids or viruses that provide no direct benefit. Accordingly, the relationship between bacteria and their plasmid and viral vectors of horizontal transfer can be viewed on a continuum from mutualism to antagonism (Levin and Lenski 1983). On the one hand, these vectors provide bacteria with new and useful functions that would otherwise be difficult to evolve, thereby benefiting their hosts. On the other hand, these vectors of horizontal gene transfer are truly parasites, utilizing the resources and machinery of their bacterial hosts to ensure the replication and infectious transmission of their own "selfish" DNA.

This duality has led to some academic disagreement and perhaps confusion concerning whether horizontal gene transfer should be viewed as an integral feature of the bacterial life cycle, or alternatively as an indirect consequence of the infectious transmission of subcellular parasites. This duality also may affect how we view the potential significance of infectious transmission of recombinant DNA from genetically engineered organisms that are deliberately released into the environment. Is infectious transmission of genetic material so pervasive that we can assume that any recombinant engineered in the laboratory has already been tried in nature, so that we have nothing new with which to concern ourselves? (See also Regal 1986.) Or is infectious gene transfer so rare that we can effectively ignore it in our considerations of the possible risks associated with the release of genetically engineered organisms?

Despite these academic arguments, there are few biologists who would not agree with the statement that rates of infectious gene transfer vary considerably. For example, genes that are found on the vectors themselves are far more likely to be transferred than are genes normally found in the host chromosome. Thus, although the spread of plasmid borne antibiotic resistance in enteric bacteria gives ample evidence for the potential for rapid exchange of extra-chromosomal genes (Falkow 1975; Broda 1979; Koch 1981; Hughes and Datta 1983; Levy 1985; Hardy 1986), detailed studies of the patterns of linkage among chromosomal variants in E. coli indicate that horizontal transmission of these genes is a rather rare occurrence (Selander and Levin 1980; Caugant et al. 1981; Selander and Whittam 1983). Similar results are obtained for the pathogens Haemophilus influenzae (Musser et al. 1985) and Legionella pneumophila (Selander et al. 1985), whereas the patterns of linkage among genetic variants in Neisseria gonorrhoeae suggest a much higher degree of horizontal transfer of chromosomal genes (Musser 1986). This variability may reflect differences in the nature of the mechanisms of gene exchange operating between taxa; differences in the susceptibility of various taxa to infection by certain types of vectors; and differences in the biological, physical, and chemical properties of the environment, which influence the degree of cell contact and the population dynamics of vectors and hosts (Stotzky and Krasovsky 1981; Freter 1984).

The significance of this variability is that there are no simple answers to the questions regarding the likelihood of infectious transfer of recombinant DNA. Perhaps the only broad generalization to be made is that infectious gene transfer is neither so rare that we can ignore the possibility of its occurrence, nor so common that we can assume its consequences to be trivial. Therefore, it is prudent that the evaluation of the likelihood of infectious gene transfer be undertaken on a careful case-by-case basis when considering the deliberate release of recombinant organisms into the environment.

A GENERAL FRAMEWORK FOR EVALUATING THE RISKS ASSOCIATED WITH INFECTIOUS GENE TRANSFER

In the preceding section, we saw that a variety of processes could give rise to the infectious transfer of genetic material, and I claimed that no broad generalization could be reached concerning the importance of these processes in nature. What, then, would we need to know for a particular case in order to evaluate fully any potential risks associated with the infectious spread of the engineered genetic material?

The hypothetical scenarios presented earlier in this chapter demonstrate that we need to understand as much basic biology as possible about the recombinant organism and about the natural community of organisms into which it is to be released. Only then will it be feasible to identify the potential risks, and seek to minimize their likelihood and their impact. It is therefore essential that we endeavor to bring as much basic biological expertise as possible into the risk assessment process.

What follows now is a general framework for assessing the likelihood of horizontal gene transfer, and evaluating alternative measures for minimizing this likelihood. It presumes that the basic biology of the engineered organism and the natural community into which it is to be deliberately released are sufficiently well understood that one can identify particular routes of infectious gene exchange that might produce undesirable consequences.

First, it is important to recognize that the likelihood of an adverse consequence resulting from the deliberate release of a recombinant organism into the environment is dependent upon scale (Levin and Stewart 1977; Alexander 1985a). That is, an adverse consequence arising from a low rate of infectious spread of an engineered gene is not likely to occur if the recombinant organisms are released into the environment in very small numbers. However, with the release of many recombinants, the same low level of horizontal gene transfer may be significant. This scale effect is especially relevant because we are considering biological entities, which are self-replicating.

The effect of scale is well illustrated by the rise of resistance to penicillin in the bacterium N. gonorrhoeae. For many years, the gonococcus was treated efficaciously by penicillin, and only occasional low-level resistance was observed. However, in 1976, this pathogen acquired a gene that encodes the enzyme beta-lactamase, which enables a cell to cleave the penicillin molecule, and resistance by the gonococcus rapidly became a serious clinical problem. It appears that a plasmid encoding this function was transferred from an enteric bacterium to the gonococcus, a very rare event (Roberts et al. 1977). Had penicillin therapy of gonorrhea been conducted on a much smaller scale, clinically significant resistance might never have arisen. Unfortunately, one difficulty with risk assessment procedures that are based solely on direct observation is that they can tell us nothing about rare events, which might still have extremely important consequences. Thus, we should be willing to include in our considerations any reasonable inferences that are based on parallels with similar systems where we have greater experience.[1]

In addition to <u>absolute</u> scale, the dynamics of horizontal gene transfer <u>are dependent</u> on the <u>local</u> population densities of the donor and the recipient. In particular, the rate of infectious spread of an engineered genetic molecule can be expected to be proportional to the product of these densities, multiplied by some factor that indicates the intrinsic rate of gene transfer (Stewart and Levin 1977; Levin et al. 1979; Levin and Rice 1980; Evans 1986). The magnitude of this intrinsic rate will depend on the properties of the particular recombinant organism and the natural community into which it is to be released. Some of the important properties will include whether an engineered gene in the recombinant is located on a chromosome or on an extrachromosomal element; the propensity of the vector to integrate into its host's genome; the susceptibility of the recipient population to infection by the vector; and the physical and chemical properties of the environment that affect the survival of the vectors, the accessibility of donors and recipients, and so on.

Levin and Stewart (1977) examined the dynamics of infectious gene transfer that would result from the hypothetical release of a recombinant organism into the environment.[2] In their calculations, they identified two critical variables. The first is the ecological fitness of the donor recombinant organism, which is expressed as the rate at which the recombinants are lost from the community. The second variable is a measure of the rate of infectious transfer of the engineered genetic material to indigenous organisms in the community. This rate is expressed so that it is independent of the densities of the donor and recipient populations. In addition to these variables, their computations require the initial density for the donor population, as well as the density for the recipient population, which is assumed to remain constant through time. One can then derive a simple integral to compute the expected number of events resulting in infectious transfer of the engineered gene prior to the extinction of the donor recombinant population. In particular, it can be demonstrated that the likelihood of infectious spread of an engineered gene is as sensitive to the fitness of the recombinant donor as it is to the rate of horizontal gene transfer. If the recombinant organism does not persist in the environment, then there can be some reasonable expectation of avoiding any adverse consequence associated with a low level of infectious transfer. But if the recombinant organism persists indefinitely, then there is an ever-increasing likelihood of eventual transfer of the engineered genetic material to an indigenous population, with its attendant risks. Thus, the fate of the recombinant organism, of obvious importance in its own right, is also inextricably linked to the likelihood of infectious spread of its engineered genes to other organisms.

What factors determine the fate of the recombinant organism? Once again, answering this question requires a detailed understanding of the biology of the recombinant organism and of the natural system into which it is to be released, which can only be attained by careful study on a case-by-case basis. However, let me repeat a widely stated explanation for why a population of recombinant organisms might fail to persist after its deliberate release. According to this argument, the introduction of foreign genes into an organism, although providing some function of biotechnological utility, is intrinsically maladaptive to the recombinant organism. That is because the engineered genes are presumed to represent the same sort of "excess baggage" associated with DNA replication and protein synthesis that was discussed when considering the parasitic nature of vectors of horizontal gene transfer (see also Regal 1986). Thus, it is assumed that natural selection will purge these ecological "misfits" from communities after they have performed their intended biotechnological function. If true, this argument should go a long way towards allaying not only those concerns about risks associated with the direct ecological effects of the recombinant organism, but also those concerns arising from the indirect effects of horizontal gene transfer.

Unfortunately, there is a dilemma to be faced in the engineering of a recombinant organism for deliberate release into the environment. On the one hand, ecologically unfit recombinants reduce the possibility of adverse consequences associated with their release. On the other hand, many of the applications of recombinant organisms require that they be able to survive and replicate in the environment in order to perform their intended biotechnological functions. Thus, there is a fine line between recombinants that are too fit and those that are not fit enough (see also Simberloff and Colwell 1985). Whether this balance can indeed be attained is likely to depend on the specificity of the traits that are engineered into recombinant organisms. That is, a high specificity of ecological function should allow a recombinant trait to be maintained only where it is needed.

Evaluating this specificity is especially difficult, however, when one considers the infectious transfer of an engineered trait from one organism to another. In each of the hypothetical examples presented early in this chapter, the engineered trait in the recombinant organism satisfied the criterion of a high degree of ecological specificity. Yet in each case, the expression of this trait in another organism had dramatically different ecological consequences. This is because the fitness effects associated with carriage of a particular gene may depend on the genetic background, as well as on the environment, in which it is found (see also Dykhuizen and Hartl 1983; Hartl 1985).

Thus, even knowing the likelihood of horizontal gene transfer tells us very little about the fate of the recombinant organisms that may arise in situ. An analogy can be made between horizontal transfer of a gene between organisms and dispersal of an organism between habitats. Dispersal of an organism to a new habitat is unlikely to have any lasting effect if it is poorly adapted to the conditions in its new habitat and cannot become established. Similarly, infectious transfer of engineered genetic material is likely to be of consequence only if it provides a selective advantage to the recipient (see also Alexander 1985b; Hartl 1985). If the engineered genetic material allows the recipient to utilize an additional resource, or permits the recipient to become less sensitive to the effects of some agent of control, then it is much more likely that the horizontal transfer will have a significant ecological impact. In fact, one can extend the analysis of the dynamics of infectious transfer of an engineered gene to incorporate the effect of the selective advantage, if any, accruing to the recipient. This analysis indicates that the likelihood that a recipient of an engineered gene will become established in its natural community is directly proportional to its selective advantage (see similar analyses by Haldane 1927; Feller 1957; and Lenski and Levin 1985a).[3]

It is sometimes assumed that ecological niches are "full." (See exchanges between Davis 1984 and Simberloff and Colwell 1985, and between Brill 1985a, b, and Colwell et al. 1985.) If valid, this would suggest that horizontal transfer of engineered genetic material is unlikely to provide the recipient with a truly novel selective advantage that allows it to proliferate with unanticipated consequences. This view ignores, however, two important considerations. First, natural communities are constantly undergoing change, and few, if any, are invulnerable to invasion by introduced species (see Chapter 4; also Sharples 1983; Simberloff 1981, 1985). Second, there are constraints on evolutionary processes that limit the ability of organisms to become "perfectly" adapted, including the simple lack of appropriate genetic material (Gould and Lewontin 1979; Lenski and Levin 1985a; Regal 1986). One simply cannot assume that organisms have long ago "solved" all the problems of their adaptation.

It has also been argued that the introduction of foreign genes is no more likely to have unintended consequences than traditional practices used in agriculture. (See exchanges between Brill 1985a, b, and Colwell et al. 1985; and among Hardy and Glass 1985, Lenski and Levin 1985b, and Regal 1985.) In fact, there are examples in which crop varieties produced by traditional means have become weeds, and there are instances of apparently very simple genetic changes in natural populations that have had major ecological effects (Alexander 1985b; Colwell et al. 1985; Simberloff 1985). Moreover, this argument ignores the primary advantage of new recombinant techniques over traditional selective breeding programs employed for many centuries: recombinant techniques enable one to move genetic material across taxonomic barriers where natural gene exchange either does not occur or else occurs only very rarely. Therefore, we should not exclude the possibility that the transfer of engineered genes in situ may provide novel genetic variation and new ecological benefits to the recipient organisms.

We must know the following in order to predict accurately the likelihood of an adverse consequence arising from the infectious spread of engineered genetic material. First, we must understand the biology of the recombinant organism and the ecology of the community into which it is to be deliberately released in sufficient depth so that we can identify the horizontal gene transfer events that could reasonably be expected to produce potentially adverse effects. Without this knowledge, the complexity of ecological communities and the number of possible routes of gene exchange make a comprehensive survey infeasible. Second, we must be able to quantify the likelihood that such horizontal transfer will occur and give rise to these potentially adverse effects. This likelihood is equally sensitive to three critical factors: the ecological fitness of the deliberately released recombinant organism, which will determine its persistence in the environment and hence its opportunity to serve as donor of an engineered gene; the intrinsic rate of transfer of an engineered gene, which will depend upon the specific characteristics of the donor, vector, recipient, and environment; and the effect of an engineered gene on the fitness of the potential recipient, which will determine whether the recipient that arises in situ can become established in the ecological community.

Finally, it must also be emphasized that one cannot assume that the various factors that are important in determining the likelihood of infectious spread of engineered genetic molecules will remain constant. While the laws of chemistry and physics are constant, the relationships between organisms and even between genes within an organism are constantly changing (Lenski and Levin 1985b; Regal 1986). For example, there may be genetic changes in recombinant organisms that modify the rates at which engineered genes are transmitted. A gene may transpose from a chromosome or a nonconjugative plasmid to a conjugative plasmid, greatly increasing its ability to be infectiously transmitted (Levy 1985; Slater 1985). A plasmid that is repressed for the production of conjugative pili may become derepressed, allowing that vector to be maintained in a population where it could otherwise not persist (Lundquist and Levin 1986). Similarly, genetic changes may be favored which compensate for the "cost" of carrying an engineered trait. This may occur, for example, as the result of mutations that alter the regulation of gene expression, so that some gene product is no longer overproduced when it is not beneficial (Dykhuizen and Hartl 1983; Moyed and Bertrand 1983). The effect of such changes will be to increase the stability of the engineered trait in the recombinant organism, and thereby enhance the persistence of the recombinant organism in the environment, which in turn increases the opportunity for subsequent infectious spread of an engineered gene (see also Roberts et al. 1977; Lenski and Levin 1985b). Thus, the heterogeneity of ecological systems in space and time, and the ability of biological populations to undergo evolutionary change, introduce further variables that must be considered.

SUMMARY

The deliberate release of genetically engineered organisms into the environment may provide a variety of

economic and social benefits. Evaluating the possible
risks associated with the release of genetically engineered
organisms into the environment is difficult because of the
complexity of ecological systems. This risk assessment is
further complicated by the possibility that an engineered
gene may be transmitted to another organism. It is possible to construct plausible scenarios wherein the spread of
an engineered gene to an indigenous organism has deleterious consequences, even though the engineered organism itself causes no direct adverse effects.

According to traditional views in genetics and evolutionary biology, recombination is limited to Mendelian segregation and reassortment, which occurs during sexual reproduction and is confined within species boundaries. Procaryotes (including bacteria) reproduce asexually, yet they
can undergo genetic recombination by a variety of mechanisms, some of which are mediated by subcellular parasites
(including viruses). These mechanisms are variously termed
infectious or horizontal gene transmission, and they form
the technological basis for genetic engineering. Infectious gene exchange may occur even between rather distantly
related taxa, as witnessed by the spread of antibiotic resistance genes in bacteria.

Many factors influence the importance of infectious
transmission as a source of genetic variation in natural
populations. There is no broad generalization that can be
made regarding the likelihood of infectious spread of engineered genes. Infectious gene transfer is neither so
rare that we can ignore the possibility of its occurrence,
nor so common that we can assume its consequences to be
trivial. Thus, it seems prudent to evaluate any possible
risks associated with the infectious spread of engineered
genes on a case-by-case basis. One difficulty in evaluating these risks arises because horizontal transmission
may often be a very rare event that nonetheless produces
important effects, owing to the self-replicating nature of
biological entities. Hence, the likelihood of observing
the infectious spread of an engineered gene will be highly
dependent on the scale of the deliberate release of the
recombinant organism.

In this chapter, I have argued that we must have the
following information in order to predict accurately the
likelihood of infectious spread of an engineered gene.
First and foremost, we must understand the biology of the
recombinant organism and the ecology of the community into
which it is to be deliberately released in sufficient

detail that we can identify those avenues of horizontal gene transfer that could produce potentially adverse environmental effects. Second, we must be able to quantify the likelihood that such horizontal transfer will occur, and this requires answers to several questions: How long will the deliberately released recombinant organism persist in the environment, and hence be a potential donor of the engineered gene? At what rate is the engineered gene infectiously transmitted to the potential recipient? And how will the engineered gene affect the ecological fitness of the potential recipient, and thus its ability to proliferate in the environment? Also, the heterogeneity of ecological systems in space and time, and the ability of biological populations to undergo evolutionary change, introduce further variables that must be considered.

It should be apparent that evaluating any possible risks associated with the infectious transmission of engineered genes requires an interdisciplinary effort (see Chapter 7; also Regal 1985; Flanagan 1986). Molecular biologists must investigate the expression and stability of engineered traits, and they must understand how these are affected by the genetic background in which the traits are found. Population geneticists must measure the rates of gene transfer in natural populations, and evolutionary biologists must determine the effects of engineered traits on the fitness of organisms. Ecologists must understand the structure of natural communities in order to evaluate changes in the selective pressures resulting from genetic modification of organisms, and they must be able to use this information to predict the effects of genetic modification on such diverse processes as the dynamics of populations and the cycling of nutrients in ecosystems. In the coming years, ecologists and evolutionary biologists may learn a great deal by observing the effects that result from the careful modification of specific genetic traits, and from this, they may be able to offer suggestions regarding how to engineer organisms that are not only safer, but also more effective in their intended biotechnological applications.

NOTES

1. It is of interest to note in this regard that Falkow and colleagues used such reasoning to suggest the possibility of plasmid-mediated penicillin resistance in Neisseria gonorrhoeae before it was actually observed.

2. In the 1970s, concerns focused on the accidental release of engineered organisms from laboratory containment. The mathematical analysis of the fate of deliberately released engineered organisms is identical.

3. It is also possible that a gene that is selectively neutral or even disadvantageous for the recipient could become established, provided that the rate of infectious transmission of that gene is sufficiently high (Levin and Stewart 1977). However, the conditions for this to occur are much more restrictive and, in my opinion, are generally less applicable.

ACKNOWLEDGMENTS

I thank Pete Atsatt, Judy Bouma, Peter Bowler, Allan Dietz, Simon Ford, Sue Hattingh, Bruce Levin, and Cliff Woolfolk for their helpful discussion and comments during the preparation of this manuscript, and Jim Musser for allowing me to cite his work prior to publication. I am also very thankful for Cheryl Adams and Dianne Christianson, who kindly retyped this manuscript after an earlier version was destroyed by the crash of the hard disk on my personal computer. NIH grant GM37105 provided support during the preparation of this manuscript.

REFERENCES

Alexander, M. 1985a. Ecological Consequences: Reducing the Uncertainties. Issues in Science and Technology 1(3): 57-68.

---. 1985b. Spread of Organisms with Novel Genotypes. In Biotechnology and the Environment, ed. A.H. Teich, M.A. Levin, and J.H. Pace, 115-136. Washington, DC: American Association for the Advancement of Science.

Barkay, T., D.L. Fouts, and B.H. Olson. 1985. Preparation of a DNA Gene Probe for Detection of Mercury Resistance Genes in Gram-Negative Bacterial Communities. Applied and Environmental Microbiology 49:686-692.

Barton, K.A., and W.J. Brill. 1983. Prospects in Plant Genetic Engineering. Science 219:671-676.

Botstein, D. 1980. A Theory of Modular Evolution for Bacteriophages. Annals of the New York Academy of Sciences 345:484-491.

Bradley, D.E. 1981. Conjugative Pili of Plasmids in Escherichia coli K-12 and Pseudomonas Species. In Molecular Biology, Pathogenicity, and Ecology of Bacterial Plasmids, ed. S.B. Levy, R.C. Clowes, and .L. Koenig, 217-226. New York: Plenum.

Brill, W.J. 1985a. Safety Concerns and Genetic Engineering in Agriculture. Science 227:381-384.

---. 1985b. Genetic Engineering in Agriculture. Science 229:115-118.

Broda, P. 1979. Plasmids. London: Freeman.

Broda, P., R. Downing, P. Lehrbach, I. McGregor, and P. Meulien. 1981. Degradative Plasmids: TOL and Beyond. In Molecular Biology, Pathogenicity, and Ecology of Bacterial Plasmids, ed. S.B. Levy, R.C. Clowes, and E.L. Koenig, 511-517. New York: Plenum.

Brown, J.H., R.K. Colwell, R.E. Lenski, B.R. Levin, M. Lloyd, P.J. Regal, and D. Simberloff. 1984. Report on Workshop on Possible Ecological and Evolutionary Impacts of Bioengineered Organisms Released into the Environment. Bulletin of the Ecological Society of America 65:436-438.

Campbell, A. 1983. Transposons and Their Evolutionary Significance. In Evolution of Genes and Proteins, ed. M. Nei and R.K. Koehn, 258-279. Sunderland, MA: Sinauer.

Caugant, D.A., B.R. Levin, and R.K. Selander. 1981. Genetic Diversity and Temporal Variation in the E. coli Population of a Human Host. Genetics 98:467-490.

Chatterjee, D.K., S.T. Kellogg, D.R. Watkins, and A.M. Chakrabarty. 1981. Plasmids in the Biodegradation of Chlorinated Aromatic Compounds. In Molecular Biology, Pathogenicity, and Ecology of Bacterial Plasmids, ed. S.B. Levy, R.C. Clowes, and E.L. Koenig, 519-528. New York: Plenum.

Colwell, R.K., E.A. Norse, D. Pimentel, F.E. Sharples, and
    D. Simberloff. 1985. Genetic Engineering in
    Agriculture. Science 229:111-112.

Curtiss, R., III. 1976. Genetic Manipulation of
    Microorganisms: Potential Benefits and Biohazards.
    Annual Review of Microbiology 30:507-533.

Curtiss, R., III, D.A. Pereira, S.C. Hsu, S.C. Hull, J.E.
    Clark, L.J. Maturin, Sr., R. Goldschmidt, R. Moody, M.
    Inoue, and L. Alexander. 1977. Biological
    Containment: The Subordination of Escherichia coli
    K-12. In Recombinant Molecules: Impact on Science and
    Society, ed. R.F. Beers, Jr. and E.G. Bassett, 45-56.
    New York: Raven.

Davis, B. 1984. Science, Fanaticism, and the Law. Genetic
    Engineering News 4(5): 4.

Day, M.J. 1982. Plasmids. London: Edward Arnold.

DeBach, P. 1974. Biological Control by Natural Enemies.
    London: Cambridge University.

Depicker, A., M. Van Montagu, and J. Schell. 1984. Plant
    Cell Transformation by Agrobacterium Plasmids. In
    Genetic Engineering of Hosts, ed. T. Kosuge, C.P.
    Meredith, and A. Hollaender, 143-176. New York:
    Plenum.

Dykhuizen, D.E., and D.L. Hartl. 1983. Selection in
    Chemostats. Microbiological Reviews 47:150-168.

Evans, R. 1986. Niche Expansion in Bacteria: Can
    Infectious Gene Exchange Affect the Rate of
    Evolution? Genetics 113:775-795.

Falkow, S. 1975. Infectious Multiple Drug Resistance.
    London: Pion.

Feller, W. 1957. An Introduction to Probability Theory
    and Its Application. Vol. 1. New York: Wiley.

Flanagan, P.W. 1986. Genetically Engineered Organisms and
    Ecology. Bulletin of the Ecological Society of
    America 67:26-30.

Freter, R. 1984. Factors Affecting Conjugal Plasmid Transfer in Natural Bacterial Communities. In Current Perspectives in Microbial Ecology, ed. M.J. Klug and C.A. Reddy, 105-114. Washington, DC: American Society of Microbiology.

Goodman, R.M., and N. Newell. 1985. Genetic Engineering of Plants for Herbicide Resistance: Status and Prospects. In Engineered Organisms in the Environment: Scientific Issues, ed. H.O. Halvorson, D. Pramer, and M. Rogul, 47-53. Washington, DC: American Society for Microbiology.

Gould, S.J., and R.C. Lewontin. 1979. The Spandrels of San Marco and the Panglossian Paradigm: A Critique of the Adaptationist Programme. Proceedings of the Royal Society of London, Series B, Biological Sciences. 205:581-598.

Graham, J.B., and C.A. Istock. 1979. Gene Exchange and Natural Selection Cause Bacillus subtilis to Evolve in Soil Culture. Science 104:637-639.

Hahlbrock, K., J. Chappell, and D. Scheel. 1984. Genes Involved in Resistance Reactions in Higher Plants: Possible Candidates for Gene Transfer? In The Impact of Gene Transfer Techniques in Eucaryotic Cell Biology, ed. J.S. Schell and P. Starlinger, 155-166. Berlin: Springer-Verlag.

Haldane, J.B.S. 1927. A Mathematical Theory of Natural and Artificial Selection. V. Selection and Mutation. Proceedings of the Cambridge Philosophical Society 23:838-844.

Hardy, K. 1986. Bacterial Plasmids. Washington, DC: American Society for Microbiology.

Hardy, R.W.F. 1985. Biotechnology in Agriculture: Status, Potential, Concerns. In Biotechnology and the Environment, ed. A.H. Teich, M.A. Levin, and J.H. Pace, 99-113. Washington, DC: American Association for the Advancement of Science.

Hardy, R.W.F., and D.J. Glass. 1985. Our Investment: What Is at Stake? Issues in Science and Technology 1(3): 69-82.

Hartl, D.L. 1985. Engineered Organisms in the Environment: Inferences from Population Genetics. In Engineered Organisms in the Environment: Scientific Issues, ed. H.O. Halvorson, D. Pramer, and M. Rogul, 83-88. Washington, DC: American Society for Microbiology.

Horsch, R.B., R.T. Fraley, S.G. Rogers, P.R. Sanders, A. Lloyd, and N. Hoffman. 1984. Inheritance of Functional Foreign Genes in Plants. Science 223:496-498.

Hughes, V.M., and N. Datta. 1983. Conjugative Plasmids in Bacteria of the "Pre-Antibiotic" Era. Nature 302:725-726.

Kellogg, S.T., D.K. Chatterjee, and A.M. Chakrabarty. 1981. Plasmid-Assisted Molecular Breeding: New Techniques for Enhanced Biodegradation of Persistant Toxic Chemicals. Science 214:1133-1135.

Koch, A.L. 1981. Evolution of Antibiotic Resistance Gene Function. Microbiological Reviews 45:355-378.

Krieber, M., and M.R. Rose. 1986. Molecular Aspects of the Species Barrier. Annual Review of Ecology and Systematics 17:465-485.

Lenski, R.E., and B.R. Levin. 1985a. Constraints on the Coevolution of Bacteria and Virulent Phage: A Model, Some Experiments, and Predictions for Natural Communities. American Naturalist 125:585-602.

---. 1985b. Genetic Engineering. Issues in Science and Technology 1(4): 13-14.

Levin, B.R., and R.E. Lenski. 1983. Coevolution in Bacteria and Their Viruses and Plasmids. In Coevolution, ed. D.J. Futuyma and M. Slatkin, 99-127. Sunderland, MA: Sinauer.

Levin, B.R., and V.A. Rice. 1980. The Kinetics of Transfer of Nonconjugative Plasmids by Mobilizing Conjugative Factors. Genetics Research, Cambridge 35:241-259.

Levin, B.R., and F.M. Stewart. 1977. Probability of Establishing Chimeric Plasmids in Natural Populations of Bacteria. Science 196:218-220.

Levin, B.R., V.A. Rice, and F.M. Stewart. 1979. The Kinetics of Conjugative Plasmid Transmission: Fit of Simple Mass Action Models. Plasmid 2:247-260.

Levy, S.B. 1985. Ecology of Plasmids and Unique DNA Sequences. In Engineered Organisms in the Environment: Scientific Issues, ed. H.O. Halvorson, D. Pramer, and M. Rogul, 180-190. Washington, DC: American Society for Microbiology.

Lundquist, P.D., and B.R. Levin. 1986. Transitory Derepression and the Maintenance of Conjugative Plasmids. Genetics 113:483-497.

Margulis, L. 1970. Origin of Eucaryotic Cells. New Haven: Yale University.

Mayr, E. 1970. Populations, Species, and Evolution. Cambridge, MA: Belknap.

Moyed, H.S., and K.P. Bertrand. 1983. Mutations in Multicopy Tn10 tet Plasmids That Confer Resistance to Inhibitory Effects of Inducers of tet Gene Expression. Journal of Bacteriology 155:557-564.

Musser, J.M. 1986. Personal communication.

Musser, J.M., D.M. Granoff, P.E. Pattison, and R.K. Selander. 1985. A Population Genetic Framework for the Study of Invasive Diseases Caused by Serotype B Strains of Haemophilis influenzae. Proceedings of the National Academy of Sciences, USA 82:5078-5082.

Muster, C.J., L.A. MacHattie, and J.A. Shapiro. 1981. Transposition and Rearrangements in Plasmid Evolution. In Molecular Biology, Pathogenicity, and Ecology of Bacterial Plasmids, ed. S.B. Levy, R.C. Clowes, and E.L. Koenig, 349-358. New York: Plenum.

Paul, J.K., ed. 1981. Genetic Engineering Applications for Industry. Park Ridge, NJ: Noyes Data.

Pimentel, D. 1985. Using Genetic Engineering for Biological Control: Reducing Ecological Risks. In Engineered Organisms in the Environment: Scientific Issues, ed. H.O. Halvorson, D. Pramer, and M. Rogul, 129-140. Washington, DC: American Society for Microbiology.

Price, P.W., M. Westoby, B. Rice, P.R. Atsatt, R.S. Fritz, J.N. Thompson, and C. Molby. 1986. Parasite Mediation in Ecological Interactions. Annual Review of Ecology and Systematics 17:487-505.

Reanney, D. 1976. Extrachromosomal Elements as Possible Agents of Adaptation and Development. Bacteriological Reviews 40:552-590.

Regal, P.J. 1985. Genetic Engineering. Issues in Science and Technology 1(4): 14-15.

---. 1986. Models of Genetically Engineered Organisms and Their Ecological Impact. In Ecology of Biological Invasions of North America and Hawaii, ed. H.A. Mooney, 111-129. New York: Springer-Verlag.

Roberts, M., L.P. Elwell, and S. Falkow. 1977. Molecular Characterization of Two Beta-Lactamase-Specifying Plasmids Isolated from Neisseria gonorrhoeae. Journal of Bacteriology 131:557-563.

Schell, J., L. Herrera-Estrella, P. Zambryski, M. DeBlock, H. Joos, L. Willmitzer, P. Eckes, S. Rosahl, and M. Van Montagu. 1984. Genetic Engineering in Plants. In The Impact of Gene Transfer Techniques in Eucaryotic Cell Biology, ed. J.S. Schell and P. Starlinger, 73-90. Berlin: Springer-Verlag.

Selander, R.K., and B.R. Levin. 1980. Genetic Diversity and Structure in Escherichia coli Populations. Science 210:545-547.

Selander, R.K., and T.S. Whittam. 1983. Protein Polymorphism and the Genetic Structure of Populations. In Evolution of Genes and Proteins, ed. M. Nei and R.K. Koehn, 89-114. Sunderland, MA: Sinauer.

Selander, R.K., R.M. McKinney, T.S. Whittam, W.F. Bibb, D.J. Brenner, F.S. Nolte, and P.E. Pattison. 1985. Genetic Structure of Populations of Legionella pneumophila. Journal of Bacteriology 163:1021-1037.

Shapiro, J.A., ed. 1983. Mobile Genetic Elements. New York: Academic.

Sharples, F.E. 1983. Spread of Organisms with Novel Genotypes: Thoughts from an Ecological Perspective. Recombinant DNA Technical Bulletin 6:43-56.

Simberloff, D. 1981. Community Effects of Introduced Species. In Biotic Crises in Ecological and Evolutionary Time, ed. M.H. Nitecki, 53-81. New York: Academic.

---. 1985. Predicting Ecological Effects of Novel Entities: Evidence from Higher Organisms. In Engineered Organisms in the Environment: Scientific Issues, ed. H.O. Halvorson, D. Pramer, and M. Rogul, 152-161. Washington, DC: American Society for Microbiology.

Simberloff, D., and R. Colwell. 1985. Release of Engineered Organisms: A Call for Ecological and Evolutionary Assessment of Risks. Genetic Engineering News 4(8): 4.

Slater, J.H. 1984. Genetic Interactions in Microbial Communities. In Current Pespectives in Microbial Ecology, ed. M.J. Klug and C.A. Reddy, 87-93. Washington, DC: American Society of Microbiology.

---. 1985. Gene Transfer in Microbial Communities. In Engineered Organisms in the Environment: Scientific Issues, ed. H.O. Halvorson, D. Pramer, and M. Rogul, 89-98. Washington, DC: American Society for Microbiology.

Stewart, F.M., and B.R. Levin. 1977. The Population Biology of Bacterial Plasmids: A Priori Conditions for the Existence of Conjugationally Transmitted Factors. Genetics 87:209-228.

Stotzky, G., and H. Babich. 1984. Fate of Genetically Engineered Microbes in Natural Environments. Recombinant DNA Technical Bulletin 7:163-188.

Stotzky, G., and V.N. Krasovsky. 1981. Ecological Factors That Affect the Survival, Establishment, Growth, and Genetic Recombination of Microbes in Natural Habitats. In Molecular Biology, Pathogenicity, and Ecology of Bacterial Plasmids, ed. S.B. Levy, R.C. Clowes, and E.L. Koenig, 31-42. New York: Plenum.

Timmis, J.N., and N.S. Scott. 1984. Promiscuous DNA: Sequence Homologies Between DNA of Separate Organelles. Trends in Biochemical Science 9:271-273.

Vitousek, P.M. 1985. Plant and Animal Invasions: Can They Alter Ecosystem Processes? In Engineered Organisms in the Environment: Scientific Issues, ed. H.O. Halvorson, D. Pramer, and M. Rogul, 169-175. Washington, DC: American Society for Microbiology.

Watrud, L.S., F.J. Perlak, M.T. Tran, K. Kusano, E.J. Mayer, M.A. Miller-Wideman, M.G. Obukowicz, D.R. Nelson, J.P. Kreitinger, and R.J. Kaufman. 1985. Cloning of the Bacillus thuringiensis Subsp. kurstaki Delta-Endotoxin Gene into Pseudomonas fluorescens: Molecular Biology and Ecology of an Engineered Microbial Pesticide. In Engineered Organisms in the Environment: Scientific Issues, ed. H.O. Halvorson, D. Pramer, and M. Rogul, 40-46. Washington, DC: American Society for Microbiology.

Yoder, D.C. 1983. Use of Pathogen-Produced Toxins in Genetic Engineering of Plants and Pathogens. In Genetic Engineering of Hosts, ed. T. Kosuge, C.P. Meredith, and A. Hollaender, 335-353. New York: Plenum.

Zambryski, P., H.M. Goodman, M. Van Montagu, and J. Schell. 1983. Agrobacterium Tumor Induction. In Mobile Genetic Elements, ed. J.A. Shapiro, 505-535. New York: Academic.

David A. Andow, Simon A. Levin,
and Mark A. Harwell

6. Evaluating Environmental Risks from Biotechnology: Contributions of Ecology

INTRODUCTION

The history of technology development is replete with examples of well-meant introductions of new technologies, followed by unexpected adverse consequences. Nuclear power plants, pesticide manufacture in Third World countries, and some Green Revolution plant varieties provide a few contemporary examples. One lesson to be gained from our past experience with new technologies is that they carry the risk of unforeseen deleterious side effects. Biotechnology represents a rapidly developing area, as yet free from such catastrophes; thus we are fortunate in having the opportunity to anticipate potential problems and to minimize potential social risks.

Biotechnology, as used in this chapter, refers to a class of techniques that can be distinguished from conventional methods of genetic manipulation such as selective breeding, crop rotation, introduction of exotic organisms, hybridization, and isolation of microbial pesticides. These technologies generally involve whole, intact organisms. Biotechnology extends these to include "genetic engineering" technologies based on the suborganismic level--for example, tissue culture, cell culture, and genetic transformation, the movement of genes from one organism to another by recombinant DNA (rDNA) techniques. These new techniques are in many respects quite similar to the more conventional genetic and breeding techniques, but they are distinguished by two characteristics: the potential to transfer genetic material between widely disparate organisms, and the potential to do this with precision.

Biotechnology has a large potential to improve the human condition, and to engender important advances in pharmaceutical production, food processing, agricultural production, and environmental management. However, accompanying such deliberate releases is the risk of undesirable side effects on human health, the environment, and society. Even if the great majority of biotechnology product introductions prove to be beneficial or benign, a single major catastrophe could harm the entire industry. By seizing the opportunity to structure a reliable system to preclude such mishaps, we facilitate biotechnology development; without a widely respected, effective regulatory system, any intended introduction faces the near certainty of litigation and other forms of opposition (Levin and Harwell 1986). It is better to develop biotechnology products carefully and deliberately than to rush and court potential disaster.

At issue in this chapter is the establishment of the principles that must underlie risk assessment methodology, not the details of particular cases. Our attention is on deliberate releases to the environment; we will not treat risks involved with accidental release of engineered organisms. This constitutes a key distinction: for accidental releases, risk assessment centers on the typically low probabilities of breach of containment and of establishment in the environment; in contrast, organisms engineered for deliberate release are designed specifically to survive and reproduce for some period of time.

FRAMEWORK FOR ASSESSING RISKS

To understand the potential for environmental impact of a genetically engineered product, we must understand the fate and transport of genetically engineered material, the potential for containment, the potential impact on the environment, and the ability to mitigate.

Fate, Transport, and Containment

Alexander (1985) and Andow (1985) review the literature concerning fate and transport of bacteria, the most likely early candidates for deliberate release into the environment. One of the first considerations is whether or not the released organism can be contained at the release site. There are, however, many technical difficulties associated with containing a bacterial population.

In the absence of essential nutrients and an adequate energy base, bacterial populations can fall to levels in nature so low that they cannot be detected. However, if nutrients and an adequate energy substrate become available, the populations can rapidly rebound to quite high densities. An important implication is that it is extremely difficult to be assured that an undetected bacterial population is absent (but see Andow et al. 1987), or will not develop explosively when conditions change.

In general, bacterial species have multiple modes of dispersal. For example, a soil bacterium could be moved with aeolian dust, be projected in aerosol from rain splash, cling to a passing animal, percolate down to the ground water, or follow several other pathways for movement. Thus, effective containment of an introduction at the site of initial release would be difficult to accomplish and evaluate, and must be treated as having some probability of failure.

The size of the proposed release affects the likelihood of being able to contain the release. The larger the population of bacteria at a source site, the more likely it is that some organisms will disperse. Releases for experimental purposes typically are limited spacially, of short duration, and involve few organisms. In contrast, a deliberate release of a genetically engineered organism would be done in expectation that it would grow and reproduce. Since populations are expected to become larger, the likelihood that there will be some individuals that disperse and escape containment is larger. Thus, while both entail risks, containment of large, deliberate releases is more problematic than containment of small experimental releases. In either case, containment never can be assured totally. Increased attention can enhance the probability of success; this increased attention, in turn, increases cost.

An additional problem is that bacteria can exchange genetic material by horizontal transfer between species, as well as between individuals (see Chapter 5). Such transfers can lead to rapid proliferation if selection pressures are favorable. While the frequency of occurrence of this process is unquantified, its existence makes containing the genetic information less likely and monitoring fate and transport more difficult.

Effects and Mitigation

Although some likely effects can be identified easily, in general, answers remain elusive and unresolved. Limburg et al. (1986) suggest that it is not possible to make long-term predictions about effects of a particular stress on the dynamics of particular populations, much less on community structure or on ecosystem functions. Consequently, attempts at prediction must be viewed as rough approximations, and reliability often decreases as predictions are made further into the future.

Indirect effects often are more important than direct ones, yet are virtually impossible to anticipate, in part because of the potentially tremendous number of possible indirect relationships, and in part because of insufficient understanding of interspecific interactions and the physicochemical conditions that influence them. In all environmental evaluations, we must rely fundamentally on extrapolations from different ecosystems, perturbations, or scales of evidence. Clearly, we cannot foresee all possible contingencies, yet we must make reasonable decisions concerning environmental protection and management even in the presence of uncertainties.

This underscores the desirability of coupling monitoring with management, so that management can be adapted as information accrues and understanding increases (Holling 1978; Limburg et al. 1984). Thus, for any deliberate release of an organism, we must expect errors, and we must have available the means for mitigation (Levin and Harwell 1985).

Because the potential for containment and mitigation will vary depending on the proposed release, assessment of this potential is part of the process of risk assessment. If containment probability is high, if likely adverse effects are extremely small, or if mitigation is possible, then the release might be deemed relatively safe (internal surface in Figure 6.1); if all three of these criteria are met, then the risk associated with release is relatively low (i.e., lower left front corner in Figure 6.1). In other words, for any particular case, trade-offs exist among containment, effects, and mitigation. However, because of the uncertain nature of predicting ecological effects, emphasis must be placed on assurances of the means for mitigation and high probabilities of containment.

Quarantine efforts in the United States are illustrative. The U.S. Department of Agriculture and many individual states take elaborate precautions against potentially catastrophic introductions of exotic species. Where anticipated effects are large, effort is placed in containment and mitigation. Accidents, however, do occur (e.g., citrus canker, Mediterranean fruit fly) under even the most care-

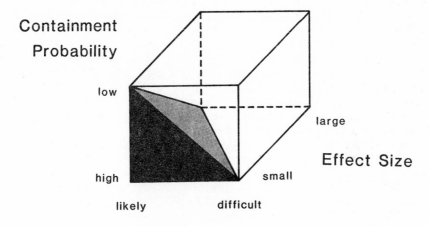

Figure 6.1 Relation between the environmental risk from a deliberate release of an organism, and (1) the probability of containing a proposed release of an organism; (2) the size and predictability of adverse ecological effects stemming from the release; and (3) the ability to mitigate a release should it be desired. The dark area represents relatively risk-free releases.

ful regulatory system, and mitigation efforts have had substantial economic costs. It is instructive to note that the Quarantine Act to guard against these introductions came as a response to the catastrophic introduction of white pine blister rust, not in anticipation of catastrophe (Horsfall 1983). We reiterate the importance of developing a sound regulatory policy for biotechnology before catastrophe occurs.

MODELS FOR ASSESSING RISK

Despite methodological difficulties, it is important and necessary to evaluate the potential ecological effects before deliberately releasing genetically engineered microorganisms, as would be the case for the release of any organism. It is certain that we cannot rely on such specious assurances of safety as the argument sometimes advanced that the genomes of organisms have been optimized by a long history of natural selection, so that any artificial alteration of the genome would be harmful to the individual and population and lessen the chance of spread. Regal (1986) labels this the "untuned engine model" and exposes its fallacious assumptions. Organisms are not optimally adapted to their environments; they are adequately adapted for survival (Gould 1979; Regal 1986). Indeed, organisms are not adapted to their environments; they are adapted for survival in those environments (Whittaker 1970). There is nothing to prevent an alteration in the genome from producing an organism better adapted to some environment than the indigenous ones, and such an organism certainly could spread. There is no more basis for the argument that all introductions will be safe than for the argument that none will be safe; the challenge is to assess levels of safety and to minimize the probability that damaging accidents may occur.

Thus, case-by-case risk assessment is essential, based on the nature of the product. To facilitate these analyses, it is necessary to rely on models derived from other experiences. No single model is likely to be generally applicable to all proposed releases, but for any particular case, appropriate models can be developed.

Laboratory Experimentation and Toxic Chemicals

The risk factors associated with laboratory experimentation with genetic engineering are fundamentally different from those relating to the deliberate release of biotechnology products into the environment. In the case of deliberate release, "escape" into the environment is a certainty; survival, at least for some period of time, is essential for the introduction to be useful. The potential growth and spread of introduced biological material offers enormous possible economic benefits, since an initially small release may spread its effects over a wide area; therein lies an obvious environmental risk. Further, many genetic alterations are aimed at modifying interspecific interactions (e.g., by modifying resistance to pathogens or predators, or by changing competitive ability) or system-level processes (e.g., nutrient cycling). It is clear that the regulatory issues for deliberate releases are fundamentally different than for controlled laboratory situations, in which risks are incurred accidentally. The probabilities of adverse ecological side effects are orders of magnitude greater for deliberate than for accidental releases because the possibilities of growth and spread are much larger (Levin and Harwell 1986).

Chemicals provide an analogy of particular relevance to regulators, because the basic considerations are the same as for biological introductions. For example, one needs a testing system to assess the fate and the potential effects of the introduced material, whether one is dealing with a chemical or with an organism. This is the primary justification for proposing that the Toxic Substances Control Act (TSCA) serve at least as gap-filling legislation for regulating the introduction of microorganisms (Gillett et al. 1985).

However, one of the major differences between chemical and biological introductions is that organisms have a great capacity for geographical spread and proliferation by reproduction and plasmid transfer. This means that the ecological impact from biological introductions can increase in severity and that the organisms can rebound from extremely low concentrations. Thus, reliance on detection thresholds for regulation would be inadequate.

Another major difference is that organisms exhibit individual adaptive behavior. This behavior leads to movement of various kinds, and greater degrees of unpredictability and uncertainty (Bateson 1972). Thus, regulatory schemes must be dynamic and adaptive.

Introductions and Invasions

Deliberate introductions of new crops, new varieties of old crops, and biological control agents, and accidental introductions of exotic organisms provide natural models for the introduction of genetically engineered species into the environment. We distinguish several models of introductions. These differ in whether the introduced organism can be found in the target environment, in another non-target environment, or in no current environment. They differ also in the ecological functions the introduced organism is expected to play in the target enviroment.

If an introduced organism is similar to species already present in the target environment, ecological information on those present provides the natural starting point in evaluating how the introduced species might fare. For

example, if crop varieties with certain agronomic characteristics are known to do well and others to do poorly in
certain environments, then the performance of new varieties
with specified agronomic characteristics could be predicted
fairly accurately.

In general, conventional plant and animal breeding
have selected for features that have little effect on the
ability of the species to proliferate in natural environments; indeed, they are usually at a disadvantage outside
the target environment. In the unlikely event of escape of
these higher organisms from controlled environments, they
can be located relatively easily and destroyed. Thus,
mitigation is possible, and the likelihood of irreversible
adverse environmental effects usually is small (Regal 1986).

However, there remain familiar potential problems: intensive selection for plant varieties with desired agronomic characteristics can result in increased susceptibility
to pests or other adverse environmental conditions. The
rapid spread of southern corn leaf blight is an obvious
case in point. In addition, rather unusual crop phenotypes
are being considered as objectives of genetic engineering.
Finally, while for many crops in many environments, individuals will not survive well outside the cultivated field,
all crops will survive well in some environments. For
example, wild landraces of dry beans (Phaseolus vulgaris)
occur commonly in the uplands of Central and South America
and probably exchange genetic material with the cultivated
beans (Kaplan 1981). Wild varieties of potato freely
introgress with cultivated potato and wild Solanum species
in Peru (Rabinowitz, 1985). Indeed, examples could be generated endlessly, and justify some attention to the safety
of introductions even of genetically engineered crop varieties.

Augmentative biological control of crop pests provides
another model. Predators, parasitoids, pathogens, and competitors of crop pests are artificially increased and released back into the target environment. Since these
organisms already occur in the target environment, information on their ecologies in the target environment generates
a sound model. For example, the performance of nuclear
polyhedrosis virus on gypsy moth populations and the effects of INA⁻ Pseudomonas syringae in suppressing INA
bacteria can be assessed by studying natural populations in
target environments (Andow et al. 1987). The primary weak-
ness in this comparison is that augmentative releases of
organisms frequently occur on much larger scales than natural populations.

If the introduced organism does not occur in the target environment, but does occur elsewhere, then ecological information concerning its biology in its native environment is useful. This information could suggest how an introduced organism would fare in the target environment and how unwanted outbreaks could be mitigated. Classical biological control is based on this premise. For example, cottony cushion scale was introduced into California and threatened to destroy the citrus industry. Entomologists determined that the scale originated in Australia, and the factors controlling scale populations in the native environment were examined. Researchers found a ladybird beetle that was a voracious predator of the scale, and introduced it into California. The ladybird consumed the scales and saved the citrus crop (Huffaker 1971). Hence, mitigation of the exotic species outbreak was based on information from the original environment.

Introduction of exotic organisms provides another good model for introduced non-native organisms. Several recent reviews (Paine and Zaret 1975; Hall and Ehler 1979; Hall et al. 1980; Simberloff 1981; Sharples 1982) discuss this problem in detail. The general conclusions are that the great majority of such introductions do not lead to the establishment of the introduced species, and many of those that do become established do not cause dislocations in other parts of the ecosystem.

This model is extremely helpful in identifying the kinds of problems that might arise in the case of deliberate releases of genetically engineered exotics, but most of the available examples involve vertebrate and insect species. It is difficult to extrapolate from studies on vertebrates and insects to derive conclusions about microorganisms and plants, which are the most likely candidates for deliberate release (OTA 1984). Such widely different taxa have very different characteristics of growth, reproduction, and dispersal, and they perform fundamentally different roles in the ecosystem. Thus, we must take steps to enlarge our current data base to include more examples of introductions of microorganisms and plants (Levin and Harwell 1986). In addition, for deliberate releases of the products of biotechnology we can expect a higher probability of successful establishment than for random introductions, since the organisms would be developed with enhanced establishment abilities. Thus it seems particularly relevant to analyze the examples of exotic introductions that have been established to determine the factors that allow some exotics to have major ecological effects.

For organisms not present in any environment and novel in ecological function, all these models break down. In this case, we do not have recourse to study an original population either before or after introduction. Most currently proposed introductions do not fall into this category. For those that do, however, the lack of an adequate model argues for the need for additional safeguards.

In addition to these comparisons, there are other bases for evaluation. Can the introduced organism sustain its own populations, or does it require continued support or replacement (Levin and Harwell 1985). Ecological function is also important. Is the introduced organism a pathogen, competitor, predator, or parasite? Is it expected to alter certain ecological processes, such as nitrification or nitrogen fixation? Factors such as these are critical to the categorization of risks.

Epidemiology, Ecology, and Evolution

Epidemics, epizootics, and epiphytotics provide an analogy deserving serious consideration (Levin and Harwell 1986; see also Andow 1985). In much the same way that hosts differ from each other, potential target environments differ; and as various disease pathogens differ in their physiological manifestation of disease, so will the products of biotechnology differ in their effects on the environment. It would be absurd to believe that the effects and incidence of all human diseases could be predicted from a few general medical principles; it similarly would be absurd to believe that the effects and incidence of deleterious environmental impacts of genetically engineered organisms could be predicted from a few general ecological principles. Risk assessment of biotechnology must proceed at least initially on a case-by-case basis, guided by general ecological principles, in much the same way that the health risks of individual diseases are analyzed as unique cases guided by the general principles of epidemiology. The assumption that ecological systems are resilient and can withstand any perturbation clearly cannot be supported on the basis of experience (Levin and Harwell 1986; Regal 1986). For specific systems, the insights of an experienced ecologist would provide more valuable counsel concerning potential effects than would reliance on any general rules.

Natural systems are evolutionarily dynamic. Microorganisms have an especially high potential for change because of their rapid population turnover rates (Levin and Harwell 1986). Strong selective forces lead to rapid evolution, just as antibiotics have led to the rapid evolution of antibiotic resistance among bacteria. Similarly, fungal pathogens can rapidly overcome the resistance bred into agricultural crops such as cereals.

The example of the versatile influenza virus illustrates how general principles can guide analysis of risk. The various pandemics of influenza that have been experienced during the past century represent only slight variations on a single theme: influenza A strains differ from one another by only a few surface antigens, and thus mutation or recombination is sufficient to produce new strains or to reintroduce very old ones. If there is insufficient immunity in the human population, these new strains have the potential to initiate pandemics. Thus, very small genetic alterations can make major ecological differences (Levin and Harwell 1986). For pathogenic microorganisms, pathogenic competence can change rapidly. For non-pathogenic microorganisms, however, simple changes are less likely to convert the organism into a competent pathogen.

The potential for rapid growth, proliferation, and evolutionary changes in populations of microorganisms is well illustrated by the history of myxomatosis in Australia (Levin and Pimentel 1981; Levin and Harwell 1985). The European rabbit, introduced into Australia, became a major pest species until the myxoma virus was introduced as a control measure (Fenner 1983). Within a few years, the virus had apparently done its work, and the rabbit population was nearly eliminated. However, shortly after the initial success, the virus evolved to a much less virulent form, and the rabbit population began to recover. This viral alteration and the subsequent evolution of resistance in the rabbit population demonstrate not only the potential for microorganisms to spread rapidly and cause major ecological effects, but also the extreme evolutionary volatility of populations of microorganisms. Natural communities are dynamic evolutionary assemblages with great potential to respond to new stresses (Levin and Harwell 1985; Regal 1985).

Many of the innovations of genetic engineering are not fixed on chromosomes, but are placed on plasmids, which have the capability to move among individuals and even among species (Levin and Harwell 1986). As mentioned earlier, how common this is in nature is unknown (see Chapter 5), but it is useful to think of the plasmids as closer to parasites than to parts of their host genomes. The potential for horizontal transfers certainly is present for many populations of microorganisms. The spread of plasmids in a population may be rapid when favored by selective pressures. For example, plasmids may code for properties such as antibiotic resistance, and may carry these properties as they move from one organism to another; this has occurred in hospitals and through animal feed. Failure to consider the community effects of the use of antibiotics has been a short-sighted strategy with disadvantageous side effects (Levin and Harwell 1986).

In summary, each analogy illuminates particular situations, but the unique features associated with deliberate releases are important.

- The targets of genetic engineering often are microorganisms that have broad geographical ranges and play fundamental roles in ecosystem processes. The wide geographical ranges and high dispersal capabilities of some of these organisms suggest that introductions might proliferate widely if they were to escape beyond the initial area of release.

- The problems of survival following escape from containment, which are the focal points of regulation of laboratory experimentation, are not at issue when release is deliberate. The organism is engineered to survive. The focus of risk assessment must shift to the potential for proliferation, to ecological effects, and to the possibilities to mitigate.

- Organism introductions differ from chemicals in their capacity to grow, multiply, and display adaptive behavior.

- Various lines of reasoning provide a strong argument for a case-by-case approach to risk analysis. This does not mean that we descend into pure empiricism, but it does suggest that we recognize the uniqueness of each situation and allow general ecological principles to guide our analysis, not determine it.

- For many of the natural introductions that have occurred, we have a good understanding of the biology of the species and some indication of the natural control mechanisms; these provide possible devices for mitigation in case an introduction leads to adverse effects.

- Experience from deliberate and accidental species introductions, both of indigenous and exotic organisms, provides good models for the introduction of genetically engineered organisms. Three models are distinguished: (1) the introduced organism is already present in the target environment (indigenous introductions); (2) the introduced organism is not in the target environment, but occurs in another environment (exotic introductions); (3) the introduced organism is not in any natural environment (no clear analogue).

- Some useful models are provided by plant variety introductions, new crop introductions, augmentative biological control, classical biological control, and exotic species invasions. All of these models are likely to provide some guiding principles for risk assessment. None of the models, however, is likely to be generally valid for all cases.

In establishing a regulatory structure to govern introductions, we have the opportunity to develop mechanisms that go beyond considering each introduction in isolation (Levin and Harwell 1986). In the case of chemicals, the sequential introduction of new materials presents a situation in which any single introduction may be considered to be acceptable in risk, but in which the cumulative risk associated with multiple low-level stresses is unacceptable. Similarly, the probability of adverse effects of any one product of biotechnology may be quite low; but there will be many introductions, and the probability that some will cause problems is not low. For this problem, there is no easy solution; but it is better to contemplate it while the slate is clean.

CONCLUSIONS: REGULATION AND MANAGEMENT

As Levin and Harwell (1985) argue, a sound regulatory system for the deliberate release of the products of biotechnology must include:

- case-by-case assessment before release of the fate and transport of the genetic information, and of possible effects on the biota and on system processes,

- monitoring of fate, transport, and effects after release,

- a plan for containment within predefined spatial and temporal limits, and

- contingency plans for mitigation in case of undesirable side effects.

These are not mutually independent. Preliminary assessment affects planning for monitoring, containment, and mitigation; conversely, the possibility of mitigation is an important factor in assessing impact.

An integrated plan involving the various components is needed. There are a variety of possible schemes for arriving at such an integration (Gillett et al. 1985; Levin and Harwell 1986). One goal should be ranking of risks associated with various introductions on the basis of immediate health or ecological effects, the likelihood of geographic spread, and factors related to the potential for limitation of effects and possible mitigation.

It should be possible to develop a safe, effective regulatory regime that will not unduly inhibit the development of an industry that holds such great promise. We must direct our efforts to designing such a system so that the promise of the industry will be realized without unacceptable societal costs generated by disastrous accidents.

ACKNOWLEDGMENTS

This chapter is ERC-095 of the Ecosystems Research Center (ERC), Cornell University, and was supported by the U.S. Environmental Protection Agency Cooperative Agreement Number CR811060. Additional funding was provided by Cornell University and the University of Minnesota.

The work and conclusions published herein represent the views of the authors, and do not necessarily represent the opinions, policies, or recommendations of the Environmental Protection Agency, Cornell University, or the Minnesota Agricultural Experiment Station.

REFERENCES

Alexander, M. 1985. Survival and Growth of Bacteria. In Potential Impacts of Environmental Release of Biotechnology Products: Assessment, Regulation, and Research Needs. J.W. Gillett et al., 63-77. ERC-075. Ecosystems Research Center, Cornell University, Ithaca, NY. (Revised version appears in J.W. Gillett et al., Environmental Management 10(4): 463-469, 1986.)

Andow, D.A. 1985. Dispersal of Microorganisms with Emphasis on Bacteria. In Potential Impacts of Environmental Release of Biotechnology Products: Assessment, Regulation, and Research Needs, J. W. Gillett et al., 78-119. ERC-075. Ecosystems Research Center, Cornell University, Ithaca, NY. (Revised version appears in J.W. Gillett et al., Environmental Management 10(4): 470-487, 1986.)

Andow, D.A., S.S. Snapp, and P.S. Teng. 1986. Potential Environmental Impacts of Widespread Releases of Non-Ice-Nucleating Bacteria in Agriculture. In Genetically Engineered Organisms in the Environment, Office of Technology Assessment, Volume 1. Washington, DC.

Bateson, G. 1972. Steps to an Ecology of Mind: Collected Essays in Anthropology, Psychiatry, Evolution, and Epistemology. San Francisco: Chandler.

Fenner, F. 1983. Biological Control, as Exemplified by Smallpox Eradication and Myxomatosis. (The 1983 Florey Lecture) Royal Society of London. (218B): 259-285.

Gillett, J.W., A.M. Stern, S.A. Levin, M.A. Harwell, M. Alexander, and D.A. Andow. 1985. Potential Impacts of Environmental Release of Biotechnology Products: Assessment, Regulation, and Research Needs. ERC-075. Ecosystems Research Center, Cornell University, Ithaca, NY. (Revised version appears in J.W. Gillett et al., Environmental Management 10(4): 433-463, 1986.)

Gould, S.J. 1980. The Panda's Thumb. NY: W.J. Norton.

Hall, R.W. and L.E. Ehler. 1979. Rate of Establishment of Natural Enemies in Classical Biological Control. Bulletin of the Entomological Society of America. 25:280-282.

Hall, R.W., L.E. Ehler, and B. Bisabri-Ershadi. 1980. Rate of Success and Classical Biological Control of Arthropods. Bulletin of the Entomological Society of America. 26:111-114.

Holling, C.S. 1978. Adaptive Environmental Assessment and Management. New York: Wiley.

Horsfall, H.G. 1983. Impact of Introduced Pests on Man. In Exotic Plant Pests and North American Agriculture, ed. C.L. Wilson and C.L. Graham, 1-13. New York: Academic Press.

Huffaker, C.B., ed. 1971. Biological Control. New York: Plenum.

Kaplan, L. 1981. What Is the Origin of the Common Bean? Economic Botany 35:240-254.

Kimball, K.D., and S.A. Levin. 1985. Limitations of Laboratory Bioassays, and the Need for Ecosystem-Level Testing. BioScience 35(3): 165-171.

Levin, S.A., and M.A. Harwell. 1985. Potential Ecological Consequences of Genetically Engineered Organisms. In Potential Impacts of Environmental Release of Biotechnology Products: Assessment, Regulation, and Research Needs, J.W. Gillett et al., 133-173. ERC-075. Ecosystems Research Center, Cornell University, Ithaca, NY.

---. 1986. Environmental Risks and Genetically Engineered Organisms. In Biotechnology: Implications for Public Policy, ed. S. Panem, 56-72. Washington, DC: Brookings Institution.

Levin, S.A., and D. Pimentel. 1981. Selection of Intermediate Rates of Increase in Parasite-Host Systems. American Naturalist 117(3): 308-315.

Levin, S.A., K.D. Kimball, eds., W.H. McDowell, S.F. Kimball, assoc. eds. 1984. New Perspectives in Ecotoxicology. Environmental Management 8(5): 375-442.

Limburg, K.E., C.C. Harwell, and S.A. Levin. 1984. Principles for Estuarine Impact Assessment: Lessons Learned from the Hudson River and Other Estuarine Experiences. ERC-024. Ecosystem Research Center. Cornell University, Ithaca, New York.

OTA. 1984. Commercial Biotechnology: An International Analysis Washington, D.C., U.S. Congress, Office of Technology Assessment, OTA-BA-218.

Paine, R.T. and T.M. Zaret. 1975. Ecological Gambling: The High Risks and Rewards of Species Introduction. Journal of the American Medical Association 231:471-473.

Rabinowitz, D. 1985. Personal communication.

Regal, P.J. 1985. The Ecology of Evolution: Implications of the Individualistic Paradigm. In Engineered Organisms in the Environment: Scientific Issues, ed. H.O. Halvorsom, D. Pramer, and M. Rogul, 11-19. Washington, DC: American Society for Microbiology.

---. 1986. Potential Ecological Impact of Genetically Engineered Organisms. Ecological Consequences of Biological Invasions, ed. H. Mooney. New York: Springer-Verlag.

---. 1985. The Ecology of Evolution: Implications of the Individualistic Paradigm. In Engineered Organisms in the Environment: Scientific Issues, ed. H.O. Halvorson, D. Pramer, and M. Rogul, 11-19. Washington, DC: American Society for Microbiology.

Sharples, F.E. 1982. Spread of Organisms with Novel Genotypes: Thoughts from an Ecological Perspective. Oak Ridge National Laboratory, Environmental Science Division, Publication No. 2040. (ORNL/TM-8473). Also in U.S. Congressional House Committee on Science and

Technology, Environmental Implications of Genetic Engineering. 1983. 157-206. June. Also in Recombinant DNA Technical Bull. 1983. 6:43-56. June.

Simberloff, D. 1981. Community Effects of Introduced Species. In Biotic Crises in Ecological and Evolutionary Time, ed. M.H. Nitecki, 53-81. New York: Academic Press.

Whittaker, R.H. 1970. Communities and Ecosystems. New York: Macmillan.

Part Three

The Future of Biotechnology— Six Perspectives

7. Safe and Effective Biotechnology: Mobilizing Scientific Expertise

It is well to observe the force and consequence of discoveries, and these are to be seen nowhere more conspicuously than in printing, gunpowder, and the magnet. For these have changed the whole face of things throughout the world. . . . in so much that no empire, no sect, no star seems to have exerted greater power and influence in human affairs than these mechanical discoveries.

--Francis Bacon (1620)

INTRODUCTION

Biotechnology holds a potential to alter human affairs that has been compared to the great historical eras of technological impact, such as the Industrial Revolution. Society may be entering an "Age of Intervention," as Clifford Grobstein has claimed, leaping to new conceptual and technical levels in the use and modification of other life forms for human ends. The technical potential exists to manipulate the human genetic blueprints as well.

In the case of recombinant DNA (rDNA) techniques, "gene splicing," and biotechnology in general, the genie is out of the bottle, for better or worse. The basic techniques are relatively inexpensive and have become "cookbook." It will not take rare talented minds to expand the capacity of the technology to new tasks. Biotechnology has become common property in the same sense that fire, gunpowder, lasers, or transistors have.

There is no great power that is <u>only good</u>, without dangers, and that cannot be misused. For all the well-

145

known and clearly merciful effects that gunpowder, movable-type, and the compass had in European hands, they also had enormous violent and bloody effects as well. In China, gunpowder was restricted to charming and benign pyrotechnic uses. But it was quickly used for killing once it fell into the hands of the warring feudal Europeans. War expanded--or was forced--to a vast new scale of bloodshed with the destructive power of explosives. Even the tiny compass played an important role in colonialism and in the destruction of many gentle human cultures.

The challenge with biotechnology will be to maximize its benefits to society and to minimize health and environmental hazards and other costs. It is a sobering fact that every book that I have seen on biotechnology includes some warning that it will present a range of new and considerable challenges to the integrity and effectiveness of our social institutions.

Economic and political competition for the most part have directed how a new technology will be used, and there is little that any group has been able to do to completely control these forces. Consider printing. Against authority, pamphlets were secretly printed in France, and revolutionary ideas spread that led to the bloody overthrow of authority itself in 1789.

Should one conclude that new technologies are impossible to control to any useful degree, and so society should not even try? This argument is plainly invalid. Some level of control of technology has plainly been possible and useful. Scientists restrict themselves from conducting certain types of experiments on human subjects. Atomic energy is fairly well regulated. Even in much of the United States, pistols cannot be openly carried. Traffic laws control the use of automobiles. Society knows a great deal about the dangers associated with certain medicines and other chemicals, and has accordingly adopted safer patterns of usage than would otherwise have been possible.

Civilized society will undoubtedly demand some assurance that the great new power of biotechnology will also be used as effectively and as safely as possible. Perhaps there can be no ultimate assurance that potent new diseases will not be built and used for blackmail, terrorism, or vandalism by mercenaries, fanatics, or sociopaths. It may be hard to stop the renewed arms race in biological warfare (Tucker 1984). It may be difficult to control the political and economic destabilization that could occur in the worldwide economic shuffle that can be expected when diverse new agricultural and industrial possibilities suddenly begin to intrude on traditional trade and economic patterns (Yoxen 1984). But it should be possible to minimize the risk that some percentage of new organisms, expected to be safe in nature, instead will turn out to be destructive once they are released or escape from the laboratory or the vats of industry.

This chapter will not try to outline a program for redirecting great historical forces or for preventing the malicious use of the new technology. Instead, it will focus on the last class of concerns mentioned. There are identifiable programs of research and industry intending to establish safe operations and to deliver safe products on a vast international scale. The closely related goals of effectiveness and safety are reasonable and very important. How can they be met?

THE SCALE OF THE TASK

Genetic engineering is not simply an issue of the day that will pass. It is only now learning to walk, and it will continue to grow and add muscle with time. One argument is that it will become safer as the techniques are refined and better understood. By analogy, electrical appliances probably are safer today than they were in their early days. Others argue that as the techniques become more powerful, the consequences of misuse will become greater. By analogy, the newer hydrogen bombs are not necessarily safer than the older atomic bombs. Their misuse would be quite terrible. Thalidomide is a newer drug, but it is not safer than aspirin. Scientific progress does not in and of itself ensure the safe use of technology. An institutional context of standards, attitudes, knowledge, and organization must also be developed. The safety and effectiveness of a technology depends on how well a society comes to terms with a new form of power, as well as on how well the engineer understands his materials and his own limitations.

Society must now begin to build the foundations of a future where projects will be evermore ambitious and diverse. With biotechnology still only in its infancy, over 300 small companies are active in the United States alone. This represents the commercial face of a multibillion-dollar national investment in research and development. The potential of the technology to alter medicine, chemical engineering, agriculture, forestry, waste

treatment, pollution management, and even aspects of elec-
tronics and mining has been well reviewed (U.S. Congress
1984). Universities around the world that do not now have
strength in biotechnology are scrambling to develop programs. The industrial nations have committed themselves to
international competition in developing the commercial uses
of biotechnology, as have some underdeveloped nations.
Society must begin to plan for no less than a new technological era.

Proper planning in the new era will require the ability to predict the biological, commercial, and macroeconomic
effectiveness of new organisms. It will require the ability to estimate biological and socioeconomic risks. Key to
all such issues will be broad advances in biology that
allow us to better understand living systems in general, as
well as provide an improved ability to focus on the implications of any given project.

Planning will be greatly complicated by limitations on
the availability of information. Research and industry are
geographically dispersed. It is relatively inexpensive to
start up an rDNA operation. Much of the activity in companies and in academic research laboratories is understand-
ably done in relative commercial secrecy. Some of this
work is reported to various government agencies such as the
National Institutes of Health's Recombinant Advisory
Committee (RAC) and the U.S. Environmental Protection
Agency (EPA), but these agencies are not in a position to
pass on much of the information to the scientific community. In short, even within the United States, it is very
difficult to plan for future releases. Information flow is
limited. Much of it is by word of mouth and lacks details
that could be properly studied, discussed, and evaluated by
an appropriate range of experts.

Planning is also difficult because of the limitations
and organization of available expertise. The scientific
issues involved in making any judgments about the safety or
effectiveness of new or highly modified reproducing populations of organisms in nature are quite complex. To evaluate a given release could in some cases require the ability
to conceptualize facts and ideas in molecular biology, population genetics, ecological genetics, epidemiology, population and community ecology, evolutionary biology, and
even developmental biology and ecosystems ecology. It
could require experts on the particular taxonomic groups
involved, such as microbes, insects, or plants. It may require experts on the local ecological communities and their
ecological processes.

149

THE EXPERTS

Diversity in the Life Sciences

Society will face the obvious need to maintain a balanced pool of experts in diverse fields of biology. This
by no means may be a simple thing to accomplish. Present
economic pressures would favor a reduction in intellectual
diversity. Universities on tight budgets too often are
planning to divert funds to popular fields, such as molecular biology or computer sciences. The "glamour" subjects
may be financed through reductions in traditional programs
such as plant or animal systematics, comparative physiology, or even liberal arts programs, without sufficient consideration of the long-term societal and intellectual costs.

Bio-brokers

Suppose that enlightenment and wisdom among unversity
administrators suddenly were to become epidemic, or that
farsighted federal programs were to emerge and a diverse
pool of experts was to be maintained. Then, among those
experts in the diverse pool, there would have to be some
with much more of an interdisciplinary capacity than is now
available. We will need scientists who can think through
the behavior of an rDNA modification at a series of levels
of organization, each of which has its own emergent properties. How will a given genetic alteration affect molecular
functions, developmental and organismal level functions,
population level functions, and community ecology level
functions? The scientist who can splice genes and who can
screen for and isolate one given new property of the new
creature will probably not have the training to predict the
full implications of his work at the higher levels of
organization.

Think of these new experts as a guild of bio-brokers
who could mediate discussions and joint research projects,
and identify and bring together available talent. Political and social skills might be very useful to members of
this guild, but these skills would not be the sine qua
non. What is needed most is intellectually creative scientists who can see connections between very different sorts
of information and concepts--abstract conceptualizations of
diverse connections that conventional scientists and administrators are not trained to make. The brokers will have
to coordinate the efforts of scientists with different

philosophies of science, curricular backgrounds, technical languages, and ways of thinking.

In some sense, the issue is not too different from expecting a scientist to understand both botany and zoology, or both molecular biology and epidemiology. But ideally, this guild would have members who would have the synthetic skills and holistic sympathies of the best naturalists and the reductionistic talents and sympathies of the best experimentalists. They would understand the principles underlying the complexity of nature and would be able to see complex interactions when confronted by an actual situation. They would have a command of the basic details of molecular biology and an ability to communicate across disciplines.

This might seem a lot of talents to expect young scientists to develop in order to contest in an uncertain job market. The problem in principle is made simpler by the fact that the practical issues overlap with a wide range of basic research topics that have great inherent intellectual interest.

The Crisis in Biology

In a very real sense, the task is nothing less than to begin to heal the ruptures in biology that began when molecular biologists and organismal biologists went off in their own directions, each with their own epistemological perspectives, disciplinary issues and objectives, and professional support and communication networks. These ruptures are quite clearly at the root of our present dilemma, in which the power to manipulate life and the dreams of the new creators have raced beyond any ability to predict realistically the results of tinkering with nature. The benefits should be not only a safer future for genetic engineering, but a more effective one. Recombinant organisms will be better designed the better they can be understood at all levels of their functioning--genetic, developmental, organismal, population, and community.

Not least, the intellectual benefits will be enormous to fundamental science if society can bring about this rapprochement within biology. George Gaylord Simpson argued this as long ago as 1967 in his essay, "The Crisis in Biology" (Simpson 1967). Indeed, from a long-range view the challenge that faces society can be no less ambitious

than this. An effective and safe Age of Intervention pre-
supposes that we can heal the philosophical and social ruptures that have fragmented the life sciences into specialized groups of experts that not only seldom talk, but that
too often cannot talk with each other.

Any university should be proud to have scientists conducting basic research programs on the topics that will be
sketched in the following section (and mentioned in Regal
1985b, 1986). The practical problem, though, is that not
all intellectually interesting topics in academia are
necessarily supported, financially or in terms of local
value systems and group perceptions. Local perceptions and
values can be (fortunately, in this case) remarkably respon-
sive to financial benedictions. So the problems of getting
talented minds to work on the intellectually challenging
problems here can be reduced largely to one of funding and
imaginative administration.

Self-Initiative and Self-Interests of Professional Groups

Winston Churchill voiced a common attitude when he
argued that "scientists should be on tap but not on top."
In "Science as a Vocation," the sociologist Max Weber
argued that scientists are generally not much different
from the greengrocers who sell vegetables. The scientist
largely is involved in selling his or her knowledge to
granting agencies, students, and institutions for a pay-
check and social approval. In this sense, both the typical
greengrocer and the typical scientist have a trade rather
than a vocation, or "calling." The difference comes only
when the scientist takes some initiative, shows leadership,
and uses knowledge and skills to offer clarity and a sense
of responsibility to society. Whether Weber is entirely
correct or not, one can argue that it is crazy to expect
people who have the habit patterns of tradesmen suddenly to
adopt effective leadership roles. Society is clearly a bit
schizophrenic in its expectations of scientists. Usually
they are expected to remain patiently "on tap," but then
they are also expected to know when it is appropriate to
take some initiative, and then they are expected to have
the talents to do so.

It is not only in the interests of society, but in the
long-term self-interest of diverse professional groups of
biologists to take some initiative now and to organize so

that their members will be able to give the best possible
advice in the Age of Intervention. Otherwise they may find
themselves being reshaped or reduced by powerful economic
forces that they do not completely understand.

The danger to society in the reshaping of professional
groups by mindless market forces or by poorly informed
bureaucrats is large and real. Academia has seen many
intellectually interesting fields of study go into decline
because of faddishness and economics.

Biotechnology will clearly need, for example, the advice of ecologists who are talented observers, who know
organisms well, who are talented at understanding the
subtle complexity of natural systems, and who can think
well synthetically. Yet many bureaucrats tend to have a
stereotyped image that a good scientist is one who always
takes a reductionistic approach, who isolates components of
a system, who strives to make rigorous predictions about
these components, and who deals more in model systems and
predictive generalities than in local and historical
uniqueness. Even within a field such as ecology, with a
supposedly "holistic" outlook, the present pressures are
such that many researchers focus ever more narrowly on
their own research and professional interests. Society
will surely need both types of mentalities in the Age of
Intervention. Yet one sees presently some leaning toward
seeking advice primarily from the more comfortably familiar
reductionistic sorts of minds in biology and even within
ecology. In the absence of foresight, this leaning could
begin to warp the balance of talents available in the community of ecologists--if the impact of biotechnology on the
job market for ecologists becomes large over time. The
good naturalist could become as rare as the good doctor who
knows the family and will make house calls. Thus, it is in
society's interest for ecologists to take the initiative
and try to work for a socioeconomic climate that will help
to preserve a diversity of talents within their profession. It is in the profession's own best long-term interest to maintain a diversity of talents, because the profession is then likely to be the most productive and exciting.

It is sobering to reflect, though, that social groups
are not typically good at focusing on their long-term
self-interests. The pattern, for example, from tribal
encounters with great new socioeconomic forces, has been
one of stubborn resistance or, on the other hand, of sequential short-sighted tactical and even venal compromises. Piecemeal responses have tended to fail. Failure

has then led to a decline in morale and to the demise of the culture. Most groups of scientists are plainly not as well organized for nontechnical discussion and action as tribal groups have been. On the other hand, the perceptions of scientific groups are sometimes less rigid. Social support for the professional groups to make the transitions is needed and should help. The fascinating story of how the physicists did manage to move from a disorganized position of social obscurity to become organized, socially respected, and virtually collegial politically is not without interest in this regard (Kevles 1978).

Ideally, professional groups of biologists will face the inevitability of their involvement with the forces that will shape the future. They will do some homework and find creative ways to make positive contributions to the goal of a safe and better world without merely trading their integrity for the survival of their lifestyles or for raw power. In the end, society would best be served by enlightened professionals who do not peddle their talents, and yet who do not monastically or egocentrically shun the larger world about them and turn away from the challenges of history.

SCIENTIFIC ISSUES

Introduction

It would be absurd to suppose that every rDNA population will necessarily be dangerous. It would be equally absurd to suppose that every rDNA form will be safe. It would be interesting, but in a practical sense irrelevant, to know if the average rDNA population will be safe or dangerous. In fact, the average rDNA population probably will be safe. But no one could convincingly argue that science and industry should play Russian roulette with the health of the public and the environment, if even only one out of eight chambers in the revolver were loaded. The odds of ill effects would be too high. Yet much of the public debate over the safety of rDNA techniques has had this absurd and irrelevant flavor. In large part this is because to the unsophisticated mind, "average" means "representative of the entire category." It embodies "essence" --a semantic legacy from Greek metaphysics.

The scientific issues are by no means whether or not the average population will be safe. They are, broadly:

● To rigorously examine the theoretical premises upon which judgments will be made of the projected biological properties of an rDNA population in nature.

● To select basic research areas for priority promotion in order to bolster the theoretical basis for engineering safe and effective forms, and as a basis for reliable evaluations of risk.

● To devise more precise techniques of gene characterization and transplantation in order to minimize reliance on "shotgunning," where many of the transplanted genes are unknown. The problems of evaluation are difficult enough if the transplanted genes are limited to a few completely known ones.

● To find effective methods to evaluate risks and screen out those projects potentially most dangerous to human health or the environment.

Various models of the potential ecological impact of rDNA organisms in nature have in effect been proposed with regard to safety. I have reviewed these elsewhere (Regal 1986). The most robust model seems to be the introduced species model. The experience of ecology has been that new organisms in an environment usually will not survive for long. Of those that do become established, some ninety percent do little damage. Of those ecologically viable populations that do damage, some do enormous and expensive damage, such as goats, pigs, rabbits in Australia, killer bees, fire ants, gypsy moths, or paper-bark trees in Florida. The costs have been in the billions of dollars. One premise of the model is that in principle it will make little difference if an ecologically viable organism differs from local species because it is from another area or because it has been artificially modified. In either case, some major new trait may give it an advantage that will turn it into a rogue species. This might include a resistance to some limiting aspect of climate, soils, competition, predation, parasitism, herbivority, or the ability to utilize a new resource.

The arguments against this model sometimes assume incorrectly that the only reasons that exotic species become rogue species is that they lack their native biotic controls in a new habitat. So, it is argued, if native species are genetically altered, they will continue to be regulated by competitors, predators, and so on. This view overlooks the known fact that very subtle factors can shift the outcome, for example, of competition or infection. Species are not necessarily locked into inflexible interrelationships with one another. There is organization in natural biological communities, but it is of a different character. Some interactions are pivotal to the stability of many species in a community, while other interactions may have little community significance (Regal 1985b, 1986).

Communities may share common structuring principles, and at the same time have important idiosyncratic properties. Living systems are like that, and this should not have become such a difficult point to grasp. Humans, for example, certainly function physiologically according to common principles, and yet one individual may be allergic to a drug while another is not, individuals may be idiosyncratic in their responsiveness to therapy, and so on.

Most of the competing models that argue for the absolute safety of virtually all rDNA organisms lean on outdated ecological and superficial evolutionary notions. They tend to involve "balance of nature" thinking of the sort that is unfortunately still too often taught to students and seen in televised nature programs. Unfortunately, the biological community as a whole has been slow to assimilate conceptual advances and subtleties in this area. Even recently, an article in Science reflected a total unfamiliarity of contemporary thought and literature on this subject (Davis 1987). Sometimes the arguments for generic safety use a merely utopian and idealistic view of rDNA research and industry activity. They may claim, for example, that genetic engineering involves only one or two gene changes. They may neglect to mention "shotgunning," the addition of regulatory sequences, the molecular additions due to the vectors themselves, and mutations and chromosomal rearrangements caused by the vectors.

It is, then, necessary to prepare to understand what the impact of specific rDNA forms may be, since generic models seem to be invalid (see also Colwell et al. 1985; Gillett et al. 1985; Regal 1985a, 1985b, 1986; U.S. Congress 1981). This in turn makes it urgent to attempt to fill a number of gaps in basic, as well as specific, scientific knowledge.

Introduced Species

One priority will be to thoroughly digest and to better organize our knowledge of the history of introduced species. Are certain types of communities more or less vulnerable to disturbance by given types of exotic species? What information or studies have been needed to make accurate predictions about the effects of an introduction? What further generalities about the factors producing rogue species can be pulled out of the scattered literature or gained by more focused research?

Ecology and Genetics of Natural Outbreaks of Pests and Diseases

Another priority will be to understand more precisely the dynamics of natural outbreaks of native as well as introduced pests and pathogens. What have been the ecological dynamics of these? In what ways might genetic novelty from mutations, recombination, or hybridization have contributed to some of these? In what ways might a changing environment have been involved? There is much information (literature, model experimental systems) on disease organisms as well as pests that can provide a start to studies from an interdisciplinary perspective.

Natural Genetic Engineering

We need more fundamental research on the natural genetic engineering that occurs as plasmids and viruses, along with insertion sequences, carry about genes in nature. What are the modes and rates of natural genetic engineering? What are its fundamental ecological and microevolutionary implications? Without advances in our conceptual foundations, we will have no base line and it will be impossible to know how anthropogenic genetic engineering will change things, if at all, in nature. If anthropogenic genetic engineering substantially increases the rates at which, or changes the means by which, this takes place in nature, what will be the significance in the long or short run?

The vectors (plasmids, viruses, insertion sequences) do have their own effects and can cause mutations and chromosomal rearrangements--as well as their more widely known abilities to locate genes, carry, and insert them in new locations in new host species. We need to know more about the unintended effects of the vectors. We need to know more about the effects that vectors which have been artificially enhanced may have in nature generally or in the human body specifically.

Microevolution and rDNA Populations

We will need to know more about microevolution in order to judge the fate of genetic additives (Regal 1985b, 1986). Too much of what one hears from the bioengineering community assumes that one can expect engineered organisms to remain stable in nature, to behave exactly as intended. But one should expect organisms to adapt to their own advantage over their generations rather than to retain any added traits unmodified and to perpetually use these exactly as the engineers intended. What internal and external selection factors maintain stable genomes? What are the microevolutionary and ecological implications of destabilized genomes? Under what conditions will selection tend to eliminate the "labels" and "leashes" that genetic engineers expect to remain in the new organism? When might a new physiological capacity give an organism a competitive advantage and when might it constitute a burden? What do we understand of "hybrid vigor?" Under what conditions might added genes produce unexpected "hybrid vigor?" If one "shotguns" large restriction fragments into a new host and the genes on these lack their normal regulators, how will their expression be regulated in the new host under various conditions? Will genetic buffering restrain the pleiotropic potentials of added genes, or will broad genetic expression become more probable in a new genetic background (Ninio 1983)? What implications might such studies have in terms of the probability of unwanted properties eventually expressing themselves in populations, and possibly in promoting the shifts of populations to new adaptive modes?

Microbial Ecology

Microbial ecology is not well understood. Since many of the first recombinant organisms to enter the environment through intent or escape will be microbes, this area must be singled out for special and priority attention.

One nagging issue seems to be: is the ecology of microbes essentially different from that of higher organisms? One hears that generalities from the mainstream of

158

ecology cannot be used to cast light on issues in microbial ecology. One also hears scientists argue the opposite. This dispute should be resolved. In any event, much more study is needed about the behavior of microbes in natural systems.

Engineered organisms will be interesting research material in fields such as developmental biology, population genetics, and even some of the environmental sciences. Ways should be found as soon as possible to encourage basic research on new organisms. This should be critical in allowing science to understand better any unusual properties of various classes of these new creations.

GETTING STARTED

One clear and overwhelming need is for a new generation of scientists who are comfortable with conceptual material in both molecular biology and in the organismal and environmental sciences. How shall society begin to move in this direction?

One obvious thing that can be done is to highlight the intellectual merit of certain research areas by organizing funding not only for interdisciplinary research projects, but also for truly interdisciplinary graduate and postgraduate training programs. One natural focus for such a program would be one that bridges the complex molecular biology of genomes and ecological genetics. Another focus might be in the application of evolutionary and ecological principles to disease organisms--and so on. Specific survey courses in biotechnology and relevant aspects of ecology and evolution, with both laboratory and field phases, are certainly possible. Such programs would meet a critical societal need and also maintain intellectual vigor and a healthy cross-fertilization of thought in universities.

There is even now interest among scientists and teachers in brush-up courses and workshops that would improve their ability to participate in the rapid changes that are going to occur in biology.

The system of competitive granting and peer review has a great deal of inertia built into it. It is often difficult for even an established investigator to begin a new line of research, even within the system of traditional disciplinary issues. It seems unlikely that science will begin, through this system and through individual initiative alone, to move quickly, in response to either the demands or the opportunities, toward safety and wisdom in the new era. It may be necessary to set up special grant-ing mechanisms to stimulate new research activity, train-ing, and possibly employment. There is tremendous pressure to come up quickly with methods of risk assessment. It will be important to keep in mind that whatever the politi-cal and practical urgency of this matter, there is a pro-found need to see that society ensures programs in basic research that will help biology in general to catch up to and keep conceptual pace with the remarkable advances in the ability to manipulate life.

One action to ensure competent expertise might logi-cally seem to be to set standards through licensing. How-ever, the problem of how to educate the variety of experts needed when talents must be pooled would remain. Genetic engineering will become much more widely practiced as the techniques improve and become less expensive. We even hear that some projects could be done now in a properly equipped high school or small college laboratory. Certainly the cost of cloning is rapidly falling and technical knowledge is more widely available. One meets teachers claiming that inexpensive cloning will soon be possible, and that classes will become more fun when students can learn to create their own new life forms. At some time in the near future, a society that licenses barbers and fishermen can be ex-pected to consider licensing to restrict the number and variety of people who create new life forms. This is a different problem, though, than the one at hand. Licensing would not be an effective or meaningful response to the pressing need to stimulate creative talents that I have outlined.

The writing of new, high-quality textbooks could be sponsored. These would be books that explore the fundamen-tals of biology and at the same time relate the knowledge of diverse fields to the challenges of the new era. These would help to stimulate and support new college courses. (James Watson made a version of such a suggestion at the Banbury Conference that John Fowle and I organized in 1984.)

A most critical need is for better information flow between those enterprises seeking profits and those seeking to understand the implications of the new creations, as well as with those seeking to ensure the effectiveness and safety of the new power. These are not always the same parties. Presently, much of the research and development

goes on in relative secrecy. It is uncomfortably interesting, to say the least, to think of many small groups of
economically constrained workers attempting the complex
goal of constructing ecologically effective and safe new
organisms in secret.

Regulatory bodies may be expected to evaluate a proposal in as little as ninety days. Independent scientists
may not have any access to the data or other materials.
This is not much time even to think through a difficult or
unusual proposal. It is certainly too little time for
independent scientists to do much of the research that may
be needed in order to understand how the population may
behave once it is released into nature.

It should not be acceptable that society is starting
to enter this new era with complex and important decisions
being made in secret deliberations, with the scope of research and industry activity largely known only from ver-
bally transmitted data, with projects advancing without the
opportunity for the community of scholars to deliberate on
scientific aspects in open journals, without the opportunity for independent examination of the actual organisms by
disinterested scientists, without a national program of
basic research that balances the rapid pace of technical
development, and with little or no replication taking place
by which to confirm scientific beliefs and assertions.
Good science is difficult under the best conditions. It is
hard to be optimistic about the quality of decisions that
will be made under the present circumstances.

A suggestion that was made to me by scientists in
industry is that an independent and respected research
study organization could realistically be set up jointly by
industry and government. This could play a central role in
coordinating the evaluation of the potential for function-
ally effective and economically effective organisms. It
could conduct the basic and generic research needed as a
background to design specific studies of the safety and
effectiveness of specific projects. Some persons in industry complain that in the present climate, where true
promise can be hard to distinguish from "hype," expensive
projects may be well under way before any independent and
proper analysis of economic prospects or of safety concerns
has been done. It is not economically reasonable for each
company to form its own staff and research programs to deal
with this issue. Moreover, the available talent is now too
limited to staff a large number of independent and dispersed high-quality programs.

The proposed organization could provide a focus for an appropriate mix of talent and for programs of professional training. It could function as a clearinghouse to help form some focused picture of the range of projects under consideration and in progress. It could help to circumvent some of the problems associated with the competitive climate among businesses and the political climate in which government agencies must operate. The working-out of a proper arrangement might have to be done in the context of the development of a truly coordinated national policy on biotechnology, with the full cooperation of industry, government, and other interested parties. I pass this suggestion along for discussion.

Whatever the details of support, certainly there is profound merit to the idea of one or more politically independent "think-tank" laboratories. These must be made sufficiently attractive intellectually so that the nation's best scientific and nonscientific minds could be coaxed to rotate through to research, meet, utilize central resources, learn, instruct, discuss, reflect, and publish on the many difficult technical, social, and economic aspects of this powerful new technological concept and era. Public confidence in such an enterprise will be no greater, and deserves to be no greater, than the quality of the minds that can be attracted and the work that can be produced. Industry, government, and the public will need to understand the full implications, both the potential costs and benefits, of specific types of projects in the new era that we are entering, if the technology is to be both safe and effective.

CONCLUSIONS

I agree with those who argue that the dangers in introducing genetically engineered organisms into nature have a low though significant probability. The best model that we now have for thinking about the consequences is the exotic species model (Sharples 1982). Most species introductions do not survive in the new habitat. Of those that do, most do no harm. However, a significant fraction cause great damage. The arguments that this model will not apply to rDNA organisms have been reviewed systematically, and were found to be based on outdated ecological and superficial evolutionary thinking (Regal 1985b, 1986). Each proposed introduction will have to be judged on the basis of

the properties of the engineered organism and the properties of the environments in which the organism may come to
live.

We are entering an awesome future. Even now, a technology of enormous power is becoming relatively cheap and
simple. It will be potentially easy for a wide variety of
parties to create a multiplicity of new life forms for
profit and amusement. Living creatures multiply, adapt,
and extend their ranges. Any mistakes will be difficult
and, in some cases, impossible to correct and contain. New
forms of life should not be thoughtlessly introduced into
the environment. Certainly, they should not be introduced
intentionally, or through unconcern, based on the useless
and misleading assumption that anything that is modified
will necessarily be unable to survive in nature. In order
to reduce the risks of genetic engineering, society must
strive to close the gap between its ability to create new
life forms and its ability to predict their biological
properties in a complex setting outside of the laboratory
(Regal 1985a, 1985b, 1986).

A primary challenge will be to maintain a diverse pool
of talents in the biological professions in the coming
decades, against the fact that economic factors favor a reduction even in the present diversity. In addition, a new
guild of interdisciplinary biologists will be needed to
give advice on the complex issues that are bound to be
continually presented to science in the future.

Another major challenge will be to find ways to expe-
dite the flow of information of the commercial activity to
groups of basic scientists and to regulatory agencies so
that they will not too often be taken by surprise, with too
little time to adequately evaluate the issues presented to
them. Sound ecological thinking should be part of every
project from its inception. Large investments of money,
time, and staking of credibility tend to keep large projects in motion. Sound planning will help to avoid situations where parties are tempted to gamble on the effectiveness or safety of expensive but ill-conceived ventures
should major questions arise late in the development process. I have talked with scientists in the industry who
feel that commercial secrecy need not be a major stumbling
block to achieving this goal. Planning would be in the
industry's self-interest and some arrangements could be
probably be negotiated.

The key to as safe a future as possible may be enthu-
siastic deliberation and action, or at least responsive-

ness, by professional groups. They will at some point require the support, participation, and cooperation of the government, as well as that of industry and the universities, if the groups are to be effective and at the same time maintain objectivity. Only with the appropriate mixture of talent and information can the public's economic hopes be fairly balanced against its hopes for health and the environment.

REFERENCES

Colwell, R.K., E.A. Norse, D. Pimentel, F.E. Sharples, and D. Simberloff. 1985. Genetic Engineering in Agriculture. Science 229:111-112.

Davis, B.D. 1987. Bacterial Domestication: Underlying Assumptions. Science 235:1329-1335.

Gillett, J.W., S.A. Levin, M.A. Harwell, M. Alexander, D.A. Andow, and A.M. Stern. 1985. Potential Impacts of Environmental Release of Biotechnology Products: Assessment, Regulation, and Research Needs. Ecosystems Research Center (ERC-075), Cornell University, Ithaca, New York.

Kevles, D.J. 1978. The Physicists: The History of a Scientific Community in Modern America. New York: Alfred A. Knopf.

Ninio, J. 1983. Molecular Approaches to Evolution. Princeton, NJ: Princeton University Press.

Regal, P.J. 1985a. Genetic Engineering. Issues in Science and Technology 1(4):14-15.

---. 1985b. The Ecology of Evolution: Implications of the Individualistic Paradigm. In Engineered Organisms in the Environment: Scientific Issues, ed. H.O. Halvorson, D. Pramer, and M. Rogul, 11-19. Washington, DC: American Society for Microbiology.

---. 1986. Models of Genetically-Engineered Organisms and Their Ecological Impact. In Ecology of Biological Invasions of North America and Hawaii, ed. Harold Mooney and James Drahe. New York: Springer-Verlag.

Sharples, F.E. 1982. Spread of Organisms with Novel Genotypes: Thoughts from an Ecological Perspective. ORNL/TM-8473, Oak Ridge National Laboratory Environmental Sciences Division Publication No. 2040. (Reprinted in Recombinant DNA Technology Bulletin 6:43-56.)

Simpson, G.G. 1967. The Crisis in Biology. American Scholar 36:363-377.

Tucker, J.B. 1984. Gene Wars. Foreign Policy 57:58-79.

U.S. Congress. Office of Technology Assessment. 1981. Impacts of Applied Genetics: Micro-Organisms, Plants, and Animals. Washington, DC: U.S. Government Printing Office.

---. 1984. Commercial Biotechnology: An International Analysis. OTA-BA-218. Washington, DC: U.S. Government Printing Office.

Yoxen, E. 1984. The Gene Business: Who Should Control Biotechnology? New York: Harper and Row.

8. Moving Toward Public Participation in Biotechnology

In 1985, I gave a workshop to a group of high school students on recent advances in genetic technologies. After a brief presentation, I asked the students to draw their vision of the world in the year 2010, when they would be in their forties. Several depicted overpopulation, environmental degradation, or postnuclear holocaust; many drew pictures of people living in domes under the ocean or in space; and a few sketched strange-looking, genetically engineered animals and people. Almost all of the drawings contained elaborate forecasts of new technologies. This was not surprising, since so many of the images of the future presented through the mass media are filled with these science fiction high-technology scenarios.

What was surprising was that when I asked whether their images showed a future that they wanted, none wished to live in the scenarios they had drawn. I then asked them what they might do now, or when they became adults, to help shape new technologies. None of the students had any ideas.

WHAT IS SOCIAL RESPONSIBILITY?

Social responsibility means that those who are formulating social policies today not only consider short-term impacts, but the impacts on today's high school students and generations to follow. As we attempt to guide the development of a technological revolution as pervasive and complex as that which is taking place in the biological sciences, we have a responsibility to ensure that it is safe, that it does not exacerbate environmental degradation and social inequities, and that it fulfills its promises of improving people's lives.

165

In order to meet the challenge of guiding new genetic technologies, all sectors of our society must participate in decision making about such radically new developments as the release of genetically modified organisms.

The high school students at my workshop could not suggest ways to address or affect the new technologies. They had no notion of how technological innovations are generated and who controls the critical decisions. Yet, their drawings showed that they had much at stake in the outcome of those choices. I do not think that these students are unique. I frequently speak with people, as individuals and as members of organizations, who are aware that genetic engineering will have a profound impact on their lives, but who know of no opportunities for participating in the current ethical, regulatory, or policy debates.

PUBLIC PARTICIPATION

In the wake of the industrial tragedy at Bhopal, India, escalating problems of hazardous waste contamination, and unresolved questions concerning the safety of releasing genetically engineered organisms, it is critical that scientists and policy analysts rekindle public concern for effective participation in technology assessment and management.

In the communities where debates over the safety of recombinant DNA research took place during the 1970s, public officials and residents demanded an active role in studying and developing guidelines. The participation was centered around a strong belief in the democratic principles that:

• those who bear the risks and consume the products of new technologies are entitled to participate in the process of regulation,

• those who live near or work in recombinant DNA facilities should have a knowledge of the unique characteristics of these environments which are important considerations in evaluating public health risks, and

• the public will only have confidence in the outcome of the regulatory decisions if public representatives are included in making these decisions.

During the 1970s, concern persuaded local and federal officials to incorporate public representatives into the regulatory process. This included the integration of public representatives into the Recombinant DNA Advisory Committee (RAC), local biohazards committees, and institutional biosafety committees (IBCs). The federal government also designed programs to assist the public in gaining access to technical information and evaluating the impact of new technology, such as the National Science Foundation's Ethical Values in Science and Technology (EVIST), Science for Citizens, and the Office of Technology Assessment. All of these institutional frameworks for public participation --the RAC, community biosafety committees, and IBCs--were unprecedented at the time of their inception. The people who participated in these activities were well aware that they were part of a social experiment.

The results of public participation in the debates about recombinant DNA (rDNA) during this period can provide invaluable insights for building models for public involvement in more complex problems, such as minimizing the hazards associated with the release of genetically engineered organisms. A number of researchers have analyzed the successes and problems with the RAC and IBCs (Bereano 1984; Krimsky 1982, 1984; Dickson 1984), and in what follows, I draw on some of their ideas.

For many years, the RAC has provided a critical forum for airing issues concerning the safety of rDNA experimentation. The majority of RAC members have been molecular biologists. In the late 1970s, during the Carter administration, the membership of the RAC included researchers and public representatives who had warned of potential dangers of recombinant DNA research, as well as those who believed that there were few, if any, hazards.

The National Institutes of Health (NIH) guidelines and proposals reviewed by the RAC are extremely technical. The effectiveness of the lay members in articulating their concerns and questions has often been a function of their ability to learn the technical language and concepts quickly. Frequently, when public representatives have been unable to express health and safety concerns in quantifiable terms and support them with experimental evidence, they have not been taken seriously by the majority of the RAC. This has also been true for outside observers of the RAC meetings who have presented proposals or raised concerns.

Since 1981, when the Reagan administration began to appoint representatives to the RAC, the participation of public and scientific members who played an active and crucial role in formulating critical debates has substantially declined. Furthermore, some of the most vocal participants on the RAC have major appointments in biotechnology firms or are actively promoting genetic engineering research (Davis 1984; Johnson 1985). The RAC has increasingly become more of a forum for those who promote the new technology and have a financial interest in its prosperity rather than a forum for active debate among those with conflicting points of view.

The issues that are now presented to the RAC are broader and more complex than before. For example, the RAC has had working groups to consider environmental release experiments and proposals for human gene therapy. The decisions of these groups require greater active participation by a cross section of ecologists, public representatives, and bioethicists who provide a critical perspective.

SORTING OUT BIOTECHNOLOGY REGULATION

As the activities of the biotechnology industry have expanded, congressional committees--most notably, the House Energy and Commerce Committee and the House Committee on Science and Technology--public interest groups, and regulatory officials are increasingly critical of the ability of the RAC to provide adequate oversight of the industry's development (Subcommittee on Investigations and Oversight Staff Report 1984). To many in the public interest sector, the positioning of the RAC within the NIH, an agency that promotes and funds a substantial amount of rDNA research, itself constitutes a conflict of interest. The NIH is not a regulatory agency, and it has no legal jurisdiction over commercial research activities.

The ability of the RAC to regulate genetic engineering research adequately was challenged in a 1984 lawsuit and decision by U.S. District Court Judge John J. Sirica [see GeneWATCH 1(nos. 3 & 4): 7]. A coalition of environmental groups led by Jeremy Rifkin, well-known critic of biotechnology, took the NIH to court because it had not filed an environmental impact assessment when it decided to approve the proposals of two researchers at the University of California to release genetically engineered "ice minus" bacteria. The court ruled that the NIH must submit an environmental impact assessment when it approves experiments involving the release of genetically engineering organisms into the environment.

During the past few years, in response to these criticisms, the regulatory agencies--FDA, EPA, USDA, and others --have been drawn into the debate over regulation of the biotechnology industry. In 1984, EPA asserted jurisdiction under the Federal Insecticide, Fungicide, and Rodenticide Act (FIFRA) and the Toxic Substances Control Act to regulate some experiments involving intentional release of novel microorganisms. The agency has reviewed under FIFRA several proposals to field test genetically engineered microbial pesticides. They approved the field tests of ice minus in California. Those field tests took place in the spring of 1987.

A new phase in federal regulation of biotechnology came over the horizon with the convening of the Working Group on Biotechnology under the Office of Science and Technology Policy (OSTP) and subsequent publication of the Federal Register notice "Proposal for a Coordinated Framework for Regulation of Biotechnology" on December 31, 1984 and a final version published in June 1986. This framework established the regulation of the products of genetic engineering research under existing legislation.

This new era also provides renewed opportunities for public involvement. However, there are a number of factors that influence the public's ability to participate in the new debates. As indicated earlier, the effectiveness of public representatives on advisory or biosafety groups is often dependent on their ability to find scientists who are willing to explain and testify on the issues. Only a few molecular biologists are willing to risk their professional reputations by providing the needed technical assistance to environmental or community groups. The abolition of programs such as Science for Citizens and the proposed dissolution of the EVIST program by the Reagan administration create a situation in which few, if any, scientists receive support or encouragement to advise and educate community or environmental groups on technical questions.

This trend is reinforced by the strong financial ties which a large number of molecular biologists have to biotechnology firms. Surveys of the relationships between molecular biologists and commercial biotechnology firms have shown that a substantial number are paid consultants, participate on scientific advisory boards or boards of directors, have equity in firms, or have research contracts with biotechnology firms [see GeneWATCH 1(nos. 5 & 6): 3].

Furthermore, few research dollars are devoted to analyzing the hazards and risks of the proposed releases of genetically modified organisms. A small number of ecologists and other environmental biologists began in 1983 to work with EPA and the RAC to develop methodologies for assessing the environmental impacts of releasing engineered microorganisms (Levin 1984; Milewski 1985). This research should be expanded. However, instead of a rigorous analysis and debate over the safety and regulation of releasing genetically engineered microorganisms, many biologists respond to those who question the safety of these procedures by making unsubstantiated assurances that they are no different from what currently goes on in nature, and that nature is resilient (Baltimore 1985; Brill 1985).

In view of the obvious and timely need for a framework to coordinate federal activities in biotechnology regulation, the OSTP has formed the Biotechnology Science Coordinating Committee (BSCC) and agency advisory boards. This structure reinforces barriers to public participation due to a lack of technical support.

It is imperative that an oversight board recognize the interrelationships of the scientific and nonscientific dimensions of biotechnology. In the interest of the overall common benefit, comprehensive discussions of these issues are necessary early in the process. Many of the public issues raised in these debates revolve around ethical and social concerns about new research in molecular genetics and its applications to biotechnology. Ethical and social impacts are embedded in the use of proposed gene therapy, in applications of the technology to agriculture, in problems of defining acceptable risk, and in determining how much risk assessment is sufficient to insure public safety.

The BSCC has many occasions to discuss consequences of biotechnology that are both long- and short-range, as well as those that fall outside the mandate of the regulatory agencies. A board embodying this level of decision-making power should consist of nongovernment scientists from relevant fields, and professionals from disciplines such as law, ethics, and public policy, and public representatives. Each of the advisory committees to which this board would make recommendations should also have a similar composition.

The BSCC should include public representatives. The agency review committees should give special consideration to consulting organizations that represent those who will be most directly affected by the actions of the committees. For example, trade union or environmental health organizations can contribute important insights and information to biotechnology policy-making. These kinds of groups should be able to offer nominations to the agency advisory boards and to the BSCC.

If the federal government fails to develop an oversight structure that is open to public participation and capable of addressing the complex technical and social nature of the issues, citizen groups will lobby local officials on these points. Few state agencies, local officials, and community groups have been actively concerned about the release of genetically modified organisms. In the New Jersey and California state legislatures, bills have been introduced to restrict or regulate such releases, but no action has been taken on these proposals (New Jersey 1984 Senate Bill 2018, California 1983-1984 Session Assembly Bill 3354). As biosafety committees and state environmental health officials face proposed releases, they will become increasingly drawn into oversight.

Following are several recommendations for government actions that will foster greater public participation in the current regulatory debates and thereby promote a more socially responsible development of biotechnology:

- The membership of the BSCC and agency advisory committees should consist of scientists, experts from fields such as law, public policy, and risk assessment, and public representatives.

- Agency officials involved in selecting representatives for the BSCC and for advisory committees should consult a broad range of public interest and environmental groups for nominations.

- The members of the BSCC, RAC and other government policy-making groups should not have direct financial affiliations with companies involved in biotechnology research and development. This could create a serious conflict of interest.

- State and federal agencies should support research on creative models for encouraging public participation in debates about new technology and for providing technical assistance to citizen groups. Models are needed for public involvement in the initial stages of risk assessment when the assumptions and questions are formulated, because these assumptions and questions are likely to determine the outcome.

- The BSCC should be explicitly charged with examining gaps in the ability of Congress and the regulatory agencies to consider the ethical and social impact, as well as the environmental and public health impact of biotechnology.

During the current period of debate over regulation of biotechnology, it is useful to think ahead to the year 2010. Those high school students mentioned at the beginning of this chapter will judge, with the knowledge of hindsight, whether the models we are now establishing were adequate. Will they believe that we should have considered the risks more carefully before rushing ahead? Will they continue to believe that while new technologies shape much of their lives, they cannot, as citizens, participate in their development? These challenging questions continue to remind us of our profound social responsibility for shaping the future of this and other technologies.

REFERENCES

Baltimore, D. 1985. A Milestone for Biology. The Boston Globe, March 2, 15.

Bereano, P. 1984. Institutional Biosafety Committees and the Inadequacies of Risk Regulation. Science, Technology and Human Values 9(4): 16-34.

Brill, W. 1985. Safety Concerns and Genetic Engineering in Agriculture. Science 227:381-384.

Davis, B. 1984. A Scientist's Opinion: Science, Fanaticism, and the Law. Discover 24-25.

Dickson, D. 1984. The New Politics of Science. New York: Pantheon.

Johnson, I. 1985. National Science Policy in Biotechnology as Impacted by Current Regulatory Policy. A presentation at the National Academy of Sciences on February 27-28.

Krimsky, S. 1982. Genetic Alchemy. Cambridge, MA: MIT Press.

Krimsky, S. 1984. Beyond Technocracy: New Routes for Citizen Involvement in Social Risk Assessment. In Citizen Participation in Science Policy, ed. James Petersen. Amherst: University of Massachusetts Press.

Levin, B. 1984. Changing Views on the Hazards of Recombinant DNA Manipulation and the Regulation of the Procedures. The Recombinant DNA Technical Bulletin 7(3): 107-114.

Milewski, E. 1985. Congressional Hearing on the Adequacy of Current Statutes and Scientific Knowledge of the Regulation of Biotechnology. The Recombinant DNA Technical Bulletin 8(1): 7-16.

U.S. Congress. House Subcommittee on Investigations and Oversight Staff Report. February 1984. The Environmental Implications of Genetic Engineering.

9. An Industry View of the Public Policy Issues in the Development of Biotechnology

INTRODUCTION

In light of the other chapters in this volume, it seems appropriate to remind ourselves about some of the rewards of biotechnology. This chapter will present an industry view of public policy issues in the development of biotechnology, and will also examine how we can verify that biotechnology has met its promise.

The key issues for domestic policies, which are outlined in Chapter 10, are to maintain U.S. leadership in biotechnology, to minimize ecological and ethical risks, and to maximize the benefits of biotechnology. Because some of those benefits have been overdramatized, people may wonder whether they actually will be realized. As a matter of fact, there are strong assurances that there will be important contributions from biotechnology. One issue, perhaps not adequately highlighted, is that policy should address the successful applications of biotechnology, which are very likely today, rather than focusing exclusively on the assessment of low-probability risks. This is particularly true if addressing those risks will cause major time delays before some of the benefits can be realized by society.

BIOTECHNOLOGY: PROMISE AND PERFORMANCE

What were the promises of biotechnology? In the early 1980s, it was suggested that recombinant DNA (rDNA) would be used to produce various types of fuels, such as ethanol and hydrogen. The change in the economics of petroleum has caused a shift of emphasis, and some of the longer time horizons place fuel development using rDNA well into the future. However, there still is great potential in the area of energy after the year 2000.

The advent of biotechnology suggested that rDNA would also produce chemical, agricultural, and pharmaceutical products. Potentially, the spectrum of chemicals includes secondary metabolites, simple organic chemicals, complicated organic chemicals, enzymes, sugars, glycols, fibers, plastics, mineral-concentrating organisms, chemical-degrading organisms (for waste disposal), oils, and lubricants. Future agricultural benefits may include lower nitrate utilization, high salt tolerance, and pathogen and insect resistance in plants; improvements in food processing; and improved health and economics in animal husbandry through vaccines and growth hormones. Potential pharmaceutical products include blood expanders, hormones, antibiotics, and vaccines. Many of these products may be available for the very first time because of biotechnology. The volume of business projections for these areas by the year 2000 has generally exceeded $2 billion (OTA 1984).

What has been delivered in the period 1980-1987? In the area of agriculture, genes that carry heritable traits which can be passed from generation to generation and exhibit controlled expression have been introduced into plants. For example, some of these gene products allow plants to achieve full nutrition with reduced fertilizer; others increase resistance to herbicides, viruses, and insects. These are remarkable achievements, and all have been accomplished within the last several years.

In animal health care, prophylaxes for a number of diseases among cattle (such as colibacillosis) have been marketed. Bovine growth hormone has improved milk production. While it is true that the United States produces an excess of milk, for the rest of the world (and even for the United States), improving the economics of milk production is a very important contribution. Interferon (an antiviral protein) and a number of recently announced natural stimulators of white blood cell production may reduce the incidence of shipping fever. A number of other potential vaccines for major diseases have been developed. In almost every case, substances being introduced into the food chain for human beings are safer than anything previously used. The safety of the process, as well as the benefit to society, is being realized.

In the area of diagnosis, monoclonal antibodies are highly specific and are rapidly changing the nature of medical practice. Hybridization probes (which use cloned nucleic acid copies of the gene itself as a marker to detect the gene in other cells or organisms) provide sensitivities down to 10^{-18} molar. With this type of sensitivity, DNA the size of a lump of sugar can be detected with ease in a volume of water of one cubic mile. The ability to measure to this minute degree is progressing very rapidly. If these techniques are used to look for the ecological consequences of the release of genetically engineered organisms into the environment, detectable alterations from the normal state may be so small that we will have to determine exactly how significant what we see really is.

Studies of oncogenes (genes whose altered expression result in tumor formation) provide insights into the biology and etiology of cancer and new diagnostic possibilities. When the structure of DNA was first elucidated in the 50s, Watson and Crick promised insight into all life processes. That promise is being realized very rapidly in cancer research because of what is now being learned about oncogenes.

In human therapeutics, many of the major human proteins targeted for study have been cloned, levels of production of these proteins by the organisms into which they are cloned approach theoretical limits, and there are major advances toward the use of rDNA techniques to develop safe vaccines. The recombinant products are proceeding through the regulatory process, and various types of "magic bullets" with antibody carriers are already being examined in human clinical studies. Tissue plasminogen activator has proven extraordinarily effective in the rapid dissolution of blood clots associated with cardiac infarcts in both animals and humans. After administration of this substance, blood flow in occluded arteries is increased in minutes.

Vaccine production is another area in which biotechnology has made important contributions to human health. For example, infected blood is the source of the vaccine called Heptavax B[TM], produced by Merck from antigens from hepatitis B-infected patients. Because of the source of this material, there is a great risk that the blood from which it is derived may carry other diseases (for example, non-A, non-B hepatitis, and possibly even AIDS). As a result, its use has been limited. The vaccine is also very costly. Recombinant DNA technology, in contrast, has produced an alternative hepatitis vaccine that reduces the cost to a potential of five dollars per vaccination. At this price, the entire United States population could be vaccinated every five years if necessary. The rDNA vaccine eliminates the risk of causing disease through the use of infected blood. It is an attractive product today, both for the United States and for other countries. In fact, the Centers for Disease Control has recommended an eradication program for hepatitis similar to the program launched for smallpox some years ago. However, there are 200 million people with type B viral hepatitis around the world, with a significant portion in Third World countries. Even the potentially low cost of five dollars is a very high price for these countries, whose citizens may not realize the benefits of an rDNA vaccine unless ways are found to cover the costs of inoculation programs.

Erythropoietin is a hormone produced in the kidney that causes the blood-forming stem cells to differentiate into erythrocytes (red blood cells). Because kidney disease inhibits production of the active hormone, persons suffering from kidney disease, such as patients on dialysis, often suffer from anemia. Treatment of anemia for dialysis patients now costs more than $100 million a year. There are 75,000 patients who undergo dialysis in the United States, most of whom would benefit from this product. Recombinant DNA techniques have enabled production of this hormone for the first time, and the rDNA product has proved effective in extensive human trials in the U.S. and several other countries. Erythropoeitin treatment will change the lifestyles of those people who are presently on dialysis and must return home to bed between treatments due to severe anemia. It should also ameliorate many other forms of anemia.

Recombinant DNA technologies have proved successful for the identification and isolation of genes of interest, but what about the ability to use these technologies to produce biological products? Isn't that the barrier? In fact, the bacterium Escherichia coli can produce high levels of foreign proteins, and the feasibility of using this organism for producing the quantities of biologicals necessary for most therapeutic purposes has been demonstrated. For example, one 300-liter fermentation batch of E. coli can produce 225,000 doses of a protein such as interferon in a few days. Thus, the production of millions of doses per week is carried out routinely for many biologicals. Because E. coli can be grown inexpensively and has been selected for its nonpathogenicity, such production can take place without enormous investment or significant risk.

For all these products, which do not require intentional releases of genetically altered material into the environment, there is still a concern about accidental releases (see Chapter 10). It is true that incidental to the manufacturing process, there are bacteria that are producing biologically active proteins, such as interferon and interleukin 2, among others. If deliberate release is the primary focus of regulation, there certainly will be concerns about nondeliberate release. If the concern that earthquakes or other such low-risk scenarios might result in accidental releases leads to major changes in regulation, it will be a long time before some of these products can produce benefits for those whom they are intended to serve.

Table 9.1 shows the statuses of eleven biologicals as of May 1987. In general the products are reaching the market as projected by Paine Webber, Inc. in 1985. As of May 1987 there are four recombinant DNA products available in standard medical practice: recombinant human insulin, currently being used to treat thousands of patients; human growth hormone, which was approved by the Food and Drug Administration in 1985 and is used to treat the 10,000 to 15,000 children in the United States who suffer from hypopituitary dwarfism; alpha interferon, approved for treatment of hairy cell leukemia, a deadly form of cancer; and a recombinant-derived hepatitis B vaccine. Five years from now, millions of patients will be treated by recombinant-derived products.

We in the United States are pleased to say that we think we are the world leaders in this field. Start-up biotechnology companies are responsible for ninety-five percent of these developments. For example, through December 1987, start-up biotechnology companies accounted for virtually all of the major new biologicals undergoing clinical studies. One demonstration of the U.S. leadership position in biotechnology in the world today is Japanese alliances with biotechnology companies; ninety-five percent of these alliances are with American biotechnology firms. This is a clear testimonial to the contention that today the United States is the global leader in biotechnology.

MAINTAINING THE MOMENTUM OF BIOTECHNOLOGY

What are the critical factors necessary to maintain the momentum of biotechnology, which in my mind represents

TABLE 9.1 Status of Selected Biotechnology Products, May 1987

Product	U.S. Regulatory Status	Company/Collaborators	Indication
Alpha interferon	Marketed 1986	Genentech, Hoffman-LaRoche, Biogen, Schering Plough	Hairy cell leukemia
Beta interferon	Human clinical testing	Cetus, Shell Oil	Anticancer, anti-infective
Consensus interferon	Human clinical testing	Amgen	Anticancer, anti-infective
Erythropoietin	Human clinical testing	Amgen, Kirin, Johnson and Johnson	Chronic anemia
Gamma interferon	Human clinical testing	Biogen, Shionogi, Genentech, Boeringer Ingelheim, Daiichi-Seiyaku, Toray Industries, Amgen, Schering Plough-Suntoray	Anticancer, anti-infective, anti-arthritic
Human growth hormone	Marketed 1985 Marketed 1986	Genentech, Kabi Vitrum Eli Lilly	Growth hormone deficiency
Interleukin 2	Human clinical testing	Cetus, Biogen, Takeda, Amgen	Anticancer
Tissue plasminogen activator	Market approval pending	Genentech, Boeringer Ingelheim, Mitsubishi Chemical, Kyowa Hakko	Thrombolytic agent
Tumor necrosis factor	Human clinical testing	Genentech, Cetus, Asahi	Anti-tumor agent
Hepatitis B vaccine	Marketed 1986	Chiron, Merck	Immune prophylaxis
Human insulin	Marketed 1982	Genentech, Eli Lilly	Diabetes

Source: Linda Miller, Paine Webber, Inc.

a responsibility for the United States at this time? The consulting firm of Arthur D. Little, Inc. (ADL) investigated this question. They looked at issues associated with commercialization, risks, legislation, the long-term impact of biotechnology, and basic research. According to ADL, university-industry relationships are probably of most concern, followed by commercialization of biotechnology, risks in biotechnology, regulation, and long-term impact, in that order. I'm not sure that there are many in the industry-- scientists or business people--who would agree that university-industry relationships, and for that matter, university-industry-government relationships present any problem. Most feel that the effectiveness of these relationships has probably been responsible for the U.S. leadership position. The university-industry relationship has been an extraordinary example of collaboration, and as far as I have seen, has caused little change in the academic freedom and the academic responsibilities of those who have contributed to the transfer of technology to industry.

It is important to note that ADL pointed out that there were a number of federal agencies active in biotechnology issues, and raised concerns about the wisdom of giving additional agencies authority to control and influence other aspects of biotechnology. This issue could be pivotal to future U.S. leadership.

How should the United States maintain its leadership position in biotechnology? We should recognize that our current position was attained partly because of the risk capital system and partly because of government support of research through the National Institutes of Health (NIH) and the National Science Foundation. The support of research should not be diminished even when the federal budget is tight. The government, through NIH and other agencies, has supported basic research for a long time. This support has increased over the years to the point where the annual budget is in excess of $500 million. This support certainly must be viewed as the foundation of modern biotechnology in the United States; it should not be curtailed.

Letting the government do the job is not always the best way. However, most of the biotechnology innovations have been made by small companies that live from hand to mouth; they have perhaps one or two years of financing and must move very quickly to prove that they can produce something viable in order to be financed beyond that time. It would be inappropriate for these companies to be funding basic, long-range research. There is a formula that the government has found to be useful, which ought to be sustained. A significant percentage of the NIH budget should be going to basic biological research, without deciding in too much detail what is good and what is bad. For example, support was provided for the scientists who performed the microbial genetic studies that laid the foundation for genetic engineering. If we look back fifteen years, their studies did not seem appropriate for the good of humankind.

Support for applied research is somewhat more questionable. Perhaps industry can take care of that. The suggestion has been made that the United States needs to develop goals such as those adopted by other countries for the development of their biotechnology industries. This has not seemed to be a particularly worthwhile approach for the United States, and it certainly has not been relevant to the success experienced to date by American biotechnology companies.

FUTURE EXPANSION

Are there real barriers to continuing the expansion of biotechnology at its current rate? Recognizing first of all that biotechnology has progressed effectively and safely over the past ten years, it seems as though expansion should continue if possible. A number of events have highlighted potential concerns of the public about the rapid development of biotechnology. In Germany, the Social Democratic Party and an environmentalist party have expressed strong objections to some biotechnology programs. In the United States, a number of experiments involving controlled release of organisms and genetically engineered viral vaccines have become issues of increasing public concern. The public was clearly surprised by some of these developments, although the Industrial Biotechnology Association and most of the companies active in biotechnology have made serious efforts to inform the public of their activities and about the technology in general.

It is evident that such concerns must be addressed promptly and openly. Equally important will be far more extensive, realistic, and informative communications to the public on a continuing basis, and possibly formal programs to provide clarification of the issues involved and a greater understanding of benefits and risks. Companies must recognize that it is extremly shortsighted to shortcut any regulations or guidelines or to initiate experiments that do not adhere to accepted practices. Only if these

issues are carefully addressed will the following suggestions for safely expanding biotechnology be useful.

Recommendations

Expediting patent actions certainly would accelerate
progress. Foreign counterparts to U.S. patent applications
are published and made available around the world. These
complete disclosures are made in exchange for a period of
exclusivity. Delays in granting U.S. patents mean that
these disclosures are made without commensurate protection.

Export barriers should be reduced. In 1985, many
products could not be exported. It was very difficult for
an American firm to contemplate developing a product involving malaria or foot-and-mouth disease without export opportunities. Export of a product without government approval for that product in the United States was considered
marketing a banned product. In these cases, many biotechnology companies decided to export the technology rather
than the product, thus eroding the U.S. leadership position. Taking note of this situation, the 99th Congress
took action in 1986 to remove export impediments. Biotechnology companies may now export their products without
restriction.

The regulatory process should be expedited. No one
wants to introduce shortcuts into safety considerations
about major risks of biotechnology. If something untoward
happens, the public and the industry will suffer, both
immediately and in the long term. Those that are in the
industry are well aware of that. At the same time, the
regulatory process today is extremely burdensome, as can be
seen from the number of federal agencies involved in biotechnology activities. I don't think laissez-faire in
biotechnology is acceptable. Risk assessment is appropriate. Alertness and discussion are important. However, we
should be examining real risks, not imaginary ones. It's a
question of what brakes are applied while risk assessment
is being done. Such assessment should be performed with
equal concern for the potential benefits as for the possible risks.

Capital is the other element that is necessary to
maintain momentum. The risk capital system has provided
the resources; the motivation is profit making.   March 1987

estimates put annual expenditures by the biotechnology industry in excess of $1 billion, with a market capitalization of about $8 billion (Industrial Biotechnology Association 1987). It appears that in the United States, the capital is available to pursue biotechnology.

Why U.S. Leadership Should Be Maintained

Perhaps underlying the question "How should the United States maintain its leadership?" is another question, "Should we maintain our leadership in biotechnology?" To answer that, let's look at the prospective benefits. In medicine, there is important progress in many areas: cancer, cardiovascular disorders, anemias, dwarfism, congenital defects, diabetes, autoimmune diseases, and pulmonary disorders. If we acknowledge this progress and consider some of the fundamental problems facing the world, what are the best alternatives other than biotechnology for addressing these problems? The scientists with whom I have talked do not see any major alternative with the same time horizon as biotechnology. Policy, then, should address the issues surrounding successful applications of biotechnology, rather than focusing exclusively on the low-probability risks.

If biomass alternatives for the production of energy and chemicals begin to function effectively, they will affect the entire petroleum balance around the world. The ecological impact of biomass expansion could be very important. Shifting sources of natural products could mean that a developing country which is just emerging with some new natural material that it can produce can have its whole economy scuttled by rDNA sources for the very same material. This would be much like the production of indigo from petrochemicals about one hundred years ago.

In the field of agriculture, there will be dissemination of a new technology, and a shifting of world food sources. The United States will be exporting some of its foodstuffs, with their nutritional characteristics, both good and bad. There will be some long-range effects as the Third World receives those imports.

Finally, in the area of human health, there will certainly be population increases, shifting age distributions, and an increase in inherited diseases as we can supply improved treatments for diseases which otherwise would fail to be propagated to future generations.

The potential to eradicate, cure, arrest, or amelio-
rate diseases prevalent in the Third World is a very serious issue. We have in our armamentarium today the ability
to address these diseases as never before. The risk of
failing to do that job would increase the disparity in
health care delivery between the United States and other
developed countries and the rest of the world.

I think that issues concerning the successful application of biotechnology are important. If we think that the
United States still might have reason not to proceed, then
be assured that this field will be pursued. Japanese firms
are engaging in biotechnology with a great deal of convic-
tion, as anyone who visits Japanese companies would know.
There is momentum in the engineering area, in the energy
and textile area, in the chemical sector, in the agriculture and food processing sector, and in the diagnostics,
pharmaceutical, and health care sectors. The United States
is the leader today. I think we can move ahead, minimizing
the risks, maximizing the benefits, and maintaining leadership. We should ensure that our society and the rest of
the world are comfortable with the way this is being done
--in a responsible and safe manner. We should be dedicated
to realizing the spectacular future that has sometimes been
described for biotechnology.

REFERENCES

Industrial Biotechnology Association. 1987. Personal
    Communication.

OTA. 1984. Commercial Biotechnology: An International
    Analysis. Washington, DC: U.S. Congress, Office of
    Technology Assessment. OTA-BA-218.

10. Federal Activities in Risk Assessment and Risk Management in Biotechnology

Measuring risk-- . . . the probability and severity
of harm--is an empirical, scientific activity. . . .
Judging safety-- . . . the acceptability of risks--is
a normative, political activity.

--William W. Lowrance, Of Acceptable Risk

The federal government has a responsibility to concern
itself with the risks and rewards of biotechnology, and
that concern has stimulated great debate. Most participants agree that the rewards and opportunities are bound-
less, but also that the risks are real and uncomfortably
uncertain. Proposals for dealing with the risks and
rewards are clearly wide-ranging. Some believe that continuous, mandatory scientific monitoring is needed to
assess the probability of deleterious effects of every
genetically engineered organism released into the environment. Others argue that molecular genetic engineering is
no more risky than traditional animal or plant breeding and
that elaborate risk assessment might just as well have been
proposed for developing hybrid corn or breeding quarter
horses. Others focus on rules and regulations that target
all relevant risks at all production stages, regardless of
whether these rules and regulations were invoked before.
These different perspectives deal with the same two
words, the same two recurrent concepts: risks and rewards.
For much of the dialogue in biotechnology, however, it is
not always clear what we are talking about. What risks?
What rewards? They are clearly not all the same. I urge
that at the outset of these deliberations, we first define
exactly what risks and what rewards are at issue and keep

these definitions in focus as we create mechanisms to assess and manage risks to society without unduly limiting the rewards that society can reap.

RISKS OF BIOTECHNOLOGY

Risk is a scary word. It conjures up images of peril and danger and the clear possibility of injury. How can we evaluate the risk of a new technology or scientific innovation? How does society cope with risk when it is threatening? First, we should recognize what we mean by risk in the context of the scientific opportunity for biotechnology. I suggest that there are at least three quite different kinds of risks; they relate to technology differently and they require different management. Risks may be nefarious, they may be accidental, or they may be incidental.

The nefarious risks are the most frightening and probably give risk the worst name. Almost any product or process, including biotechnology, can be used in evil ways for purposes of war, terrorism, or other madness. We have seen criminal uses of life-saving drugs and surgical procedures, of cars, computers, and even candy bars. Nefarious acts are evil, unexpected, clandestine, extralegal, and typically do not fall into the scale of balancing risks and benefits. One could not control nefarious risks by regulating weapons, by maintaining registries, or by controlling scientific exploration. One does control such activity via assorted intelligence gathering and law enforcement efforts.

The second kind of risk is the accidental. The risk of accidental harm comes with many, if not most, rewards. Whether it is an established procedure or an innovation, technology involves risk. We speak of accidental risk as a probability estimate. Regardless of how established a procedure, and how good our probability estimates, we can never be sure of a specific adverse event developing in a specific situation. The element of uncertainty cannot be eliminated, and depending on a variety of factors, may or may not be tolerated. Generally, the greater the benefit, the greater is the public's tolerance of accidental harm. At the individual level, risk tolerance is displayed all the time: the decision to drive a car, to fly in an airplane, to smoke a cigarette, to live at a high altitude, or to undergo a surgical procedure. At the level of society where benefits are diffuse and there is little or no personal choice, determining action based on risk of accidental occurrence becomes the business of government, includ-

ing the local, state, and/or federal authorities. Within
the federal government that responsibility lies within the
regulatory agencies.

The third type of risk is the incidental. Incidental
risks are the perterbations of the immediate environment,
the community, and the world which accompany most major
scientific and technological advances. Incidental changes
were protested in nineteenth century England by the Luddites as anticipated evils of the industrial revolution.
Changes in the world which accompany technological advances
may be viewed as either progress or decay, depending upon
one's personal perspective. Highways, smokestacks, house-
hold chemicals, motor vehicles, and assembly lines of ro-
bots bring incidental changes, not all nice. Therapy with
antibiotics runs the risk of producing "incidental" antibi-
otic-resistant organisms that may be far more dangerous
than the organisms for which the antibiotic was administered. Technological triumphs do not please or benefit
everyone. Although in general incidental risks may be better anticipated than either accidental or evil risks, they
are more difficult to label ahead of time as being definitely good or definitely bad now and in the future. What
seems clear, however, is that attempts to label incidental
changes as either good or bad and to control the ones that
are bad should be performed with utmost care and with input
from many sectors of society. Much of the angst that sur-
rounds the current debate on biotechnology relates to the
great difficulty of placing this most uncertain of all
risks in balance.

RISKS AND REWARDS

How do these risks relate to the rewards of biotechnology? Again, all rewards are not the same. Practically
viewed, there are already different emerging "rewards," and
they clearly do not all carry the same risk or the same
benefit. Many rewards are the inert proteins and chemicals
produced by biotechnology and bioengineering. Insulin,
growth hormone, tissue plasminogen activator, and ethylene
glycol are produced more safely, better, and in some cases,
in larger volume by engineered microbes than by extraction
from either pig pancreas, human cadaver brain, malignant
melanoma cell lines, and petroleum, respectively. It is
hard to deny that these are rewards for man's cleverness
which benefit many and have very low risk of either accidental or incidental harm. How we approach regulation of

such inert products is a simpler and less controversial task with considerable new product precedent, and should not be brought into the dialogue of special and unique concerns surrounding biotechnology.

The next level "reward" of biotechnology that we are facing is that of living microbes harnessed to help man. Although alive, they are altered so as to be used in a fashion similar to conventional inert products for targeted benefits. Microbes that serve as a herbicide, or depollute the environment, or open clogged drains are engineered to survive in a narrowly limited time frame, to be overcome by sturdier types, and to be benign and brief habitants. The main challenge in assessing risks and benefits of these engineered microbes being used as chemicals is to assess their potential for accidental contamination, for spontaneously reverting to a hardier form, and for incidentally altering the ecosystem. These risks can be estimated, and adverse effects usually prevented. In general, for these crippled organisms, we know the questions to ask and, if answered, the kind of research that needs to be done to find the answers.

The third level of anticipated biotechnology rewards brings improved plants or animals. These rewards represent an approach well known to agriculture and animal husbandry. They are designed to benefit man. The main challenge here is to be sure that those plants and animals are, in fact, better. Although the incidental changes accompanying breeding raise some vague concerns, the concerns tend to be dispelled by the fact that animals and plants are, after all, under man's control, are visible, are contained within designated spaces, and can be destroyed if need be without ethical quandary.

A fourth, most remote, most exalted, and surely to be most anxiety-provoking reward encompasses the genetic engineering feats which could result in a better man or woman. Human genetic engineering holds the promise of eliminating sickle cell anemia, thalassemia, cystic fibrosis, and Huntington's chorea, as a start. But the accidental and incidental consequences of tampering with the human gene pool make even the heartiest of souls a bit queasy. The Frankenstein fear, after all, is really directed toward this very specific level of biotechnology effort, and not toward inert chemicals, crippled microbes, hybrid corn, or megamice. Here, in particular, are the concerns about all three potential risks, and here the dialogue balancing risk and benefits must, of necessity, be broad.

Regulation of biotechnology is a challenge of the decade. It must proceed with full intent to protect public safety, while assuring the public of the benefits of its multibillion dollar investment in molecular biology. In the process of balancing the rewards for individuals and for society with the potential for accidental harm, for criminal abuse, and for incidental change, it seems wisest to proceed case by case with the best available data, full recognition of the uncertainties, and appreciation of the differing magnitudes of risk and reward.

FEDERAL ROLE IN DEALING WITH THE RISK AND REWARDS OF BIOTECHNOLOGY

What is the federal government's role in these issues of risk and reward? The federal government has had a long nurturing partnership with biotechnology. It has invested billions of dollars in the basic research which has taken us this far to the promise of widespread benefit. Well over ninety percent of the basic research in molecular biology that has led to biotechnology and engineering has been funded by the National Institutes of Health (NIH) and the National Science Foundation (NSF). On the brink of realizing the practical benefits to medicine, agriculture, and assorted industrial and consumer applications, issues of risk and regulation confront us as never before. There is clearly a need to reap the benefits and particularly to maintain American leadership in this field, which the United States has largely been responsible for creating. A report of the President's Commission on Industrial Competitiveness (1985) posed the question, "What are the strengths and weaknesses of the United States with regard to our future economic and industrial leadership?" The list of weaknesses is long. It includes capital costs, monetary exchange rates, cost of American labor, U.S. trade laws, and international trade laws. On the strength side there are only two major advantages: our technology base, the technology which propels our economy; and our talent base, the innovators who create and renew technology. In biotechnology, the United States is now leading the world because of these two strengths in research and talent. The leadership is not an accident or a genetically determined fact of life. It results from a strong federal investment and a well-nurtured talent pool. It also results from the entrepreneurial spirit and strong efforts on the part of industry. A widespread concern that has been voiced repeatedly is that American leadership could be harmed by overregulation. In the words of the President's Commission on Industrial Competitiveness (1985), "The net result of our cumbersome and complex regulatory environment has been that innovative products are more easily and quickly introduced abroad. The issue is not whether regulations should exist, their benefits are clear, but improper or ineffective regulation can inhibit innovation."

This desire to reap benefit does not mean, however, that biotechnology should not be regulated. Just as it has taken upon itself to encourage the growth of biotechnology via research, the federal government also must make sure that biotechnology can develop safely. The concern dates back to the time when biotechnology was still in the research phase. The history of the Recombinant DNA Advisory Committee (RAC) at the National Institutes of Health is a testimony to federal responsibility for risk assessment and management of laboratory-based research that it funded. As biotechnology has entered the commercial world, many other government agencies become players: the U.S. Environmental Protection Agency (EPA), the U.S. Department of Agriculture (USDA), the Food and Drug Administration (FDA), and the Occupational Safety and Health Administration (OSHA). They have taken and must assume a growing role in assessing the risks of biotechnology. In addition, because of overlapping issues and perceived needs from the community, a work group on biotechnology was established in 1984 at the White House under the Cabinet Council system to focus on many important issues in biotechnology, including regulation, but also research, manpower, and trade laws.

The first task that the White House Work Group undertook was regulation, since it seemed to be the most pressing. In approaching this issue, the Working Group operated under three premises: first, that biotechnology is a desirable technical innovation and progress should be encouraged in biotechnology research as well as commercial application; second, that the safety of a new application of biotechnology must be adequately assessed, particularly with regard to accidental and incidental risk; and third, that the current U.S. leadership in biotechnology must be maintained as commercial applications grow.

The first written public statement of the Working Group's efforts was published in the Federal Register notice of December 31, 1984, and the final notices with revisions after public comment, in November of 1985 and June of 1986 (see Federal Register 1984, 1985, 1986). The

notices present a cohesive statement of the Reagan administration's approach to biotechnology. The documents provide
a matrix that describes existing laws and regulations applicable to biotechnology at each stage of development.
The stages include research, developing, manufacturing,
marketing, shipping, and disposal, and comprise nineteen
pages of rules and regulations, suggesting that there is
both abundant and at times overlapping authority to deal
with biotechnology. In addition, the EPA, USDA, FDA, and
OSHA present policy statements on exactly how they will
individually approach the emerging field. The differences
in the policy statements among the agencies have caused a
great deal of comment. The differences, however, largely
reflect the varied kinds of biotechnology benefits the
agencies review. The FDA has been dealing mainly with inert proteins and other compounds that are the products of
biotechnology, and can be handled much like any other drug
or pharmaceutical produced by conventional chemical processes. Not surprisingly, their approach is the least controversial. USDA has been dealing mainly with whole plants
and animals, and has long expertise in dealing with genetic
manipulations, although not necessarily the bioengineered
type. Its most uncertain tasks include transgenic exchanges among living animals and handling microbial growth
promoters. The EPA statement, the longest and probably the
most controversial, deals with one of the most difficult
areas of commercial biotechnology, namely, the release of
genetically altered microbes into the environment. Despite
the differences in these notices, however, all agencies
agree that the benefits and risks should be approached case
by case. Indeed, most of the perceived differences among
the agencies are not differences in philosophical bent, but
rather differences in the kinds of cases the agencies face.
    A third and important part of the notice is the devel-
opment of a biotechnology interagency coordinating committee to provide communication and coordination among the
regulatory agencies in the development of their policies.
This committee was established using the organizational
structure of the Federal Coordinating Council for Science,
Engineering and Technology (FCCSET). The FCCSET is a statutory interagency coordinating mechanism housed within the
Office of Science and Technology Policy, Executive Office
of the President, with the mission and authority to coordinate federal science activities among federal agencies.
    The Biotechnology Science Coordinating Committee
(BSCC), established in October 1985 under FCCSET, plays a
major role in coordinating the scientific issues related to

research and commercial applications of biotechnology. Individual agencies' committees provide detailed, case-by-case scientific review of applications under statute and in accordance with their own policies that respond to the needs of the individual agencies. The BSCC is centrally located and is aware of reviews being conducted by the various agencies. It reviews final reports when appropriate, and in time will develop generic scientific guidelines that can be applied to similar applications received by various agencies.

The BSCC serves as a forum for addressing broad scientific problems, sharing information and achieving consensus. It serves to promote consistency in the development of agency review procedures and assessments, facilitates continuing cooperation among the federal agencies on emerging scientific issues, and also identifies gaps in scientific knowledge that may need attention. The coordinating group receives information regarding the scientific aspects of biotechnology applications submitted to the federal agencies for review, and conducts analyses of broad scientific issues that extend beyond those of any one agency. With this process, generic scientific recommendations are developed that can be applied to similar recurring applications. The core membership of the BSCC includes senior policy officials from USDA, EPA, FDA, NIH, and NSF. The committee seeks input from the public on issues of generic concern, and for such issues, meetings will be open to the public.

The major goal of the Biotechnology Scientific Coordinating Committee is to provide coordination among the regulatory agencies in their scientific risk assessment and to provide and ensure good science. At the basic science level, the National Institutes of Health Recombinant DNA Advisory Committee (NIH RAC) has done this superbly. For the expanded needs of commercial biotechnology, an expanded mechanism is necessary. The working group considered many times using the present NIH-based RAC alone. It has the scientific expertise and has performed its function extremely well, although it has been questioned in the environmental area. The NIH, itself, felt that it could and would not extend its responsibilities and capabilities to deal with issues beyond biomedical research. That the existing NIH RAC, expanded to accommodate more environmental expertise, might in some fashion be elevated to the parent board to provide a broad capability was also considered, but again rejected because of concern about individual agency needs, confidentiality, and the risk to the RAC of moving it out of NIH.

Under the present system, the Biotechnology Science Coordinating Committee is advisory in nature. Its effectiveness depends on its scientific credibility, its usefulness to the individual agencies, and the quality of its leadership. The BSCC's separate identity from the regulatory agencies hopefully gives it added credibility. Since the BSCC is not reviewing individual applications submitted to the agencies, issues of confidentiality and added delays in decision making are not a problem.

Coordination among the agencies regarding regulatory policy is yet another matter. To a large extent, such policy is dictated by agency statute and management and is more difficult to coordinate at an interagency level. Surely, consistent scientific risk assessment will help promote consistent policy making. However, there is also a major need for ongoing dialogue among the agencies on their regulatory policies as they are formulated. For a while, the White House Domestic Policy Council Work Group in Biotechnology played this role, since it was comprised of the high level policy makers within the agencies. Careful attention must be paid to continuing this kind of policy coordination in the future.

The formation of a coordinated program in the federal government should provide a means for weighing both the risks and benefits of biotechnology as an integrated effort across the many government agencies concerned, regardless of their mission or statutory responsibilities. All participants must be aware that as biotechnology progresses, rewards and risks as yet unimaginable will present themselves, and there must be adequate mechanisms to deal with them. New laws may have to be added, and new regulations may have to be promulgated. What we need now--and will continue to need--is the commitment of all parties to make the regulatory system work to protect our health and environment without denying the benefits and rewards of this exciting field. The final judge, the public, should expect no less.

REFERENCES

Federal Register. 1984. Proposal for a Coordinated Framework for Regulation of Biotechnology; Notice. 49:50856 ff. December 31.

---. 1985. Coordinated Framework for Regulation of Bio-
technology; Establishment of the Biotechnology Science
Coordinating Committee; Notice. 50:47174 ff.
November 14.

---. 1986. Coordinated Framework for Regulation of
Biotechnology; Announcement of Policy and Notice for
Public Comment. 51:23302 ff. June 26.

Lowrance, William W. 1976. Of Acceptable Risk. Los
Altos, CA: William Kaufmann, Inc.

The Report of the President's Commission on Industrial
Competitiveness. 1985. Global Competition, The New
Reality. 2 vols. January.

11. Biotechnology and the Public Purpose: A Public Agenda for Biotechnology in the Congress

INTRODUCTION

For the last several years, the revolution in molecular biology has shown us a new face: commerce and profit. Genetic engineering has moved rapidly from a science capable of unlocking the secrets of life to a science that is ballyhooed for its immense industrial potential. This chapter describes some special problems faced by the public health and environmental communities as they formulate responsible positions for the public policy debate that will accompany congressional action on biotechnology. We will consider the problems associated with the introduction of novel, genetically engineered organisms into the environment. We will also show that the public interest requires public health and environmental groups to advocate exploitation of biotechnology for public purposes.

INTENTIONAL RELEASES INTO THE ENVIRONMENT

The first phase of the debate about hazards to the environment from genetically engineered organisms is ending. The debate began in 1975 at Asilomar, the now-famous conference called at the University of California to discuss the hazards of genetic engineering. At that time, distinguished molecular biologists took upon themselves the responsibility to conduct the early research with manipulated DNA in a manner that would not create unnecessary risks. Until safety could be demonstrated, these university researchers opted for careful containment of the genetically manipulated organisms. The National Institutes of

Health (NIH) and their Recombinant DNA Advisory Committee have dominated the self-regulatory, pre-industrial, containment phase of the debate. During this phase, most environmental and public health organizations remained silent, and only a few vocal critics questioned the judgments of scientists, who appeared to be proceeding in a cautious manner.

As industry enters the picture and new plans call for intentional releases of new organisms, the debate must change. Profit motives can push collegial trust to the side. No one can ignore the multitude of examples in which industry has chosen to dismiss scientific predictions of disaster and where we are now counting the bodies. It has taken fifty years for us to consider banning the introduction of new asbestos into the environment. Industry still questions the utility of toxicologic predictions each time these predictions suggest that a new chemical is likely to cause cancer in humans.

Scientific doubts and concerns are being expressed today about the harmful potential of introducing novel organisms into the environment. The risks are not well understood. It is now possible to take an organism adapted to a particular environment and insert into it certain genetic characteristics--characteristics that were not previously associated with the organism, and which would be unlikely to be transferred to it in nature. Thus we have the ability to increase the likelihood of radical introductions into our environment. It is the small chance of making truly radical introductions and the small chance that the new organism or the genetic trait will survive in the new ecosystem that cause scientists to be worried about unlikely ecologic disasters.

When it was first proposed that the major problem facing regulators and policy makers was the absence of an adequate scientific base for making predictions about genetically engineered organisms, two responses were most common. Many molecular biologists, representatives of the nascent industry, and officials in the U.S. Department of Agriculture said that there was no risk because there was nothing new in genetic engineering that Mother Nature or the Almighty had not tried already. Others invoked natural law or the Deity to explain that the hazard was clear and extreme because scientists were tampering with species.

The dilemma about how to regulate intentional releases of genetically manipulated organisms into the environment is still unresolved. But rather than reinforcing either extreme of dogmatic certainty, scientific opinion seems to be coalescing around the need to reduce the uncertainty of predictions. In August 1984, a group of ecologists challenged the conclusions of the molecular biology community at a meeting at the U.S. Environmental Protection Agency (EPA). The ecologists' manifesto was a challenge to open scientific exchange and intercourse between the previously distant disciplines of ecology and molecular genetics. The American Society of Microbiologists took up the challenge, and there was standing room only for a special meeting in Philadelphia in June 1985 that discussed the same issue: the scientific base for predicting the consequences of introducing genetically manipulated organisms into new environments. The Keystone Center in Colorado organized a broad group of scientists and others to create a research agenda capable of improving predictive capabilities for the purpose of risk avoidance. In November 1985, the National Science Foundation and the congressional Office of Technology Assessment brought a group of scientists together to examine the ecology data base for predicting the behavior of engineered organisms. The results were brought to the second Brookings Institution conference on biotechnology in February 1986.

The Legislative Task

The legislative task is far simpler when it is acknowledged that no one knows exactly how regulatory decisions should be made. Congress can and will respond to the new pressure to develop a scientific basis for prediction of the public health and environmental consequences of genetic engineering. Congress can design legislation that forces the development of a scientific knowledge base and supports the research that is needed. Although Congress cannot invent standard methods for assessing the safety of new microorganisms, it can demand that the development of methods go forward, and that the executive agencies agree to interpret the same predictive tests in the same manner. The model for this cooperation is already in place with the National Toxicology Program. Finally, Congress can establish a single statutory standard for the protection of human health and the environment. Thus, biotechnology can be regulated so that existing statutes do not result in laxity at the Department of Agriculture and strictness at the EPA.

Industry remains intent on having the federal government regulate biotechnology under existing statutes. This seems like a fading hope. The view is no longer credible, and the ecology, public health, and environmental communities deserve credit for creating the new milieu. Congress was never disposed to accept the idea that statutes written before anyone ever spliced a gene could be applied to gene-splicing technology, but the comments generated by the Reagan administration's December 31, 1984, regulatory proposal revealed more problems than anyone dreamed existed. It should now be possible to draft effective new regulatory legislation that establishes clear objectives and demands the scientific information needed to make good predictions.

Before concluding that effective regulation is just around the corner, the major obstacle that could derail Congress should be noted. Biotechnology is based on complex science, but requires only rudimentary equipment--new organisms can be grown in someone's kitchen. Thus, the United States must pursue the regulation of biotechnology internationally as well as at home. The Organization for Economic Cooperation and Development (OECD) has been working on the issue, and some of the best American thinking guided OECD's working group during its early months. (It is interesting that U.S. federal agency representatives to this working group seemed to think more clearly about regulatory issues when they were not trying to fit their ideas into the constraints of existing U.S. laws.) If international efforts fail to get all industrial countries to establish "harmonious" regulatory programs, Americans face two threats: the risk of dangerous activities abroad, and a growing danger at home from industries that argue that they cannot compete in world trade while living up to U.S. safety standards.

PUBLIC PURPOSE

When Congress approached the issue of environmental and public health regulation, it was recognized that the growing commercial interest in biotechnology represented a greater hazard than the early days of academic research. As biotechnology is exploited by industry, commercial objectives will lead to increasingly varied uses and increasingly varied hazards. Less caution may be used when entrepreneurs see sizeable profits on the horizon.

The second part of this chapter deals with a very different problem associated with commercial development of biotechnology: the risk that socially useful products will not be developed if they are not anticipated to be sufficiently profitable. Congress is concerned that commercial objectives will not assure that all the benefits to mankind possible through biotechnology will be achieved.

Vaccines

The best-understood example of a use for the new technology which may not be fully exploited is that of vaccines. For the last several years, Congress has wrestled with this problem. Vaccine prices have increased severalfold, causing cutbacks in state and local immunization efforts. Manufacturers blame the price increases on the cost of lawsuits and liability insurance related to vaccine reactions. Some firms have dropped out of the vaccine business altogether, causing public health officials to worry that some vaccines may become totally unavailable. However, an investigation by the Health and Environment Subcommittee of the House Committee on Energy and Commerce (a report prepared by the Congressional Research Service, "Childhood Immunizations," was printed by the Committee in September 1986) revealed that investment in vaccine development was declining even before anyone recognized a liability problem.

Unfortunately, new genetic engineering techniques for vaccine development, capable of producing new and safer vaccines quickly and often cheaply, came as both government and industry were cutting back on research to produce new vaccines. A hearing in March 1985 by the House Energy Committee's Subcommittee on Oversight and Investigations drew attention to the prescience of researchers at the National Institute for Allergy and Infectious Diseases, and to a report from the Institute of Medicine of the National Academy of Sciences which confirmed the NIH's prediction that within five years, it should be possible to have at least ten new vaccines ready for use. (Compare this with the rate of sixteen widely used vaccines developed during the first 200 years since Jenner.) Despite the promise of immense savings in lives and disability, as well as in medical care costs, the Reagan administration has not increased funding for vaccine development; further, inflation means a true decrease in government funding. The traditional vaccine firms, which were already moving out of the vaccine business, do not appear to have reinvested when genetic engineering appeared on the scene.

The failure to produce a safe pertussis vaccine is a relatively minor problem for the United States, but the failure to produce vaccines against rotavirus or malaria is to miss a truly dramatic opportunity for helping developing countries. One of the characteristics of many of the biotechnology opportunities that may be neglected is that they are more important to the developing world than to the industrial countries that now possess the technology.

Contraceptives

Commercial investment may not be directed at research into new and more effective contraceptives. Safer, longer acting, and male-targeted contraceptives are now possible with genetic engineering. A greater variety in contraceptive techniques seems to be required to meet the needs of all members of every population group in the world. Again, this research is directed at the problems of some of the poorest people in the world and does not appear to be attractive to commercial enterprises.

Food

Food production is a natural target for the new technology. However, industrial countries tend to suffer from overproduction of food and have often created complex schemes to protect the livelihoods of farmers. Poor countries, without the immediate capacity for using biotechnology or the cash to buy either food or the technology, often have starving populations. Although the problems may be largely ones of distribution, using biotechnology to develop food resources in close proximity to today's starving people would be a great step forward. There is little or no commercial investment to attack this problem.

There are special problems even when it comes to improving conventional crops through biotechnology. For example, rice is the world's largest food crop. It would be very helpful to improve rice strains using genetic engineering, but very little is known about its biochemistry and physiology. It will take many years of basic research on rice before molecular biologists understand how to intervene to increase productivity.

Most of the early firms to enter the field of biotechnology had little capital and were interested in products that could reach the market very quickly. Even the larger firms entering the field now appear to have a relatively short horizon for their product development or possess established product lines which they do not wish to expand.

Toxic Waste Management

Environmental uses of biotechnology have also suffered at the hands of industry and the Reagan administration. Before President Reagan was elected, EPA believed that it had a mission to study the best disposal methods for toxic wastes. Neither land treatment nor incineration was an adequate solution for existing wastes, already in the environment and causing frightening health hazards, or for new wastes that would be produced each year by industry. Biotechnology seemed to offer at least two attractive possibilities. It might be possible to create special organisms that could digest toxic wastes. Alternatively, enzymes produced in large quantities by genetically engineered organisms in fermentation processes might catalyze much more complete and rapid degradation of particular wastes. Biotechnology, with an intense research program, may provide promising solutions. Some firms, such as General Electric, which dumped millions of pounds of PCBs into the Hudson River, are working on biotechnological solutions, but progress is far from optimal. The Reagan administration chose to shut down the EPA research program in 1982, claiming that industry would do the job. Neither EPA nor the Office of Management and Budget bothered to determine whether industry was doing enough research on microbial approaches to toxic waste management.

Energy

In a nation where energy production is organized into large-scale power networks and giant oil refineries, it is not surprising that little research has been done on microbial approaches to energy production and the use of biotechnology to improve small-scale systems. But local, small-scale energy production may be essential to many developing countries. Here again, the profit motive is not likely to generate research in industrial countries to assist countries that lack hard currency to buy industrial products. (It is worth noting that Japan appears to be an exception to this rule. Japanese companies and the Japanese government are assisting the developing countries of

Asia to learn about and use biotechnology. The Japanese foresee future Asian reliance on Japanese expertise and equipment. More important, they see today's assistance producing future prosperity and thus markets for other Japanese products.)

Skeptics on Technology

Each new technology has had enthusiasts who promote it, and a familiar cast of scientific skeptics who ask the difficult questions. Repeatedly, these skeptics have asked about the risks and hazards, and whether society is doing everything it can to prevent them.

The skeptical attitude toward new technologies has moved beyond looking at the direct hazards--carcinogens, reproductive hazards, neurobehavioral toxins, and acute toxicity. Public health professionals are now vocal critics even where a technology may be safe but has been permitted to consume health-sector social resources inappropriately. For every Medicaid patient who receives a liver transplant, a state will lack funds to immunize at least a thousand children. The tendency to aim technology at expensive treatments for disease rather than at effective prevention has produced an "allergic" reaction to almost any new technology.

A New Role

The reasons should be clear why public health and environmental groups must be concerned both about neglected development and the hazards of unwise development. The uses of biotechnology that will be neglected by the profit-making sector of the economy are often those that serve important public purposes. For example, preventing disease through vaccination is overwhelmingly preferable to treating many diseases with drugs. However, a successful preventive technology inevitably shrinks the demand for existing treatment products. Similarly, a microbial pesticide may be far more specific and safer than popular, broad-spectrum chemical brews, but development of such specific pesticides poses the same dilemma for the chemical industry that vaccines do for the pharmaceutical makers. Companies choose new products based on the principles of corporate economics, not public health, or they risk destroying the market for their own products.

This is a lesson that scientists might have learned as they fought the hazards of "progress" in other fields. Public interest groups can improve their position to counter the profit imperative of new technologies and their concomitant hazards. Where doubts nag the public conscience about whether industry is assiduously promoting all the social opportunities inherent in a new science, there is leverage. In this instance, the argument for serving the public should be particularly solid: it is the taxpayers who have supported nearly all of the molecular biology research from which industry is gleaning future profit makers.

Legislative Prescription

Congress can provide a legislative antidote to the commercial logic which results in social neglect. It is possible to encourage industry through a program of grants and tax breaks. The Orphan Drug Act is a small example of such a program. The military research and development programs, despite certain basic questions about their social utility, are gargantuan examples of the encouragement of activities which would not occur if the market were limited to private citizens. Two recent examples have contributed in a small way. The 1986 Superfund reauthorization contains a new university grant program for developing new technologies in waste management. The National Vaccine Program, also enacted by the 99th Congress, directs the Public Health Service to promote industrial participation in the production of needed vaccines.

Legislative action must begin with a constituency ready and able to define the public purposes. This role is ideal for environmentalists and public health professionals. Both academic researchers and industry can provide technical and political support, but, based on past experience, they are unlikely to take the lead.

Congress needs a constituency to speak for the people-oriented uses of biotechnology; environmentalists, scientists, and public health professionals should take this role. Without a new presence in the public debate about development, drain cleaners and cosmetics will undoubtedly be among the first products to be developed, while vaccines, contraceptives, toxic waste digestion systems, and small biomass generators will be among the last. Without pointed warnings, the government will wait for many years to discover that industry had no interest in efficient protein production to prevent the waves of famine that repeatedly strike the developing world. Without public-spirited insistence on taking the longer view, the United States will find a remedy for the liability exposure of vaccine manufacturers for untoward reactions, but will not assure that new and safer vaccines are developed.

The risk Americans face from failing to assure the proper development of biotechnology seems more palpable and more important than the hazards that can be prevented by total opposition to the technology. The strongest position for the public interest community would be not only to demand a scientific basis for predicting public health and environmental risks, but also to demand that government assure the development of biotechnology for public purposes.

12. Reviewing the National Policy Issues Associated with the Commercial Development of Biotechnology

INTRODUCTION

In these waning years of the twentieth century, it is becoming increasingly questionable whether or not American economic leadership is also on the wane. U.S. global competitiveness has declined in numerous manufacturing areas, and American industry is now facing substantial challenges in high technology innovation, once its area of clearest advantage. Nowhere, perhaps, is the challenge to American technological dominance more apparent than in the realm of biotechnology. While the United States has enjoyed a significant lead in basic biological research capability, that lead is now diminishing. Moreover, American ability to translate research findings into efficient industrial processes and competitively priced products is noticeably deficient. More important, uncertainty about the resolution of a number of critical policy issues intensifies these deficiencies.

This discussion cannot hope to bring resolution to any of these issues, but it can provide a useful review. These observations are fairly impressionistic; however, they are based on extensive interviews with scientists, government officials, and industrialists in Boston, the San Francisco Bay Area, and Washington, DC. While atheoretical from a social science standpoint, this descriptive analysis is not without important implications for understanding both technical change and regulatory economics. These matters are, unfortunately, beyond the scope of this chapter. Suffice it to say that the biotechnology industry presents a number of factual incongruities to reigning theories of the political economy of technological innovation (for elaboration on this point, see Daneke 1986).

MAPPING THE BIOTECHNOLOGY TERRAIN

The term biotechnology specifically denotes the manipulation of living organisms such as recombinant DNA (rDNA) for the express purpose of engendering new products and/or more efficient processes. The end result of these manipulations is assumed eventually to have some sort of commercial value; thus, biotechnology is generally thought of as an industry. However, unlike other technologies, if one compares biotechnology to, say, computers, it is like the programming concepts without the hardware. Biotechnology still connotes many activities which are very far removed from the marketplace. Nevertheless, the assumption is widely held that all activities, from basic biological research to regulations about environmental release, have a relationship (even if remote) to commercial viability. Thus, when the issue of aiding commercial development is raised, a vast variety of activities can be evoked. In reality, not all of them yield equal returns in terms of commercial enhancement. Moreover, commercial development for global competitiveness is often tempered by other conflicting policy objectives (for example, full employment and/or environmental health and safety). In this complex and convoluted policy realm, institutional and ideological factors may play a more significant role than technological and market forces. Mapping all these domains demands more than conventional economic wisdom. Groups like the Office of Technology Assessment (OTA) were conceived for the purpose of providing Congress a broader vision. Legislators, however, are easily inundated, and increased information often clouds as well as clarifies the issues.

Surveying Without Conveying: The OTA Report

Recognizing biotechnology's importance and its many unresolved issues, OTA launched a major study of biotechnology in the early 1980s (OTA 1984). This study is a comprehensive international review of issues associated with the development of a globally competitive, commercial biotechnology industry in the United States. In the executive summary of its 600-plus page report, the OTA issued the following warning: "Although the United States is currently the world leader in both basic science and commercial development of new biotechnology, continuation of the initial preeminence of American companies in the commercialization of new biotechnology is not assured" (OTA 1984, p.

3). However, specific data cited and the general tone of the report are guardedly optimistic. It suggests, for example, that the United States has a ten-year lead on the Japanese, its nearest competitor in both the basic science and commercial development of biotechnology. Other sources in government and industry suggest that the lead is narrower: five to eight years. All these estimates are highly subjective, and past experience suggests that specific catch-up projects (for example, the Manhattan Project) can leap a five-year gap in ten months. Regardless of which estimate one accepts, both Japanese and American policies (or non-policies) are causing the gap to close more rapidly than had been estimated previously. For the U.S. economy, the implications of losing yet another global market battle could be significant, since biotechnology promises to be a $200 billion-a-year industry before the year 2000. More important, perhaps, the loss of the biotechnology battle would signal a further loss of control of the "innovation process" itself (Daneke 1984).

Somehow the OTA report did not adequately convey the crucial nature of this contest. This may not necessarily be the fault of the study itself. Actually, the failure to grasp the urgency says more about Congress than it does about its technology advisors. Congress can only respond in an ad hoc fashion to immediate problems; it doesn't realize that a five- or even a ten-year lead is negligible. In addition, when the OTA report came out, Congress was preoccupied with short-term crises, such as the budget.

OTA might have been more direct in making its case, however. It could have isolated more specific policy options, rather than vague fields of options. Furthermore, it could have separated these distinct options from vague, ideologically charged issues of general "industrial policy."

Factors Affecting a Biotechnology Industry

Nonetheless, the OTA study provides an excellent yardstick for assessing current trends, especially when one compares its list of priorities and issues (see Figure 12.1) to the perceptions and activities (both implicit and explicit) of industrialists and government officials. In judging issues, one must be aware of their potential impact both on American competitiveness and the possibility for real programmatic change, given existing institutional and ideological barriers.

Figure 12.1 Relative importance of factors affecting
the commercialization of biotechnology according to
the OTA report (1984)

Most Important Factors:

1. Financing and Tax Incentives for Firms
2. Government Funding of Basic and Applied Research
3. Personnel Availability and Training

Factors of Moderate Importance:

4. Health, Safety, and Environmental Regulation
5. Intellectual Property Law
6. University/Industry Relationship

Least Important Factors:

7. Antitrust Law
8. International Technology Transfer, Investment, and Trade
9. Targeting Policies in Biotechnology
10. Public Perceptions

A final important caveat is that as the industry con-
solidates, the salient issues will change. (This will be
amplified later in the chapter.) The OTA analysis is predicated on the notion that the most important factors are
those which promote an optimal mix of large- and small-firm
involvement in biotechnology development.

It is possible, and in fact highly probable, that
national policy makers confuse the entrepreneurial phase
with later phases of development. Policies proposed on the
behalf of small start-up firms will often actually provide
more aid to large, established enterprises. When global
competitiveness is the ultimate goal, oligopolistic consolidation, fueled by government programs which promote capital intensiveness and standardized production over agility
and creativity, is worse than self-defeating.

Infant industries are often faced with a legislative
"Catch 22." Stated simply, when an industry is small and

fragmented and can use the most help, it doesn't have any political clout; when it is large and organized, it has the clout, but doesn't want the same type of help. This phenomenon warrants its own studies; for now, suffice it to say that small biotechnology firms have hardly been in a position to challenge existing bureaucratic relationships that adversely affect their industry, and by the time the biotechnology industry is itself the beneficiary of relationships conducive to its business, its needs will be vastly changed. In sum, it is no surprise that virtually no hearings were held on the OTA report. Biotechnology, as an industry, has a relatively small lobby, and by the time it emerges as a major industry, it will probably demand deregulation rather than aid for entrepreneurial activity.

Real Issues Versus Red Herrings

Thus far, federal priorities, as evidenced by existing policies and activities--for example, recommendations and initiatives spearheaded by the White House Office of Science and Technology Policy (OSTP) and pursued by the Task Force on Biotechnology in the Department of Commerce-- suggest a growing recognition of the importance of biotechnology. Unfortunately, the focal points of current policy tend to be those issues which are least important to global competitiveness. For example, activities have been directed toward antitrust and some minor trade issues. Antitrust proposals from other units within the Reagan administration (such as the Economic Planning Council) have interesting implications for industrial policy in general (Kutzmann 1985; Miesing 1985) and may eventually accelerate consolidation in biotechnology, but at present the entire antitrust issue is of minimal significance. Looking at the emergence of new government-encouraged research consortia (such as MCC in Austin), one might conclude that antitrust enforcement is already fairly relaxed.

What is of greater potential consequence is the current pattern of international cooperation. The Japanese and Germans, and now the French and British have been especially aggressive in pursuit of joint ventures with small American research firms. These cooperative agreements raise significant questions about the transfer of economically sensitive expertise. To date, little official concern has been expressed about these joint ventures. International patent and trade laws are fairly vague on issues of joint research, and biotechnology is generating some interesting test cases. However, by the time intellectual property rights are established internationally, it is likely that the U.S. global position will have already been substantially weakened.

Relative Quiet on the Regulatory Front

The OTA report suggests that regulatory issues are only moderately significant. While this assessment is more or less accurate from a purely economic standpoint, these issues are far from unimportant. Moreover, if left unresolved, they could greatly impede the development of the American biotechnology industry.

Environmental health and safety issues are by far the most potentially explosive set of concerns floating just below the surface of current policy awareness. Moreover, small groups, such as the one headed by Jeremy Rifkin, have successfully delayed experiments such as Lindow's frost-controlling bacteria. In this particular case, procedural guidelines were invoked, but substantive challenges were also organized. The issue of environmental release of engineered organisms remains hotly contested, and the existing regulatory apparatus is being called into question.

It is not even altogether clear who will ultimately regulate biotechnology. Obviously, the Food and Drug Administration (FDA) will review certain products, and other agencies will review other types of products. However, if Congress becomes convinced that biotechnology may involve unforeseen hazards, it could well place many biotechnology products in the "toxic substances" category, and subject them to the laborious review procedures of the U.S. Environmental Protection Agency (EPA). The Reagan administration, in accordance with its general deregulatory posture, has been attempting to "get all the ducks in line" on biotechnology. As one official put it, the administration wants to "avoid regulations that could cost the U.S.A. its leadership among industrial nations" (Business Week 1984, p. 40). However, since the Japanese and Germans have even more stringent environmental requirements for biotechnology than the United States does, the argument for lax regulation for purposes of gaining a competitive edge may eventually prove imprudent. Most responsible industrialists realize that it is better to set up reasonably strict, but hopefully expeditious regulatory procedures at the outset. Moreover, as Harvey Price, former director of the Industrial Biotechnology Association, explained, "the public deserves a certain amount of regulation" (OTA 1984). Uncertainty about regulatory requirements is usually more of a problem than the regulation itself, and currently that uncertainty is high.

The University Connection

Another area in which the rules remain murky is that of university-industry relationships. A recent report by a distinguished group of scholars and industrialists concluded that "the ties that bind corporations and universities are not only valuable for the welfare of the economy but for the health of the university" (Sproull et al. 1984, p. vi). However, this report, which relied on biotechnology for its examples, included horror stories in which a number of serious issues were raised.

Cases in which a single firm is allowed to enter into a contract relationship with a university present the most significant of these issues. While these firms do not necessarily have a proprietary claim to all research results, their relationship is far different from the multisubscriber research consortia, which are nonproprietary by their very nature. More troubling perhaps than the issue of proprietary claims (which has yet to be completely resolved) is that these firms were allowed to utilize knowledge generated from research which was funded with public monies. One might argue that all universities (even private ones) are public infrastructure. Sole-source profiteering from these public resources is certainly a cause for concern, especially when some of the firms involved are foreign. Undoubtedly, these and other issues of academic integrity will continue to be problematic as long as the ad hoc approach to university-industry relationships prevails (see Ruscio 1984).

LARGER PROBLEMS AND PROSPECTS

The university-industry relationship is actually a small subset of a larger and more pressing set of issues, which the OTA report only deals with indirectly. OTA lists as important factors: government funding of basic and applied research, financing and tax incentives for firms, and personnel availability and training. One cannot effectively deal with these factors without raising questions about the entire political economy of innovation within the United States. The OTA report implies, but does not sufficiently elaborate upon, a significant gap between science and technology in publicly supported research, and various inadequacies in the financing and management of innovation within the private sector. The report is even less illuminating about the management problems, and it does not quite go far enough in either exploring weaknesses in current institutions or in prescribing viable solutions. This may have been beyond the OTA mandate, and may also be a function of OTA's somewhat optimistic appraisal of the problems. Nevertheless, it is unrealistic to consider biotechnology policy outside of the larger issue of technology policy in general. Moreover, a scaled-down approach to revising research priorities, leaving existing institutions intact, may be advisable only if substantial and complementary changes are brought within financial institutions and in large-scale corporate research and development divisions.

The Science and Technology Gap

Despite the best efforts of the early organizers of American science policy following World War II, recent years have witnessed a widening gap between basic and applied research efforts (Shapley and Roy 1985). Given the nature of biotechnology, the actual empirical difference between these realms is very slight. In fact, the emergence of a biotechnology industry provides clear support for the often overstated value of basic science. Nevertheless, these apparent payoffs are also a major impediment to policy change. A number of intermediate and applied research areas (for example, bioprocess engineering) may be substantially underfunded because basic laboratory technique is mistakenly thought to be able to produce commercially viable products.

Biotechnology is part of a growing national debate over the need for greater balance between basic and applied research. This debate has caused some critics to call for major reorganization of the American public research enterprise. Some have called for the establishment of a separate government foundation for technology (Brown 1985). Still others, including many industrialists, suggest that the nation ought to have a cabinet-level agency which blends scientific research and technological development (President's Commission on Industrial Competitiveness 1985).

In describing the need for more "generic applied research," the OTA was not necessarily endorsing these separatist arguments. In fact, the report explicitly states that basic research is essential, and implies that full-scale commercial development is not the business of government. However, in recognizing a gap between basic and applied research efforts, the OTA provides tacit support for certain changes in funding priorities. The question thus arises, can such changes be achieved within existing institutional arrangements?

The primary vehicle of biotechnology research is the National Institutes of Health (NIH), a large and fairly autonomous agency that grew out of public concern about cancer during the 1960s. Like any bureaucracy, NIH has developed a vast network of clientele relationships dedicated to continued funding for basic biomedical research. It is these networks that determine what will be funded. The validity check on this system is known as peer review, a process through which proposals for funding and research reports are evaluated by leading scientists in the field. Critics contend that the peer review process is often a useful cover for self-rewarding cliques. In any case, some bias toward retaining the status quo is institutionalized in the agenda-setting process.

One can imagine that difficulties might arise in reorienting research toward radically different domains (for example, solving problems en route to large-scale manufacturing). For instance, Channing Robertson (1985) identifies a number of problems involved in putting real engineering into the term "genetic engineering." He and his Stanford students have developed bioreactors modeled after mammalian systems, which deal with such problems as oxygenation, convection, and viscosity in industrial processes. This research, while invaluable and very basic, is hardly the stuff of NIH grants.

In an era of diminishing civilian research budgets, a "zero-sum-game" mentality is hard to resist, especially in agencies with such a strong orientation toward the maintenance of adequate funding for important knowledge base building and medical applications. Periodically, representatives from the White House (OSTP) provide pep talks to NIH aimed at changing priorities (Healy 1985). However, such talks are generally followed by those of more conventional scientists who admonish that NIH stick to its knitting. This pattern is often augmented by representatives from larger commercial firms, who also support a basic research line (Cooper 1985). Large firms with large labor-

atories, of course, can do most of the intermediate research themselves, and don't want the supply of free fundamental information cut back. These types of arguments,
coupled with the fact that so much of biotechnology is
still at the basic stage, tend to confirm institutional
inertia. Nevertheless, recognizing that the process of innovation is not linear and that elements of American intermediate research are far less developed than those of its
global competitors, tensions for reorganization are likely
to continue. These tensions could be reduced, however, if
funds for upgrading applied domains were taken from defense
research, rather than from civilian budgets.

The Training Lacuna

The gap between basic and applied research is also
manifest in the area of support personnel required to speed
technological development. An often-cited statistic in
reports on U.S. global competitiveness is the number of
engineers per college graduates, the notion being that the
inordinately large number of engineers per capita in Japan
is part of the growing competitive advantage of the Japanese. Alan Kantrow (1983), referring both to engineers and
to a vast array of semi-skilled positions, contends that
human capital is the San Andreas Fault of American innovation policy. Biotechnology is particularly deficient in
the number of skilled technicians.

As in the past, government training and fellowship
programs can play an important role in augmenting the pool
of skilled personnel. Likewise industry, with or without
government encouragement, can provide its own in-house
training if shortages become so acute as to drive up labor
costs unreasonably. However, these strategies usually
don't come into play until a crisis point is reached, and
the inevitable lag could considerably impede development.

A related and potentially more significant issue is
that the exact package of biological and process engineering skills which is critical to the scale-up phase of
research and development does not fully exist within a
defined professional channel. Moreover, the mix of technical and managerial skills required to husband biotechnology (or any high-technology operation, for that matter)
from research and development to commercialization is an
even rarer commodity. What is needed, and fairly soon, is
for biochemistry and engineering departments on the one
hand, and engineering and business management colleges on

the other, to develop a series of hybrid programs. However, given the disciplinary turf conflicts and resource scarcity at many leading universities, these melding processes are not taking place.

Overcoming these academic attitudes will require more than the mere provision of government grants to fuel hybrid curricula. New programs must be carefully designed to fully integrate industry needs. Where possible, corporate sponsorship should be a prerequisite. Once again, the model of the multisubscriber research consortium might pertain. In fact, it would not be too difficult to cull portions of the training functions inherent in these consortia and develop them into more formalized course offerings and programs.

Another tangential yet potentially critical issue might be call the "train drain" of foreign nationals. Given the scarcity of U.S. postgraduate doctoral researchers, many research laboratories rely on hard-working foreigners to fill their fellowship positions. Many of these publicly supported fellows are actually on leave from their companies in Japan and elsewhere. Thus, the U.S. is not only giving away its gene-splicing expertise, it is paying people to take it. However, university scientists are particularly recalcitrant when asked to consider any proposals which might reduce this supply of "slave labor."

The Fickle Financial Environment

The most problematic policy area identified by the OTA is that of financing. While the current configuration of financial institutions is a highly political contrivance, its connection to the sacred canons of capitalism makes it nearly immune to meaningful change. Moreover, relatively minor changes can produce unintended consequences of such magnitude that even the most foolhardy legislator will tread lightly, and usually limits attempts to influence financial policy changes to such things as tax incentives. It is precisely this delimiting of policy parameters which makes the financial domain so difficult.

Of course, an additional reason the U.S. system for financing technological innovation is sacrosanct is that it is relatively successful. Comparisons with the "bank-dominated" Japanese system notwithstanding, the somewhat chaotic capital formation and entrepreneurial system of the United States generally outperforms all others. Thus, attempts to impose guidance are usually quite delicate, and only marginally influential. For example, arguments made for the renewal of the so-called Danforth research and development investment tax credits are generally couched in terms of potential rather than actual performance (Gravelle 1985).

Assuming that the government can sustain a reasonable interest rate (which is linked to the debt and the value of the dollar), the financing of research and development and/or small research start-up companies is relatively easy in the United States. Investment tax credits, low capital gains, sub-chapter and limited partnership provisions all fuel the entrepreneurial and the "intrapreneurial" environments, and seed, venture, and equity capital pools sustain them. In fact, with specific reference to research-oriented entrepreneurship, no other nation can generate the volume and diversity of the American system. It has been this environment which has sustained economic growth in the wake of increasingly myopic behavior by major corporations. Most of the innovation and nearly all of the new jobs are developed by new "start-ups." (see Tornatzsky et al. 1983). Thus, maintaining this environment is critical.

When it comes to small biotechnology firms, the entrepreneurial system has had certain failings. Initially, it tended to violate some of its own cardinal rules in the excitement over biotechnology's still-remote potential. Venture financing, which is more conservative than many think, was given to some research endeavors essentially on the strength of scientists' credentials. Some of this excitement spilled over into early stock sales, and a few scientists with no appreciable assets became instant millionaires. Once everyone realized that the much-ballyhooed breakthroughs were still a decade away from products, stocks fell and second-round venture funding returned to more customary criteria. Start-up companies found resources by either hastily producing short-range products (for example, a biological drain opener), and/or entering cooperative arrangements with large conglomerates, many of which were foreign--mostly Japanese-owned. Some firms, of course, had more significant products (such as insulin and aspartame) almost ready for the consumer, but by and large had to rely on larger firms for testing, licensing, and marketing expertise.

While this pattern of large corporate guardianship is certainly not unique to biotechnology, its implications may be more far-reaching in such a research-intensive realm. The reason for increased concern is the generally poor performance of large firms in the management of research-oriented enterprises. Leaving biotechnology at the mercy of major corporate sponsors, especially when many of these are Japanese, may not be the best way to build a globally competitive American industry.

Recognizing a significant finance gap as small biotechnology firms move toward the marketplace, government programs might be devised to extend the "patience" of financial systems, without either absorbing all of the risks or picking winners. With the types of clientele arrangements alluded to previously, government is not a very good investment counselor. It can nonetheless provide inducements and allow individuals to choose the directions. This is the raison d'etre of the various tax programs. However, existing programs have little effect on small biotechnology firms. With no products and hence no profits, there are few taxes to write off.

More government funding for applied research (of the generic, problem-solving type) will free up the resources of some small firms for more advanced product development. Furthermore, reduced antitrust pressure will allow many small firms to pool their limited research funds. However, more continuous access to capital may still be needed. While the stock exchange has become re-enchanted with biotechnology, there is no guarantee how long such interest can be sustained. In addition, the high cost, via managerial and securities requirements, of "going public" in the U.S. market (for example, three years of auditing by a "Big Eight" accounting firm) is considerable. Perhaps Lester Thurow (1985) and others are correct in calling for new government programs which foster more direct bank involvement. Duplicating the Japanese system of long-term bank support (in which research firms only pay the interest on loans) might avoid the "quarterly report" pressures of shareholders (both venture and equity), but it should be noted that American banks are not necessarily blessed with the same judgment and patience as their Japanese counterparts.

Whatever set of changes the government might choose to consider must be carefully assessed in terms of the overall impact on the entire entrepreneurial system, a system which certainly is worth sustaining, even with its numerous imperfections. In addition, any changes designed to aid a particular industry like biotechnology must factor in lag times in policy impact, and forecast where the industry is likely to be when the programs are actually in operation. It may well be that the entrepreneurial stage of biotechnology research is nearing its close. New rounds of spin-offs will occur as product lines and specialty items emerge, as with the components industries that arose out of microprocessing. Whether these successive rounds and/or the consolidation stages of an industry require the same types of financing supports as the entrepreneurial stage has yet to be carefully analyzed. This initial assessment suggests that access to capital continues to be a problem, but it may not be nearly as pronounced in later phases of development.

Learning to Manage Biologists and Enhance Innovation

Another pressing problem, if one accepts a consolidation scenario, is that of sustaining innovative activities within large corporate structures. A few major American firms (from the chemical, food processing, and pharmaceuticals industries) are buying into biotechnology in a big way. In several cases, however, they still have very little idea what role the technology will play within their spheres of enterprise. Since many of the products are still unknown, standard models of diffusion and adaptation of innovation simply don't apply. Therefore, the interest may prove to be more flirtation than thorough-going incorporation. How these large firms manage what is essentially still very much a research activity may largely determine biotechnology's overall penetration, and ultimately the U.S. share of the resulting industry.

By nearly any standard, American firms, especially large ones, are poor research managers. A recent study of sixty top corporations by the Engineering Administration Group at George Washington University (Szakonyi 1985) concluded that sixty-six percent had ineffective research and development management. Stanford engineering professor Henry Riggs, in his book Managing High Technology Companies, defines the dominant and disfunctional managerial strategy as follows (Riggs 1983, p. 9):

1. Proliferation of product lines offered in many industries with little stimulation of primary demand for the industry's output.

2. Corporate conglomeration, the combination of fundamentally dissimilar businesses in the often vain hope of gaining some financial advantage.

3. Reliance on acquisition rather than internal product development as a result of management's preoccupation with short-term financial results.

According to Riggs, escaping this mind set is the essence of high-technology management. The state of the art in innovation management is crude at best, and in many firms nonexistent. This issue, while perhaps the most critical to the future of American biotechnology industries, is virtually ignored in the OTA report (although this is understandable, given the stage at which OTA conducted its inquiry). Moreover, aside from government encouraging universities to establish joint programs between business and engineering (for example, through grants), most of the effort needed on this issue must come from the private sector.

For the typical American manager to manage innovation better, a great deal of individual and organizational learning must take place. With specific reference to biotechnology firms, Dubinskas (1985) identifies a serious "culture chasm" between scientists and managers. Some rare individuals, such as Genetech's President Robert Swanson (trained in both chemistry and management at MIT), can bridge the worlds. However, many executives (especially those with multiple product responsibilities in large multinational firms) may never learn how to communicate with molecular biologists, whose high status, autonomy, egalitarian values, and ill-measured productivity make them virtually unmanageable by traditional methods. But learn to manage them they must, and if American firms are to be competitive, executives must learn to nurture their research teams in ways that go far beyond even the advanced concepts of organizational enhancement. At present, the lack of such effective organizational learning systems may well be the blackest hole in the biotechnology universe. More generally, the effective management of innovation within mature industries may be the single most important key to American global competitiveness.

Conclusions

In the final analysis, biotechnology, while important to the economic future of the United States, is not necessarily typical of the process of technological innovation, which itself is the key to continued American prosperity.

The "fifth-generation computer" or some other readily applied hardware may ultimately emerge as the real battle-ground for technological superiority. Nevertheless, American leadership in the basic biological sciences and general competitive strength in several applied domains (agriculture, chemicals, etc.) suggest that biotechnology could provide a significant, if not decisive, victory. Furthermore, the lessons that the U.S. political economy could glean from such a victory would obviously spill over into other domains, making the entire economy both more efficient and more effective in the translation of scientific knowledge into commercial advantage. If these lessons can be learned without damaging either the integrity of the scientific process or the energy of the entrepreneurial system (and this discussion suggests they can), then aggressive public policy experiments are called for. Moreover, if this discussion has illuminated where some of that experimentation might begin, it has more than achieved its modest objectives.

REFERENCES

Brown, G. 1985. National Technology Foundation Act. Congressional Record (January, m 28) E.230-231.

Business Week. 1984. May 21, 40.

Cooper, T. 1985. Address to the 51st Meeting of the Advisory Committee, National Institutes of Health. Bethesda, MD. June 24-25.

Daneke, G.A. 1984. The Global Contest over the Control of the Innovation Process: The Case of Biotech. Columbia Journal of World Business 83-87. Winter.

Daneke, G.A. 1986. Towards a New Political Economy of Technological Innovations. Working paper. Terman Engineering Center, Stanford, CA.

Dubinskas, F.A. 1985. The Culture Chasm: Scientists and Managers in Genetic-Engineering Firms. Technology Review 88(4): 24-33.

Gravelle, J.G. 1985. The Tax Credit for Research and Development: An Analysis. U.S. Congress, Congressional Research Service, Report N. 85-6E.

Healy, B. 1985. Address to the 51st Meeting of the Advisory
    Committee, National Institutes of Health. Bethesda, MD.
    June 24-25.

Kantrow, A.M. 1983. Management of Technology. Harvard
    Business Review 66-73. July/August.

Kutzmann, R.A. 1985. The Changing Course of Antitrust.
    Conference Paper. American Political Science
    Association. New Orleans.

Miesing, P. 1985. Antitrust: A Neglected Aspect of
    Industrial Policy. Working paper. School of Business,
    State University of New York, Albany.

OTA. 1984. Commercial Biotechnology: An International
    Analysis. U.S. Congress, Office of Technology
    Assessment. Washington, DC. January.

President's Commission on Industrial Competitiveness. 1985.
    Global Competition: The New Reality. Vol I. Washington,
    DC: Government Printing Office.

Riggs, H.E. 1983. Managing High Technology Companies.
    Belmont, CA: Wadsworth.

Robertson, C. 1985. The Maturing of Genetic Engineering. The
    Stanford Engineer 8(2): 2-9.

Ruscio, K. 1984. Prometheus Entangled: Academic Science and
    the Administration State. Public Administration Review.
    353-359. July/August.

Shapley, D., and R. Roy. 1985. Lost at the Frontier.
    Philadelphia: ISI Press.

Sproull, R.L., et al. 1984. The Science Business. New York:
    Twentieth Century Fund, Inc.

Szakonyi, R. 1985. American Industry and the Management of
    Technology. Report. Engineering Administration, George
    Washington University, Washington, DC.

Thurow, L.C. 1985. The Zero-Sum Solution. New York: Simon
    and Schuster.

Tornatzsky, L.G., et al. 1983. The Process of Technical Innovation. Washington, DC: National Science Foundation.

About the Contributors

DAVID A. ANDOW is an assistant professor in the Department of Entomology at the University of Minnesota. Dr. Andow received a B.S. in biology from Brown University and a Ph.D. in ecology from Cornell University, and did postdoctoral work at the National Institute of Agricultural Sciences in Tsukuba, Japan. He is interested in evaluating the ecological risks of deliberate releases of biotechnological products.

GREGORY A. DANEKE is professor of Public Affairs, Business Administration, and Environmental Studies at Arizona State University, and is currently the 1907 Foundation Professor of Planning and Management at Stanford University. Dr. Daneke taught previously at the University of Michigan, and was a fellow with the U.S. General Accounting Office. He received his B.A. in social sciences from Brigham Young University and his Ph.D. in political economy from the University of California. Dr. Daneke is the author of a number of books and articles on technology and natural resource policy.

JOHN R. FOWLE III is director of the Environmental Health Research Staff in the Office of Health Research, U.S. Environmental Protection Agency (EPA). Dr. Fowle earned his Ph.D. from George Washington University and after graduation was a guest worker at the National Cancer Institute. Before coming to the Office of Health Research, he worked for EPA's Reproductive Effects Assessment Group, performing mutagenicity risk assessments and helping to develop EPA procedures and guidelines for mutagenicity risk assessments. In 1983 and 1984, Dr. Fowle coordinated the initial development of EPA's research and development program in biotechnology, guiding the preparation of a multidisciplinary plan and having it peer reviewed by panels established by the American Association for the Advancement of Science. He has also co-organized several symposia on biotechnology, including the one that led to the publication of this book.

PHYLLIS FREEMAN is an associate professor of law at the Law Center of the University of Massachusetts at Boston. At the time of the AAAS symposium, Ms. Freeman was counsel to the Oversight and Investigations Subcommittee of the Committtee on Energy and Commerce of the U.S. House of Representatives, where she worked with Dr. Robbins and Congressman John Dingell (D-MI) on federal biotechnology policy, among other subjects. In January 1986, Ms. Freeman left Congress to become a Scholar in Residence at the Institute of Medicine of the National Academy of Sciences. Currently, she is examining policy issues related to preventive health applications of biotechnology, with a focus on vaccines. Her research interests include exploring the potential contribution of biotechnology to the production of new vaccines for United Nations' global immunization programs. Ms. Freeman earned her B.A. at the State University of New York at Old Westbury and her J.D. at Northeastern University.

TERRI GOLDBERG, at the time of the AAAS symposium, was the executive director of the Committee for Responsible Genetics (CRG), a national nonprofit educational organization concerned with the social impacts of biotechnology. She was a founder of the CRG, and a publisher of GeneWATCH, the bulletin of the CRG, for three years. Ms. Goldberg recently graduated from the Harvard School of Public Health.

MARK A. HARWELL is associate director of the Ecosystems Research Center at Cornell University. He received his B.S. in biology and his Ph.D. in systems ecology from Emory University. Dr. Harwell's scientific interests include stress ecology and the environmental consequences of nuclear war. He is a leading authority on nuclear winter. At the Ecosystems Research Center, Dr. Harwell is a member of the biotechnology assessment group, and has worked on the application of ecosystems theory to environmental regulation and environmental risk assessment.

BERNADINE P. HEALY is currently chairman of the Research Institute at the Cleveland Clinic Foundation, Cleveland, Ohio. At the time of the AAAS symposium, she was deputy director of the Office of Science and Technology Policy (OSTP), Executive Office of the President. While at OSTP, Dr. Healy coordinated life sciences and regulatory issues, serving as the OSTP representative on several panels, including the National Cancer Advisory Board. She also chaired the White House Cabinet Council Working Group on Biotechnology. As chair of this Cabinet Council workgroup, Dr. Healy guided the development of federal policy for the regulation of biotechnology. She earned her M.D. at the Harvard Medical School. She was a professor of medicine at the Johns Hopkins Hospital and School of Medicine, and president of the American Federation of Clinical Researchers. Dr. Healy is the author or co-author of numerous medical and scientific articles.

SHELDON KRIMSKY is an associate professor in the Department of Urban and Environmental Policy at Tufts University. He is the author of Genetic Alchemy, a social history of the recombinant DNA controversy. Dr. Krimsky is a member of the Committee for Responsible Genetics and a consultant to the Congressional Office of Technology Assessment for Biotechnology Studies. He served as a member of the National Institutes of Health Recombinant DNA Advisory Committee from 1978 to 1981. Dr. Krimsky received his M.S. in physics from Purdue University and his Ph.D. in the philosophy of science from Boston University.

RICHARD E. LENSKI is an assistant professor in the Department of Ecology and Evolutionary Biology at the University of California at Irvine. He earned his Ph.D. at the University of North Carolina in ecology, and did postdoctoral work in evolutionary biology at the University of Massachusetts at Amherst. Because of his interest in evolutionary processes that can be studied in an experimental time frame, his current work is with microbial populations. This work led to an interest in investigating the potential short-term evolutionary impacts resulting from environmental uses of genetically engineered organisms. Dr. Lenski has participated in several workshops in this area, including one sponsored by the National Science Foundation in 1986 to discuss research needs in microbial ecology. He is the recipient of a cooperative research grant from the U.S. Environmental Protection Agency to study the effects of specific recombinant traits on the competitive ability of microorganisms.

SIMON A. LEVIN is director of the Ecosystems Research Center and Charles A. Alexander Professor of Biological Sciences at Cornell University. He is a member of several national scientific committees, including the Committee on the Release of Genetically Engineered Organisms of the National Research Council's Board on Basic Biology, the Department of Energy's Health and Environmental Research Commmittee, and the Commission on Life Sciences of the National Research Council. Dr. Levin is the managing editor of three scientific journals and book series for Springer-Verlag, and the author of numerous articles and book chapters on a variety of subjects, including ecology, environmental toxicology, and mathematical biology. Dr. Levin has been concerned with the potential ecological consequences of deliberate releases of genetically engineered organisms into the environment; he has also addressed more general problems in ecological risk assessment. He received his B.A. in mathematics from Johns Hopkins University and his Ph.D. in mathematics from the University of Maryland.

ELIZABETH MILEWSKI joined the U.S. Environmental Protection Agency in 1986 as a special assistant to the Assistant Administrator for Pesticides and Toxic Substances, where she provides guidance and advice on biotechnology matters. Previously, she was an assistant to the director of the Office of Recombinant DNA Activities (ORDA) at the National Institutes of Health. While at ORDA, Dr. Milewski was editor of the Recombinant DNA Technical Bulletin, and helped organize meetings of the Recombinant DNA Advisory Committee (RAC). She served as executive secretary for many groups responsible for the development and recommendation of policy to the RAC, including the Working Group on

Toxins and the Working Group on Release into the Environment. Dr. Milewski earned her B.S. in biophysics from Pennsylvania State University and her Ph.D. in biochemistry from the University of Poitiers in Poitiers, France.

GEORGE B. RATHMANN is president and chief executive officer of Amgen, a California-based biotechnology company that conducts research and development in gene synthesis, recombinant DNA, and hybridomas. Under Dr. Rathmann's direction, Amgen has cloned and developed a variety of human and animal therapeutic product candidates. Before joining Amgen, Dr. Rathmann was vice president of Research and Development in the Diagnostics Division of Abbott Laboratories and president of Litton Medical Systems, Inc. He has held various scientific and management positions with the 3M Company. Dr. Rathmann received his B.S. in physical chemistry from Northwestern University and his Ph.D. in physical chemistry from Princeton University. Since 1982 he has served on the board of directors of the Industrial Biotechnology Association and is currently chairman of that group.

PHILIP J. REGAL is a professor in the Department of Ecology and Behavioral Biology at the University of Minnesota. He has organized or co-organized several key workshops about the potential ecological consequences of the release of genetically engineered organisms into the environment. These have included the first workshop of the Short-term Evolutionary Consequences of Biotechnology Conference held in August 1984 at the Banbury Conference Center, and the AAAS symposium that led to the publication of this book. Dr. Regal earned both his M.S. and Ph.D. degrees in zoology from the University of California at Los Angeles. He is the author of numerous publications in evolutionary biology and ecology.

ANTHONY ROBBINS is a professor at the Boston University School of Public Health. He has held a broad array of public service jobs at both the federal and state levels. When the AAAS symposium was conducted, he was a professional staff member for the Committee on Energy and Commerce of the U.S. House of Representatives, working with Congressman

John Dingell (D-MI) to oversee federal biotechnology policy and to develop congressional policy. Dr. Robbins was appointed by President Carter to be director of the National Institute of Occupational Safety and Health. Prior to that, he served as state health commissioner of Vermont and state health director of Colorado. Dr. Robbins is past president of the American Public Health Association. He earned his M.D. at Yale University and his M.P.A. at Harvard University.

FRANCES E. SHARPLES is a Research Staff Member in the Environmental Sciences Division at the Oak Ridge National Laboratory in Oak Ridge, Tennessee. She earned her M.S. and Ph.D. degrees in zoology at the University of California at Davis. In 1981 she was an AAAS Science and Engineering Fellow at the U.S. Environmental Protection Agency. She was also a recipient of an AAAS Congressional Science and Engineering Fellowship in 1984-1985, and was a legislative assistant for Senator Albert Gore, Jr. (D-TN) during that time. Dr. Sharples is a member of the National Institutes of Health Recombinant DNA Advisory Committee.

LIDIA S. WATRUD is Research Manager for Microbial Products in the Monsanto Agricultural Products Company, St. Louis, Missouri. She received a B.S. in biology from the City College of New York and a Ph.D. in mycology and genetics from Michigan State University. Prior to joining Monsanto, Dr. Watrud did postdoctoral work and taught microbiology at the University of Illinois. At Monsanto, she initiated efforts to screen microbes for useful agronomic activities. More recently, she has initiated and coordinated molecular biology and environmental studies leading to the development of genetically engineered pesticides. Dr. Watrud has been an active spokesperson for agricultural biotechnology. She has been a participant in numerous workshops with academic, federal agency, and industrial personnel to help define research and regulatory needs for responsible uses of genetically engineered organisms.

Index

242